TAKING THE MEASURE

Martin L. Keefe

TAKING THE MEASURE

Contact information: martykeefe@aol.com

ISBN: 1534775919
ISBN 13: 9781534775916
Library of Congress Control Number: 2016910250
Createspace Independent Publishing Platform
North Charleston, South Carolina

Oct 27, 2016.

My Dear Cousin Maryellen:
I am so happy that we see each other with some regularity. I hope you like the book. You will certainly recognize some of the "characters"! Love,
Marty K.

To Anna and Casey,
for all the love
they made possible.

And the end of all our exploring
Will be to arrive where we started
And know the place for the first time.

—T. S. Eliot, *Four Quartets*

CONTENTS

ACKNOWLEDGMENTS

Of the many people who have helped and encouraged me in this endeavor, I wish to especially thank in alphabetical order: Lenore Gavigan, for her critical reading and meticulous editing of multiple versions of the manuscript; Bill Grogan, for his profound and insightful guidance born of his many years of teaching English literature; John McCaffrey, accomplished author, coach and counselor, for his guidance and inspiration; and Michael Scanlon, journalist, author, and confidant, to whom I owe a great debt for much sage advice.

Not only did these good friends and wise counselors provide me with seasoned insight and professional direction, but they also offered me their unfailing support from beginning to end. This book, nurtured by that support, would not have been possible without them.

Finally as will become evident, my wife, Anna, my daughter, Casey, and the love they made possible have been the fundamental and inspirational source of this effort.

GOING HOME

On the day after Memorial Day in 2011, eleven months after her diagnosis, Anna called me from her office and asked me to pick her up and take her home. "It's over," she said. I went to her office and helped her into the car. We drove over to the FDR Drive and north toward home.

Driving together had always been something special for us, a chance to talk, sometimes without words. In our forty years of marriage, commuting to country homes had afforded us the weekly opportunity to share those thoughts and feelings that had deferred to the demands of busy workweeks. As we drove home that day, however, we shared a profound hurt in disbelieving silence, so painfully different from every moment that we had ever spent together.

We had sold our last weekend house, at Anna's request, six months after her diagnosis with stage-four colon cancer. "I can't deal with the weekend house anymore," she confided when she asked me to sell it. As an investment when our daughter Casey came along, we had purchased a beautiful piece of land in Amagansett, in the Hamptons. Years later in 2000, we built a large ranch house, which, under Anna's supervision, we would continue to extend and embellish during the following five years. Anna was a visionary designer and decorator, pursuits that, I believe, provided restorative relief from her work as a psychotherapist.

Our second country house in the Poconos, however, remained Anna's favorite. She had designed it with an architect and purchased all the furnishings during the nine months required to build it. When we moved in, our empty house was completely decorated, top to bottom, in twenty-four hours. The living space, surrounded by huge windows and skylights, was on the second floor, while all the bedrooms were on the first.

Since she loved to cook, Anna's favorite room was the kitchen, in the middle of which she had placed a huge butcher-block counter, across from two stoves with eight burners and two ovens. On the outside of the house was a large deck with a screened-in porch.

To celebrate our new Pocono house, as we had celebrated our one-month wedding anniversary years before, I came home one day with another schnauzer puppy, which we named Jacques.

Unfortunately, Jacques had the same struggle with obedience as our first schnauzer, Pumpkin. To nip this problem in the bud, Anna called in a dog psychologist, who took Jacques out for an hour of observation. Upon her return, she said to us, in solemn tones, "He seems to be sensitive and immature." Anna then inquired if the dog psychologist was talking about Jacques or about me. Jacques, like Pumpkin before him, never did learn to obey.

More importantly and most memorably, our second country house in the Poconos was the home into which we welcomed our daughter Casey, whom we adopted in 1989, just six months after we moved in and a month after the arrival of Jacques. Casey was nine months old when we picked her up at the New York Foundling and strapped her into the new baby seat. Never had we driven along Route 80 so slowly. I was afraid to go any faster than forty miles per hour in the right lane. We were suddenly parents of an infant. I was scared and more than slightly in shock. With Casey's arrival on that June day, we suddenly had a crowded and confusing house, riddled with unfamiliar responsibilities, all of which somehow blended together into a very happy home.

Many June days had come and gone since Casey had come into our lives. And daily life, after Anna's diagnosis the previous June, strangely, almost surreally, continued as it always had, with its same rhythms and responsibilities. Except for a brief hospital stay for some surgery and biweekly chemotherapy treatments, Anna had continued with her practice of psychotherapy at her office in Manhattan. During those months, we kept postponing telling Casey of Anna's illness longer than we should have. In fact, we told no one, except our closest friends, about our struggle, as we hoped and waited for some good news in which to couch the announcement of the truth. The good news never came.

We crossed over the Willis Avenue Bridge, from the FDR Drive to the Major Deegan Expressway, in continuing silence.

When we arrived home in Bronxville, Anna said she was tired and wanted to lie down. I brought her a cup of tea. She wanted to be alone. I closed the bedroom door and went to the living room. Through the French doors that led onto the balcony, I stared out at the nearby lake. Outside it was spring, with trees newly green standing amid clusters of yellow daffodils. Chirping and singing, flocks of birds were overflying the ducks and Canadian geese in the lake. There were two swans paddling along together, like a committed couple, in the far corner of the sun-drenched lake. All was beauty, serenity, and life, a world to which we now no longer belonged.

Anna had been receiving chemotherapy for about nine months. Every other Thursday, our good friend Bonnie, whom Anna had known since graduate school, would insist on driving to Westchester from Long Island just to accompany Anna to her treatments in Manhattan. Sadly, despite the chemotherapy, there had been no substantial reduction in the malignancy. Yet there were bursts of new energy from time to time. These bursts of energy were as short-lived, however, as was the hope they engendered.

One week after closing down her practice, Anna was scheduled for her biweekly chemotherapy treatment. We drove into Manhattan with our dear friend, Peggy, who is also a nurse. Anna had become progressively weaker during the preceding week and needed support to walk. On the way into the doctor's office, she suddenly collapsed. There would be no more chemotherapy.

The doorbell rang that evening. It was Betsy, the nurse who came to our home to administer further treatment to Anna after her biweekly chemotherapy. She was a lovely, dedicated woman. Anna appreciated her so much that she had given Betsy our timeshare in Aruba for a week several months before. I explained to Betsy what happened. She spoke briefly with Anna, and they exchanged good-byes, for what would be the last time.

The next morning, Anna had difficulty breathing, and I called 911. The ambulance came and took her to Lawrence Hospital, just blocks away. I sat with her in the emergency room, and she seemed to respond to whatever it was they were administering to her through the IV. We sat there chatting as normally as we could under the circumstances.

Then Anna asked me to call Casey. She wanted to talk alone with her. I knew what that meant. She also asked me to call her brother, Anthony, and ask him to come to the hospital that evening. I did as she asked. In a quiet moment together, without nurses and doctors, I tearfully blurted out to Anna that, if it were possible, I would happily take her place. I begged God to somehow make that possible. Anna pretended not to hear me.

Anna had an extraordinary ability to speak reassuringly yet directly and honestly. Casey came and spoke alone with her; wiping tears from her cheeks, she emerged from the room about an hour later. So, too, did Anthony and his wife, Josie, later that day. Anna remained in the hospital for several more days before going home, for the last time, to hospice care.

At home, I looked for opportunities to do something for her. Anything. I was drowning in helplessness. But she no longer asked for anything. The nurses who work in hospice care don't have a job; they have a vocation. For the next eight or nine days, a hospice nurse was at Anna's bedside every hour of the day and night. So was our friend Peggy. Before Anna slipped into a coma, I asked the local parish priest, Father Dawson, to come to our home and to pray with us for Anna.

Father Dawson ends every service with his best wishes for a day or an evening with "someone who is most near, dear, and special to you." Anna was that someone. We stood around her bed, Casey, Peggy, the hospice nurses, and I. Grief cannot be dispelled, but it can be transformed. That was Father Dawson's gift to us. He came to our home and said Mass, and we all shared in Communion. We cried and became one, the living and the dying, joined together in a loving farewell.

As Anna slipped into a coma and we could no longer speak with her, every hour became longer and more painful. She was there, but she was gone. At three thirty on Thursday morning, June 23, 2011, the hospice nurse came into the room where I was sleeping and woke me. Anna was near death. I woke Casey and Peggy, and we went into Anna's room. It was terrible to say good-bye, but I was glad Anna's suffering was over.

She had been so brave, so strong, so much more concerned for others than for herself. Now she was gone, and there was an unfillable hole in the world. All of us standing around Anna's bed embraced each other. A special being, an irreplaceable source of goodness, had slipped out of this world. We shared a silence we had never shared before. Casey and I wrapped our arms around each other.

Summer had just begun. The next day was Friday, the day of the week that would always find us on the road, driving together to our house in the country for the weekend. But there were no more country houses. There was only the right here and the right now, the world without Anna, a world quickly filling with emptiness.

Four years later I was driving through the Poconos, returning from a funeral in Minersville. Suddenly I felt compelled to turn off Route 80 and visit our old houses. They were there but changed, lived-in but, for me, still empty. Outside our first house on Lehigh Circle was a white pine tree about forty feet high. I remembered planting it as a six-foot tree in 1973. For a brief moment, the emptiness dissipated.

Then I heard myself quoting Anna. "It's over," I said to no one.

I lingered a while longer, not wanting to leave that little tree that had become so big. But the sun soon began its slow slide down the sloping wall of the sky and into the horizon.

It was time to go back, to go home.

ALONE

If we had remained living in that apartment after my father died, I would have continued, night after night, waiting for the empty chair to be filled. For me, absence was absence, whether by something called death or by just not coming home after work, which was the norm as far as I can remember. The idea of "never" was not something I understood. After all, the chair had once been filled on that special night, why not again?

On that night, the door, which was to the right of the radio, opened, and he entered. He walked past me and over to the empty chair, saying "hello" to nobody in particular along the way. The chair was to the left of the big Philco radio that my mother was listening to. I was sitting on the floor in front of the radio, hearing the words, sounds without meaning.

He sat and opened his newspaper. The top half of him disappeared. That night the empty chair was filled by my father for the one and only time I can remember, and it is the only memory I have of him. After that special night, whenever that chair would be empty, which it always was, I would wonder where he was and when he would come back to fill it. I was three years old, and he would die before I was four.

His chair, too, would disappear along with him when my sister and I left that apartment. As soon as my father was diagnosed with TB, a socially stigmatizing disease in June 1942, he disappeared into the hospital and was placed in isolation, an event that we didn't really understand. My six-year-old sister asked my mother when he would come back home. My mother replied that he would be back soon and "in the pink," her expression for "getting better," something she always said to us when we were sick.

Then came undeniably bad news. The doctor told our mother that my sister and I had to leave home or we would be in danger of being infected as well. For my sister and me, or at least for me, the danger of infection was beyond my understanding, and I can't remember how or if my mother tried to explain it. I don't remember leaving home or traveling, but I do remember arriving at St.

Agatha's, an orphanage in Nanuet, New York. The first thing I saw and remember was a big semicircular driveway, wrapped around a big, green lawn in front of a deep-red stone building. We entered, and the world I knew, the only one I had ever known, vanished. Immediately. Totally.

There were lots of rooms, but they were all very big, bigger than any I had ever seen before, no small rooms like those in our apartment. Everything was big, very big. And all the rooms were filled with other children of all ages. My sister and I were separated and sent to different large rooms called dormitories. I was assigned to a bed in one of the big rooms, full of boys my age or a little older. Nuns were in charge of St. Agatha's, but our big room was the responsibility of a woman older than my mother; she wore glasses, skinny, and unsmiling. My immediate reaction was fear.

I don't recall any other details of that afternoon until the approach of night. It was not yet dark outside when the lights were turned out by the skinny, unsmiling lady with glasses. Her strong, threatening, unseen voice pierced the enveloping darkness, reminding us to be quiet and to go to sleep. There was nothing, and nobody I knew that I could see, hear, or touch. For a while, no one made a sound. Then one of the boys near me started to cry, but he tried to muffle the sound. I don't remember crying. I only remember being in a world by myself, a world in which I knew no one and no one knew me. I didn't know if I would ever again see the world I had left. Even my sister had been taken away.

I was alone. I was scared. I wet the bed.

The next morning after awakening to my first sunrise in St. Agatha's, my crime was discovered by the skinny, unsmiling lady with glasses. She was shocked at what I had done and angry with me for having done it. She said nothing, at least not to me. Not directly anyway. Instead she ordered all the boys in the room to stand in front of their beds while she described to them the shameful deed I had done.

The skinny, unsmiling lady with glasses then took me by the arm and escorted me to the middle of the dormitory. "Here's what happens to boys who wet the bed," she announced.

With those words, she pulled a pink dress over my head and made me stand on my bed. I can feel my back pressing against the wall behind the bed. I can feel the metal bedpost that I clutched with my hands as she instructed the other boys in the room to file past in a line that kept looping back unendingly while they chanted, "Little girl in the pink dress wet the bed. Little girl in the pink dress wet the bed."

I held on to the bedpost, squeezing it as hard as I could, while trying to push my back through the wall so that I could disappear. But the wall pushed back, and I had nowhere to go, nowhere to hide. I had to stay and listen to what all the other boys thought of me. With nowhere to go physically, I climbed inside myself. I willed myself invisible and deaf. I willed myself immune to needs. I didn't need to eat. I didn't need to drink. I didn't need friends. I didn't need my sister. I didn't need my mother. I didn't need my father. The only need that I could not will away was the need to cry. And when I did, I couldn't stop. I only made things worse, proving the point that the skinny, unsmiling lady with glasses was trying to make: I was not a real boy.

I don't remember much after that humiliation. Later in the summer, I got the whooping cough, a contagious disease that meant isolation. How do you isolate someone who is already alone? The outside world was catching up to the inside world. I was taken to a tiny cottage with a single bed in it. It was the summertime, and it was very hot. The still air only moved when the screen door slammed after a nurse's visit or a food delivery. Strangely I was happy to be in my tiny cottage. Isolation was less lonely than feeling lonely in a crowd of lonely people. Besides, the skinny lady with the glasses never came here.

I don't remember how long it took to be cured of the whooping cough. Another stretch of time transpired. My next memory is of a fall afternoon (I would later learn it was November). I sat on a blanket with my mother and sister in the middle of the driveway-enclosed lawn in front of what I had come to know as the Main Building. We were having a picnic. My mother said she had something to tell us.

"Daddy is gone to heaven after being ill these past months." I heard the words, understood the words, but felt nothing. My sister, however, now just past her seventh birthday, burst into tears. My only thought was that, despite what my mother had promised, Daddy never got back "in the pink."

Daddy was gone. But not just Daddy. Home was gone. When my sister and I arrived home from St. Agatha's at Christmas, it was not to the home we had left. Our mother now lived with her sister and brother at our grandmother's home. No more would there be that skinny, punishing lady with glasses. No more pink dress. No more parading lines of scornful boys. No more slamming screen door. There would be no more home with the empty chair. There would be no more Daddy to wait for. A few days after Christmas, we celebrated my fourth birthday, and I think it was at that moment that I first began to understand the idea of "never."

My grandmother's railroad-apartment, on 100th Street and Columbus Avenue, was even smaller than the apartment my sister and I had left on Amsterdam Avenue between 101st and 102nd Streets. To go from the kitchen to the living room (we called it the "front room"), you had to walk through the three bedrooms. We had a woodburning (instead of gas) stove and something called DC current, which, as far as I could understand, was just something that made it impossible to buy any new electrical appliances.

World War II was raging, and soon my uncle was drafted into the army. That left me with my mother, sister, aunt, and grandmother, all of us financially dependent on my mother, who worked full-time as a telephone operator while managing the household. After the war ended, my uncle returned home and helped out financially, but by that time, my grandmother, who was now in her seventies, was not in very good health. When she went into the hospital, however, my mother assured my sister and me that my grandmother would soon be "in the pink" and back at home. That never happened. My grandmother died in the hospital at the age of seventy-five.

I remembered the empty chair in our old apartment. I had stopped waiting for someone who would never come back.

There are many ways to make ninety-four cents out of coins, but the only combination of coins making ninety-four cents that I remember well was the one composed of two quarters, three dimes, two nickels, and four pennies. All these coins were once poured from the hand of a sailor into the hand of an eleven-year-old kid, me, shining shoes on a sunny afternoon somewhere near Times Square in the year 1950.

My shoeshine kit cost about five dollars, money I had saved up by selling newspapers in bars along Columbus and Amsterdam Avenues. Selling newspapers was a good job, but because the *NY Daily News* and *Daily Mirror* came out the night before the date on the newspaper, it was night work. It was good night work, because the people in bars seemed to be more generous than the people on the street. I concluded that generosity and alcohol went together, since the biggest tips came from the guys who apparently had drunk the most.

But selling newspapers in bars was still night work, while shining shoes was a day job. I had shined shoes for a while and borrowed shoeshine kits from friends. But now I had my own brand-new kit that I could carry, holding it by the footrest, onto the Broadway IRT downtown local. Two stops, and I was at Times Square, where I hoped more shoes needed shining than anywhere else.

I knew that I looked inexperienced and therefore of questionable ability. I would have to compete on price or else just depend on the goodwill or blind faith of the passersby. (I learned later in life that I had been grappling with what are known as market forces.)

Many older shoeshine professionals had set up shop in the immediate vicinity of Times Square, so I looked around for a spot that had a lot of potential customers but no competition. I found such a place on the corner of Broadway and Forty-Fourth Street, just outside the Criterion movie theater and waited for my first customers. That's when I discovered a basic rule of marketing: if the customers don't come to you of their own free will, you have to reach out to them. So I started yelling to the passersby, "Great, great shine. Just a thin dime."

I soon learned another component of marketing: patience and perseverance. Customers don't show up just because you show up. You need a good product, but timing is really important. I worried that all the customers who might have gotten a shoeshine from me had already walked by the corner of Broadway and Forty-Fourth Street before I arrived. Who knew? But I kept telling anyone who would listen, "Great, great shine. Just a thin dime."

Finally, a well-dressed, middle-aged man stopped for a shine. As he put his right foot on the footrest, he asked if I had been shining shoes for very long. I embellished the truth and said, "About a year," which was off by about eight months. I had discovered another component of marketing strategy: exaggeration.

I wanted to shine his shoes perfectly, so I brushed, polished, brushed again, polished again, and buffed and buffed the man's shoes until the sunlight overhead was staring right back at me. "How's that?" I asked.

"Fine," he said. "What did you say, son, a dime?"

"Yes, sir, a dime."

"Well, here's fifteen cents. Nice work."

As he walked away, I looked at the nickel and dime in my hand and thought about the guy at the bar who had given me a quarter for a copy of the *Daily News*, for which I had only paid three cents. That profit had required a lot less effort. But selling newspapers is night work. Anyway, fifteen cents is fifteen cents. And a 50 percent tip. Back to work.

A few more shouts of "Great, great shine. Just a thin dime," and I had another customer and another fifteen cents. Then my third, fourth, fifth, and sixth customers appeared. A seventh customer even said he would wait while I finished shining the shoes of the sixth customer. They all gave me either fifteen or twenty cents, except for the guy who waited. He gave me a quarter.

While I looked at the quarter in my hand and contemplated my climbing profits, a voice from behind asked, "Are you still shining shoes, kid?" I turned around and saw a sailor in his white summer uniform.

"Sure, I am," I said.

With his right shoe up on the footrest, I began to brush his shoe with gusto. "Give me a great shine, kid. In the Navy, we have to have well-shined shoes."

"No problem. That's what I do," I said. I brushed his right shoe vigorously while the sailor kept looking intently at the passersby. As I started to buff, he let out a loud whistle and kept on whistling with a big smile on his face. I turned around to see what he was whistling at. Nearby stood a beautiful woman, and she was smiling back at him.

"Listen, kid," he said, "that's great. Good job. Here take this." He reached into his right pocket and took out some change. He grabbed my hand and poured the change into it.

"I'm not finished," I yelled. "I've only done one shoe."

"I know, kid," he said, "but I gotta go now. She won't wait forever. Great job. See ya around."

I turned to watch him hurry over to the pretty blond lady in a yellow dress. She was standing there, near the corner, smiling at him as he approached her. I yelled after him, "But I only did one shoe!" He waved back without turning around. By that time, he had reached her, and they were both smiling as they walked off, arm in arm.

I looked at the coins in my hand and counted them. Ninety-four cents! That was almost as much money as I had received from my first six customers combined! And it was for only one shoe. I couldn't quite understand it. It was like the first time I got fifty cents for a three-cent newspaper from a guy in one of the bars along my newspaper route.

But this was different. At least the guy in the bar got a complete newspaper for fifty cents. The sailor got only one shoe shined. I thought that the Navy was tough about shoes being shined. He might get in trouble. I couldn't stop thinking about it for the rest of the day, at the end of which I had earned $5.14. Not bad for a day job.

As I held onto the pole in the subway train back to Ninety-Sixth Street and Broadway, clutching my shoeshine kit, I thought of the sailor, the lady, and my shoeshine business. Maybe the best place to shine shoes would be outside a navy base instead of Times Square. If I got ninety-four cents for one shoe and if you multiply that by two and then multiply that by all the sailors on the navy base, I could be a millionaire.

But then I would need a lot of gorgeous, blond ladies in yellow dresses.

Mr. Claus was in a big hurry to turn around and drive back to the Catskill Mountains, from which he had just come to pick us up in New York City. He took our luggage, put it in the trunk of his car, and told us, in German-accented English, where to sit. My mother, sister, and I followed his orders in silence on that sunny July day in 1947. Mr. Claus put the car in gear, and we were off to the Catskills for a vacation.

However it happened, parts of the Catskills became Irish or Jewish or maybe Italian, and other parts became German. We were going to the German part, even though we were Irish. For a whole week. And we were going by car rather than by bus because Mr. Claus had volunteered to drive us, door to door, for a small fee.

Mr. Claus didn't talk much. He was very proper and business-like. I figured that was because he was German. Germans were very rigid, planned everything, and liked to fight wars. I picked up all those facts at the movies and from listening to the grown-ups talk about the war that had just ended two years before. The grown-ups called German-Americans "Dutchmen," which, I later learned, had nothing to do with the Dutch but was just neighborhood English for "Deutsch."

I knew only two German kids, Tommy Hecker and Franklin Borchardt. They were both in my class at Holy Name School, but I didn't know them well. I never went to their houses, which is what we used to call the apartments in which we lived. I really didn't think of them as German, not like the Nazis and Hitler. Their families were German, but they couldn't do anything about that. Most of the men in the neighborhood had fought in the war. They were the good guys. The Germans and the Japs were the bad guys. The war might be over; but the good guys were still the good guys, and the bad guys were still the bad guys.

After about three hours on the road, Mr. Claus pulled into the driveway of his guesthouse in the Catskills. There were five or six cars parked along the driveway. Mr. Claus opened the doors of the car, and we climbed out while he unloaded our luggage. I noticed a number of people sunbathing on a large lawn in the back. I asked Mr. Claus if there was a place to go swimming, and he said there was a creek right behind that house.

I wanted to go swimming right away. So did my sister, but my mother said we would have to have lunch first. Swimming suddenly became less important when we sat down at the table and saw what was being served, pancakes rolled up around centers of jams and jellies, smothered in butter and syrup. I don't think I had ever eaten German food before. It was wonderful. I couldn't stop eating those pancakes, which were called something else, German words I couldn't pronounce.

After lunch, we went up to our room and put on our bathing suits. As Mr. Claus had said, there was a creek behind the house, not very large but big enough, with a small waterfall. Some people, including children, were in the water, but most were sunbathing on the large lawn. I immediately ran into the water. It was cold and not very deep. I swam toward the waterfall, where several adults and some children were standing and talking. In German. They stopped talking when I arrived, and one man said to me in heavily accented English, "Good afternoon, how are you, young man?" I said, "Fine," and dived under the water.

I surfaced behind the curtain of water pouring down the waterfall and, for a moment, felt happily alone, as if I were invisible to the others in the creek. Then I heard the man who had said hello to me yell in English, "Hello, young lady." I immediately emerged from behind the waterfall and saw my sister approaching. The man asked if we were related, and we responded, "Yes."

He introduced us to his two daughters and spoke to them in German. They smiled and nodded to us. He told us that he was going to take his daughters on a hike and asked if we would like to come along. We said we would have to ask our mother. "If she agrees," he said, "come back here in fifteen minutes wearing your hiking shoes, and we will be ready to go."

We received permission and were back in less than fifteen minutes. The man spoke briefly in German to Mr. Claus, who walked off and quickly returned with his dog, a big, beautiful German shepherd. The man told us that he thought it would be a good idea to bring the dog along with us on the hike. We were happy to have him, and off we went, up the hill behind the creek. It was a beautiful day but hot. After a half hour of walking, we stopped by a rock beneath which a stream of clear water flowed downhill. "Here," said the man, "is the clearest, coldest water you will ever drink." Thirsty, we drank and drank. He was right. It was so clear and so cold.

We continued uphill onto a big, open meadow, flowers everywhere. The dog was running far ahead of us. I was out in front following the dog, with everyone else far behind me. As I approached a tree, I was suddenly surrounded by bees, the kind we called yellowjackets. Apparently the dog had trampled a nest on the ground. By the time I approached, the bees had stirred and were ready to attack. The dog was gone, and I was the target. The bees were all over me, inside my shirt and even in my sneakers. I started screaming, and everyone came running. Seeing all the bees attacking me, the man, without hesitation, pulled off my shirt, threw me to the ground, and rolled me into a nearby mud puddle. As he swatted the bees, he rubbed mud on me, telling me that mud was like medicine for bee stings. I did not know that. He said it was something he had learned back in Germany.

When the bees had finally disappeared, the man told me that he had counted over fifty bee stings while he was rubbing the mud on me. The stings didn't seem to hurt any more once he had applied the mud. He said that we should return to the guesthouse right away, which we did. By the time we arrived, I was feeling much better and wanted to go for a swim in the creek. I didn't want to tell my mother about the bee attack because that might be the end of hiking. So we removed our sneakers and jumped into the water.

While the German man played with his daughters, picking them up and dropping them back into the water, my sister and I stood under the little waterfall. It felt so good to wash off the mud and run the cool water over the sting marks. Everything was OK. This was a good place, and our vacation had just begun. We stayed under the waterfall for a long time. Almost everyone else had already gone back onto the lawn. When my sister and I came out of the creek, the German man came over to us and asked how I was feeling. I said, "Fine," and thanked him for his help.

It was at that moment that I noticed his right foot. He had no toes on it. I said to him, "You have no toes on your right foot," as if he didn't know. "What happened?" I asked, although it was none of my business.

He smiled kindly and said that it had happened during the war. "You see," he said, "I was on the other side during the war, in the German Air Force. Luftwaffe, we called it. And one day one of your pilots shot up my plane. That's how I lost my toes."

I was speechless. All I could say was "Oh." I thanked him again for helping me with the bee stings and walked away.

I walked around to the front of the house and saw that there was no one on the front porch but the dog. I sat down and petted him. I was confused. I had to think this out. That German man was a nice guy, even though he was German. But he had shot at American planes and pilots. That's what the bad guys did. The Americans shot back and took off his toes. They were the good guys. He was one of the bad guys. But he was a nice guy. He saved me from the bees. I bet his daughters love him the way we love our mother. But he was fighting for the bad guys and shooting at the good guys. How could he be a good guy? He had to be a bad guy. But he was a nice guy.

I thought I was going crazy. This was worse than all the bee stings. Before we went on our hike, I had known that there were good guys and bad guys. We were the good guys, and they were the bad guys. Now one of the bad guys who had been hurt by one of the good guys turned out to be a nice guy. He helped me a lot, and he treated my sister and me the way he treated his own daughters. So he had to be a good guy. But he was one of the bad guys. But he was a nice guy.

As the late-afternoon sun slipped slowly behind the hills, huge, dark clouds moved across the horizon, blurring the line between day and night, light and darkness. The world was turning gray. I started to think about tomorrow and the pancakes we would have for breakfast. Maybe we'd have pancakes for dinner, too. I liked German food.

I was madly in love with Loretta Lambert. She lived on the third floor of our building with her mother, who spoke with a beautiful accent that I loved to hear. When she pronounced her name, she stressed the "bert," while everyone else in the building stressed the "Lam." Loretta said that they were French Canadian, but Loretta didn't have an accent. If she had had an accent, it would have made me love her even more. She was the most beautiful girl I had ever seen. She was really a woman, in fact, not a girl like that annoying Helen on the fourth floor.

Loretta was just perfect in every way. And so kind to me. One day I asked her to marry me. I knew there was an age difference—Loretta was twenty-three, and I was eight—but I believed she could wait until I caught up. I was getting older every day. She smiled and said that it would not be possible because she had met someone and was about to be engaged to be married. Besides, she came from a family of Huguenots, French Protestants. Protestants and Catholics rarely married in those days. "You will meet a lovely Catholic girl one day, Martin," she assured me with a hug.

I had lost my first love, but a few years later I would meet another Lambert, far away in upstate New York, through an organization called the Fresh Air Fund. That organization arranged for city children who couldn't afford to go away to camp to spend several weeks during the summer in the country with families who volunteered their homes and care. So there I was, in my eleventh summer, at Grand Central Station with lots of other kids. We said our good-byes to our families as the Fresh Air Fund staff tied big tags around our necks. These tags identified us, our destinations, and the names of the families waiting for us. Reading upside down, I saw that on my tag had been written, "Mrs. Lambert, Booneville,

New York." I thought that was a good omen. Maybe she was related to Loretta.

Later that morning we were on our way. It was a long trip up to Watertown, New York, the nearest train station to Booneville. About six of us got off the train in Watertown, along with a chaperone from the Fresh Air Fund. We stood on the platform next to our suitcases, our neck tags flapping in the breeze. I saw several adults approaching us. Smilingly they examined our tags and declared, "Welcome," to the children who had been assigned to them. The adults picked up their luggage and walked off with them.

Soon there were only two of us left waiting on the platform. I saw a woman in the distance walking toward us with a teenage boy. She wasn't smiling. I already didn't like her. I found myself hoping she was there for the other boy standing next to me. She came to me first and lifted the tag from my chest. "You're mine," she said. My heart sank. "Come with us," she ordered as they began to walk off. I picked up my suitcase and followed them.

In the car, the boy asked me my name. I answered, "Martin." He replied, "Mountain?" I said, "No. Martin." His mother, still unsmiling, turned to me and said sternly that her son, George, had trouble pronouncing certain sounds. "Just accept it," she ordered. I said nothing. I would soon discover, however, that pronunciation wasn't George's only problem. I started praying that Loretta might be a relative and that she might suddenly walk through the front door and rescue me from this family.

Except for those few times when we were able to play ball with some other boys in the neighborhood, each day seemed like a week. Mrs. Lambert's cooking was awful. Everything was powdered. Powdered milk, powdered eggs, powdered everything. Fortunately some next-door neighbors often invited us into their home for a snack. They were very kind and generous to us. But it was obvious—not only to me, an eleven-year-old—that there was something off about George. He was fourteen years old, but the neighbors treated him as if he were even younger than I was, as if he were a very young boy.

My vague and confused intuitions about George were confirmed on the day before my departure for home. I couldn't wait to leave. During the afternoon, George's uncle came by to take us for a ride in his car. It proved to be a ride *on* his car. It was an old convertible with running boards on both sides. George and I stood together on the passenger-side running board as his uncle drove us around Booneville. At an intersection, George yelled to me, "Mountain, look at that!" I looked in the direction in which George had been pointing. As I did, the car made a left turn into the intersection, and George pushed me off the running board into the street.

I rolled along the street through the intersection. Luckily no cars came my way. Some pedestrians rushed over to help me. I was scratched and bruised but otherwise all right. George's uncle pulled up in the car. George was smiling. "Wasn't that fun, Mountain?" he yelled.

Why couldn't I have been born a Protestant? Loretta would have married me, and I would never have come to Booneville, New York. I was still in love with Loretta, but Lambert was no longer a magical name.

One year later despite my protests, I was back at Grand Central Station with a tag around my neck. Again reading upside down, I read, "The Jones family, Green Corners, New York." The train ride was not as long as my trip to Watertown, New York. When we arrived at Elmira, New York, the station for Green Corners, we again lined up on the platform with our luggage. There were about eight of us this time. Chatting and smiling, a man and woman approached us. They checked the tags of the first three boys and then checked mine.

"Welcome, Martin," the man said. "My name is Bill Jones, and this is my wife, Mary." I nodded hello. I was nervous and shy, but they seemed like nice people.

Mr. Jones picked up my suitcase, and we walked to his car. It was a very old car, with a big, long gearshift. In the back, there was something called a rumble seat, a sort of one-seat convertible. Mr. Jones asked if I would like to sit in it for the ride home, and I said yes. He and his wife got into the car, and we drove off. Riding along in the rumble seat past farm after farm, I already felt at home.

Home for the Joneses was also a farm, with a house, a barn, a chicken coop, a tractor, tools, and cows grazing in fenced-in fields as far as I could see. The Joneses had no children of their own. They treated me like a son who had just returned home from a very long trip to some faraway place. Mr. Jones asked if I would like to help him feed the chickens. “Oh, yeah,” I said. That was the beginning of working on a real farm. He even let me milk the cows.

There was no indoor plumbing, just an outhouse. But in a room in the main house, there was a big barrel, which served as a bathtub once a week when Mr. Jones filled it with warm water. It was the best bath I ever had. One afternoon one of his neighbors came by with his son, who was about my age. Mr. Jones and his neighbor took us over to a hill and put us inside the inner rims of two big tractor tires. They pushed us down the hill, and we rolled head over heels. It was the best ride of my life.

The two weeks flew by. Suddenly, it seemed, I was saying goodbye to Mrs. Jones. I thanked her for everything, and I really meant it. Then Mr. Jones and I were back in the old car, along with another one of his neighbors, whom Mr. Jones was dropping off at a garage on the way to the station. As we drove along, Mr. Jones’s neighbor talked and talked, unable to complete a sentence without cursing. I didn’t mind. I had heard all those words before. But I could tell that Mr. Jones was becoming uneasy and upset with his friend.

When we arrived at the garage, his friend shook my hand, wished me good luck, and got out of the car. He thanked Mr. Jones for the lift, and they exchanged farewells. Mr. Jones got back into the car, and we drove away in silence. After a few minutes, he turned to me and said that he was sorry that I had to listen to all the cursing that his friend had done. I told him that it was OK. I didn't mind. He seemed like a nice man, and anyway it wasn't the first time in my life that I had heard those words. Mr. Jones smiled at me and said, "He is really a nice man, Martin, and a wonderful friend. Please forgive him. He couldn't help it. He's a Protestant."

The Protestants were back. I had always associated that word with Loretta, who never cursed. Now I had discovered that being Protestant was a mixed blessing. It might have won Loretta for me, but I might have wound up cursing a lot as well, like Mr. Jones's friend.

There were two guys on my block whom my mother didn't want me to play with or be with, Pat (Sonny) Dolan and Richie (Crumb) Norris. Why Sonny was Sonny, I never knew, but Crumb was Crumb because what he loved to eat most were the crumbs of buns and cakes. Even as a kid, "Sonny" sounded all right as a nickname, but "Crumb" didn't seem like something that you wanted everyone to call you. Sonny and Crumb were always a step ahead of the rest of us in diagnosing how the world worked, what was a scheme, who was a sucker, and how to put something over on someone, preferably an unsuspecting someone.

We were all in the eighth grade and almost the same age, thirteen or fourteen. When they weren't playing hooky, however, Sonny and Crumb attended public school, while I attended Catholic school. I was a good student, well-behaved and obedient. Maybe that was what attracted me to them so much. They made their own rules and obeyed no others. At least it seemed that way to me. They were everything I wasn't, which I found exciting.

One summer day Sonny asked me if I wanted to help them do something really exciting. I agreed without thinking. The next day,

I met with both Sonny and Crumb, and we discussed the "something exciting." We were going to rob the PAL, the Police Athletic League. The PAL was and is an organization that provides recreational opportunities to New York City kids who do not have access to wide-open spaces, swimming pools, ball fields, and gyms. In the summertime, the PAL sponsors "play streets," streets that are closed to traffic and used as large playgrounds for kids of all ages.

In order to provide recreation and games for hundreds of children, the PAL supplies dozens of volley balls, basketballs, footballs, and softballs. Each evening the play-street supervisory staff collects all these balls and other supplies and stores them in a safe place in one of the buildings on the block. Sonny and Crumb, ever alert to opportunity, had discovered where these supplies were being stored. This was the something exciting that they presented to me as a great opportunity.

They had already planned how to get into the building (the door was left open during the day for staff access). And they had already planned how to make their getaway (over a fence in the backyard leading to another street). I was wondering why they needed me until Crumb said, "There will be a lot to carry."

I asked them what we were going to do with all those balls and supplies. "We got somebody to sell them to," answered Sonny. Anxious to be part of this exciting plan, I asked no more questions. The big day would be the next afternoon at three, when the staff usually took a soda break down at the corner of the play street.

The next afternoon came, and I was more nervous than excited. I even began to think of dropping out, but I knew Sonny and Crumb would give me a hard time and call me a chicken. I was afraid of being scorned more than I was of getting into a lot of trouble if we were caught. At three, as the staff drank their sodas at the corner of Manhattan Avenue, we entered the building one by one, with Sonny in the lead. Everything was stored downstairs, just outside the superintendent's apartment.

Under our shirts and inside our pants, we had stuffed large onion sacks that Sonny had collected. We would quickly fill the sacks with the loot and make our way out the back and over the fence. We found piles of basketballs, volley balls, and softballs. Even some checker games. Nobody was around. Everything was going according to plan. We quickly filled up the bags and tied the tops so that they could be dropped over the fence. Then we went out into the backyard and rushed over to the fence.

Crumb climbed halfway up the fence, low enough for us to hand him the bags and high enough for him to throw them over the top and onto the street. With only three bags left, we tied them to our pants and started to climb the fence. Out of nowhere materialized a police car in front of us and a screaming PAL staff behind us. The great getaway had been foiled. We were trapped, caught in the act and in a whole lot of trouble. Now it was really something exciting.

While the cops in the police car guarded our loot that lay on the street, the PAL staff marched us back into the building with the three remaining sacks of stolen goods on our backs. They made us walk out the front door of the building, where a crowd of kids was waiting and yelling at us for trying to steal the sports equipment from their play street. With the bags on our backs, the PAL supervisor and two staff members marched us down the block, across Columbus Avenue, and over to the police station two blocks away.

By the time we arrived at the police station, the patrol car had already brought over our intended loot, which was piled up in front of the sergeant's desk. The desk was quite high. To a thirteen-year-old, it resembled a small building. We were immediately surrounded by police officers. The sergeant banged something on his desk and told the surrounding police officers to take us into the detectives' room. He would decide what to do with us.

We were escorted into the detectives' room and told to sit on three chairs in a corner. After a few minutes, a detective walked in and introduced himself. "Are you the guys who robbed the police?" he asked. I nodded in the affirmative while Crumb and Sonny stared into space. "Robbing the police is a very serious crime," he continued. "In this case, I would guess you could go to prison for about ten years."

Ten years in prison! I started crying. Crumb and Sonny gave me a dirty look.

"The last guy who stole from us got twenty years, but he was older. Right now the sergeant is deciding what to do with you. When you steal from the police, it is up to the sergeant to sentence you. All I can say is that this sergeant is the toughest guy I ever worked for, and I've been a cop for fifteen years."

Crumb and Sonny were still staring into space, apparently unconcerned and not paying attention to what the detective had been saying.

An officer entered the room and said the sergeant wanted to see us for sentencing. I continued crying. We stood up, and the officer and detective escorted us out to see the sergeant for sentencing. Once again the sergeant banged something on his desk that sounded official, like a judge. He didn't ask us any questions. He just sentenced us.

"I hereby sentence you three boys, Patrick, Richard, and Martin, to bring your mothers down here to the police station to see me so that they and I can discuss your behavior and your crime. Bring them here before six this afternoon."

We left in silence and went our separate ways home. Ten years in prison was beginning to sound all right, compared to what I thought my mother's reaction might be. She usually returned home from work (she was a telephone operator) around five fifteen or five thirty. What would I tell her? Postponing the inevitable, I wanted to get her down to the police station before she found out what I had done. Waiting for her was sheer agony.

Finally, at five twenty, she walked down the block with a shoe box under her arm.

"Hi, Mom."

"Hi, Marty. Were you waiting for me?"

"Yes, because you have to come down to the police station…to sign a permission slip so that I can go on a PAL trip next week. It has to be signed today before six, or I won't be able to go."

The police station was only a half block away, on One Hundredth Street between Columbus and Amsterdam Avenues. We walked down the street while I tried to act like I didn't have a care in the world.

We walked up the iron steps that led to the entrance to the station house. When we entered, the sergeant called over to us, "Good afternoon, Mrs. Keefe."

"Good afternoon," my mother responded. "Marty said that I have to sign something so that he can go on a PAL trip."

"Well, I'm afraid that's not true, Mrs. Keefe, and that's not the only wrong thing that your son has done today."

"What do you mean?" asked my mother indignantly.

"Mrs. Keefe, your son was just arrested for stealing basketballs and other supplies from the PAL."

"Impossible!" yelled my mother in reply. "Not my Marty!"

"Yes, your Marty, Mrs. Keefe. I'm afraid that it's true," said the sergeant slowly and solemnly.

The dreaded moment had arrived. My mother turned to me and asked if what the sergeant said was true. I nodded silently in agreement.

"I can't believe this," she said in disgust.

The sergeant then said we were free to go. There would be no record of what I had done because the sergeant, addressing my mother, was sure that "You will convince Marty of the error of his ways. Good evening to you, Mrs. Keefe."

We walked out the front door of the station house and proceeded down the iron stoop. Before we reached the bottom of the stoop, my mother had opened her shoe box and had begun pummeling me over the head with a new high-heeled shoe.

"You will never do that again!" she yelled. "You will never again drag me down to a police station to be embarrassed by your behavior. You are a disgrace!" This was followed by another whack on the head.

Our walk home was punctuated by these periodic whacks, my reward for a short-lived career of crime. I couldn't blame her. It was so stupid to have done what I did.

Sonny and Crumb never showed up at the police station.

The building on Morningside Heights was old and very beautiful, with a mahogany-lined elevator, which took me to Franklin's sixth-floor apartment. (An elevator in an apartment building was itself a new experience for me.) I rang the bell. Franklin opened the door and welcomed me. I took a step in and suddenly entered a new world. I had never seen such a large apartment, such high ceilings.

I was in the eighth grade, a student at Holy Name Catholic School on Amsterdam Avenue and Ninety-Seventh Street. I was visiting the home of a classmate, Franklin Borchardt, whose father was a professor at Columbia University. His home was like no home I had ever visited or seen before, except perhaps in a movie.

Franklin was named Franklin as a sign of respect and gratitude to President Roosevelt, for welcoming his family to America. They fled Nazi Germany, where Franklin's father had been a professor of philosophy at the University of Göttingen. Because Professor Borchardt was Jewish, he had been forbidden to teach. Franklin's mother was a Lutheran who had converted to Catholicism, which explained why Franklin was sitting next to me in Holy Name Catholic School.

Franklin was the smartest student in the class. He also spoke German, which impressed me to no end. I have always found, and still find, the incomprehensible to be not only mysterious but impressive. It has always been a marvel to me that sequences of totally different, seemingly random sounds could mean exactly what I meant by the English words that I used.

It was not uncommon to hear Spanish and Italian spoken in my neighborhood, but German was rare, especially since World War II had just ended a few years earlier, leaving most things German avoided and unpopular. Except for a few Spanish and Italian phrases that I had learned, foreign languages remained foreign to me in grammar school. Only in high school would the strange sounds of other languages, Latin and French, be transformed into meaning.

What impressed me most was Franklin's missal, which he brought to the nine o'clock mass every Sunday. The pages on the right were in Latin, and the pages on the left were in German. Latin and German together presented a combination of incomprehensibility and mystery that left me dazzled.

My first impression of Franklin's apartment was of the thick carpeting everywhere I looked. Next, invisibly filling the room, was the soft sound of classical music. I knew it was classical music because I had heard something similar in Miss Fisher's music class at school. Then I saw flickers of candlelight coming from the two candles on the dining-room table. I had only seen such apartments in the movies. I didn't think anyone actually lived this way. But obviously Franklin did. And he was totally unpretentious about it. It was his normal world. I felt welcomed and intimidated at the same time.

Franklin's parents asked me to take a seat next to the coffee table in the living room, where the four of us proceeded to have a conversation, another novelty to me. Franklin's parents actually asked for my opinion about school, the Korean War, President Truman, and my plans for high school. I was not accustomed to having my opinions solicited with such interest by adults who seemed to value and respect what I thought. I was both nervous and grateful for the opportunity.

It was during this conversation that I noticed the book on the coffee table. It was a large book with a beautiful photograph of Chartres Cathedral, with "Cathedral" spelled "Kathedrale." At first I thought it was a misspelling, but then I realized that German words must use *K* instead of *C*, at least sometimes.

One of the Christian Bothers in Holy Name School had once told us a story about Chartres Cathedral, a story that, for me, brought the cathedral to life. He made me realize that monuments, simple stones upon stones, could have meaning and tell a story, like words in languages. The Chartres Cathedral that we know was rebuilt after the previous cathedral was destroyed by a fire in the year 1194. Between that time and the consecration of the new cathedral in 1260, artisans and workmen came from all over Europe to assist in the rebuilding. Generations of stonemasons, sculptors, stained-glass-window makers, and other artisans carried on the work over six decades. The cathedral would be completed by the grandsons of those who had begun it.

As I heard this story, the stones and windows transformed, for me, into the people who made them. Chartres Cathedral became a living thing, a community of shared purpose, of people who, in a sense, had worked together even though they had never met. And because of the book before me on Franklin's coffee table, Chartres Cathedral would always be Chartres Kathedrale.

I can't remember who died. I think it might have been a cousin of my mother. I do remember returning from New Jersey to Manhattan after the funeral. We were riding in my Uncle Marty's 1936 blue Ford, which he always polished to a shine, making it look newer than a brand-new car. The year was 1946 or 1947, not long after the war.

We returned to Manhattan through the Lincoln Tunnel. Uncle Marty pulled the car over to the curb somewhere along Forty-Second Street. He, my aunt, and cousins had to go over to the East Side to go home. We would take the subway to the Upper West Side from Forty-Second Street.

I think my Aunt Mary and my two cousins, Marty and Maryellen, were happy to see my mother, uncle, sister, and me get out of the car. The 1936 Ford had been tightly packed with four adults and four children. As we walked along Forty-Second Street and stretched our legs on the way to the subway station, my mother asked if we were hungry. My sister and I screamed, "Yes!"

Somewhere around Ninth or Tenth Avenue, we saw a diner. It looked old and somewhat run-down, but we went in anyway. It had been a long morning, and we were all hungry. We sat in a shabby booth and waited for the waitress, who seemed in no rush to serve anyone. When we finally got her attention, she came to the table, gave us menus, and walked away.

Something about that diner must have done something to our appetites. When the waitress returned to take our orders, my mother, sister, and I each ordered just a slice of apple pie. Not even with ice cream. Only my uncle ordered something from the menu, franks and beans. Soon the waitress returned with coffee for my mother and uncle and a glass of milk for my sister and me.

A few minutes later the three slices of pie arrived, followed by the franks and beans, which were served on a large, old, and battered metal plate. It looked like a plate that I had seen in prison movies, where desperate prisoners seemed happy to eat anything served on anything. For some reason, looking at that plate made me sad. Looking at my uncle eat off it made me even sadder.

He ate hungrily, sitting next to us yet far away in a small universe centered on that old, metal plate. He had no idea that watching him eat made me sad. And I didn't know exactly why observing him made me sad, which, in the end, might have been the saddest thing of all.

Hell's Kitchen was the neighborhood in which my mother and uncle, her brother, had been born and raised. The neighborhood had a reputation worthy of its name. There were a lot of Irish immigrants, most of whom worked on the nearby Hudson River docks as longshoremen. It had been and still was a tough neighborhood, where my family still had roots and friends, like Betty Truby, the owner of Truby's Bar and Grill on Tenth Avenue. Betty organized annual pilgrimages back to the old neighborhood in the form of bus-ride picnics that began and ended in front of her saloon. Having been suspended during the war, these bus rides had just resumed during the past summer.

My mother's family had lived on west Forty-Fourth Street between Tenth and Eleventh Avenues, a stone's throw from the docks where my grandfather had been a longshoreman. It was a neighborhood of shoulder-to-shoulder tenement buildings, punctuated here and there by a school or a vacant lot. My mother and father had both lived on Forty-Fourth Street before they were married. Many buildings housed small businesses on their ground floors, mostly grocery stores, bars, candy stores, and some newly arrived laundromats.

On Forty-Second Street between Eighth and Ninth Avenues stood Holy Cross Roman Catholic Church, the religious center of Hell's Kitchen, where my father had once been an altar boy. Like the neo-Gothic, red-brick church, it was a neighborhood where time seemed to stand still, yesterday and tomorrow indistinguishable from today.

Hell's Kitchen was also a neighborhood that didn't let go, even when you moved away. For decades after leaving, my aunt Dolly would ride the subway back down to Hell's Kitchen once a week to visit her friend, Mrs. Kelly. This was a neighborhood that you carried with you, one that would always define you.

My uncle had been in the Army during the war. In fact, for a number of years before the war, he had been an enlisted man in the National Guard, the Fighting Sixty-Ninth, a primarily Irish

American reserve unit, housed in an armory on Lexington Avenue and Twenty-Seventh Street. Uncle Tommy eventually was commissioned as a second lieutenant in 1940, just before the war. But something, forever secret and never explained, happened. He lost his commission and left the National Guard. He was later drafted back into the Army during the war.

Ironically the Army and the Fighting Sixty-Ninth remained the center of his life, at least in his mind. He spoke about the Army constantly, even though he went to work each day at Con Edison. Tommy never married. He would spend the rest of his life living with his two sisters, all the while becoming increasingly bitter and argumentative about his life's problems, which were, he was convinced, the fault of others.

When he was fired from Con Edison for poor performance, it was a crushing blow to his sense of self-worth, and he spiraled into an ever more profound bitterness. Simply because he was a male, however, he was a sort of fatherly presence in my life, although we rarely spoke and almost never did anything together. I do, however, have a fond memory of one Sunday afternoon in Central Park at 102nd Street, where he tried to teach my sister and me how to ride bicycles, a skill he himself never acquired. But, most of all, I remember that metal plate covered with franks and beans.

If you had been sitting at the bar in Kelly's saloon that Sunday afternoon five years after we had moved into my grandmother's apartment, you would have seen the faces of a girl and boy, noses pressed to the window, knocking on the glass, trying to get the attention of someone at the bar. Then a man sitting nearby would have turned to the sound of the knocking on the glass, nodded to the searching faces, got up from his stool, finished his glass of beer, and walked to the door.

Perhaps you might have known the man as a regular customer of Kelly's saloon. Perhaps you didn't. In any case, he was our uncle Tommy, who had promised to take my sister Rosemary and me bicycle riding in Central Park. We were interrupting his usual, Sunday-afternoon ritual of noon Mass at Holy Name Church, followed by a few beers at Kelly's. But he had promised to rent bikes for us and take us to Central Park that Sunday. A promise was a promise.

Squinting in the bright, early spring sunshine, Tommy emerged from Kelly's bar. He wasn't too happy. "Can't I have a beer in peace on my day off from work?" he asked.

"You promised to take us bike riding," my sister replied.

Tommy murmured something inaudible to himself and yelled, "OK! OK! Let's go."

Two smiling faces and one really grumpy one marched off, down Columbus Avenue to the bicycle store on Ninety-Seventh Street, where Tommy would rent bikes for us for forty cents an hour each, the going rate during the years immediately following World War II.

Central Park was just one block east of Columbus Avenue. We walked our bikes into the park, since we were forbidden to ride them on the street. My sister, three years older, was able to ride her bike, but I was just learning and needed help. That was Tommy's second task. Having paid for the bicycle rentals, he now had to hold me up as I learned to ride a bike on the traffic-free transverse of Central Park at 102nd Street.

As Tommy trotted along in his small-stepped stride, holding on to my bicycle seat to keep me from toppling over, I could hear his huffing and puffing. When we stopped periodically for him to catch his breath, which was already challenged by his constant cigarette smoking, I could see the sweat streaming down his forehead. In the meantime, Rosemary continued to happily ride her bike in circles, taunting me now and again for not mastering bike riding faster.

After about forty-five minutes, Tommy, drained and drenched, said that it was time to return the bikes to the store. Rosemary and I objected to no avail. We, with Tommy holding on to my bicycle seat, rode our bikes to the edge of the park. From there, we walked our bikes back to the store. As we strolled along Columbus Avenue, Tommy continued wiping his brow with his handkerchief, all the way to the bike shop.

He didn't like sports or going to baseball games, so we didn't share much in common. He would one day buy bicycles for my sister and me, but he would never again be interested in being a part of our bike riding. Tommy and a friend of his did, however, once take me to see a boxing match. He even bought me two pairs of boxing gloves. But my mother soon took them away after I challenged a friend to box with me and he knocked me out.

That day in the park, the first and last time that Tommy and I ever really did anything together, would be the closest we would ever be to each other for the rest of our lives. I would have to find a father or a big brother somewhere else. And I did, in the Christian Brothers who taught me at Holy Name Grammar School.

They could do everything. They were not only the smartest, most educated men I knew. They were also the best athletes. Most of all, they cared and seemed to have all the time in the world for us boys. They gave up their weekends to take us hiking, to practice sports, to improve our grades, or just to give us whatever support we needed. They became my idea of what it was to be a real man. I wanted to become one of them, and I did. Or at least I tried to become one of them.

On Tuesday, September 2, 1952, at the age of thirteen, I boarded a train for Barrytown, New York, home of the Junior Seminary of the Christian Brothers. There I would spend three blissful years of study, prayer, and sports, surrounded by many virtual fathers and brothers. I learned to love learning and self-discipline, even though I often struggled with the latter. What I absorbed during those years, mostly unconsciously, would guide me for the rest of my life, despite frequent lapses and failures.

Until that fateful day in high school, I had always assumed that I could sing. I didn't know anyone who couldn't sing. Or maybe I couldn't tell if somebody could or couldn't sing. In any case, it came as a complete shock to me when I was told I couldn't sing. Worst of all, I learned this at age thirteen, the age when you are threatened on all sides with absolute uncertainty about absolutely everything.

The person who made me aware of this missing talent was Brother Benjamin Benedict, the Music Director at St. Joseph's Normal Institute in Barrytown, New York. St. Joseph's was a religious school, a sort of minor seminary for the training of Christian Brothers, the teachers who staffed many of the Catholic schools in the New York area. These Brothers were my heroes in grammar school, and I wanted to become one of them.

So there I was one day at the beginning of freshman year, in the middle of the large chapel at St. Joseph's, singing along with about three or four hundred Brothers and Brothers-to-be. We did a lot of singing in Barrytown because we spent a lot of time in the chapel. We sang primarily Gregorian chant, a simple musical form that I still love to this day, despite my painful experience in trying to master it.

Along with the other hundreds of Brothers and would-be Brothers, I was singing the "Gloria" loudly and confidently in Latin. Our eyes were directed to the front of the chapel where we followed the direction of Brother Benjamin Benedict, who stood upon a podium so that all in the chapel could see him no matter where they were seated.

I saw Brother Benedict slowly raise his right hand to his right ear, cupping it into a sort of hearing aid. His eyes, moving quickly left to right, intensely perused the congregation. He looked as if he had been betrayed, as if an enemy had infiltrated his choir. As he descended from the podium, the look of betrayal suddenly turned to one of determined action. Whoever the culprit was, he didn't have a chance.

Brother Benedict, right hand cupped to ear, continued directing with his left hand, as he walked slowly down the center aisle of the chapel. We continued singing and following his direction. He arrived at my row and stopped walking forward. Instead he slid, as silent and slippery as a serpent, across my row and stopped in front of me. His hand fell from his ear, and the look of concentration disappeared from his face, as he commanded, "Do not sing; just move your lips."

Several other offenders were rooted out that day by Brother Benedict. We became the newest members of a group called the "nonsingers," composed of a half-dozen upper classmen, some of whom had already been moving their lips for three years. At least once a week, the entire school was reminded of the existence of our special group, since each weekly choir practice began with Brother Benjamin Benedict commanding, "Nonsingers, please leave the room."

Several years later I was on the altar as a server one Sunday morning, turning missal pages for a quirky, old priest, whom we called Pop Carol. He could be a bit threatening, but I liked him because he couldn't sing a note, either, something that I could identify with and found comforting. In the middle of the Mass, as I turned to a new page, a large fly landed on the passage that Pop Carol had begun to chant with his usual atonality.

Suddenly he stopped chanting. Stealthily he put his right hand into his left sleeve and slowly pulled out a flyswatter. With a single, quick, sharp, accurate swat, he dispatched the fly and brushed it off the missal. Turning to me with a mischievous smile of self-satisfaction, he said solemnly, "Protestant fly."

I quickly and earnestly prayed that Loretta, my first and only love, might be alive and happy, wherever she was.

My first encounter in the chapel with Brother Benedict did not presage future harmony in our relationship, which only worsened over time as he discovered that I was totally inept at everything he taught, such as piano and arts and crafts. Painful as this sometimes was, I soon learned that all pain is not the same. Some pains are so bad that all other pain fades away. Three years later I encountered one of those pains.

We had just eaten the kind of enormous lunch that only hungry teenagers can devour effortlessly: multiple grilled cheeseburgers, corn on the cob, potato salad, baked beans, and, to add healthy balance, fruit salad. We sat on the beach talking and laughing, hoping for speedy digestion so that we could return to the refreshing waters of Lake Taghkanic, a beautiful lake about ninety miles north of New York City.

It was a warm, sunny, July day in 1955 with no homework and no stress, a fun day of swimming and boating on the lake. The major attraction was a big raft anchored about thirty yards from the beach. A wooden tower with a ladder had been erected on the raft. It was possible to climb up and jump off the tower into the lake from several different levels. All morning long there had been an endless sequence of climbing, jumping, splashing, swimming back to the raft, and climbing the tower once again.

At noon, we were whistled in for lunch. We were awaiting the next whistle to tell us we could return to the water and, most of all, the raft with the tower. For our own protection, we were each assigned a buddy for the day. It was the responsibility of each of us to be aware of our buddy's location and to be attentive to his safety, particularly in the deeper water between the beach and the raft.

As we sat on the beach waiting for the whistle, we bragged or lied to each other about the number of times we had jumped off the raft tower during the morning. Danny, a soft-spoken guy from Rhode Island, said, with his funny New England accent, that he would like to try it but was afraid of deep water. His buddy, Mike Payne, told him he would do fine. I said that I would swim to the raft with him. We would all help him and keep an eye on him. "Nothing to worry about, Danny. You will love the raft," we all seemed to say in unison.

The whistle finally sounded, and most of the boys went running into the water. The six of us surrounding Danny were still trying to persuade him to come out to the raft with us. He declined at first, then wavered, and finally, with our increasingly insistent encouragement, agreed. We told him that there would be no problem since we would surround him on the way out to the raft and back to the beach. Once on the raft, he could jump in close to the ladder, climb back up, and do it again and again. He would love it, and Mike Payne would be happy because he had not been able, as Danny's buddy, to go to the raft in the morning.

A few minutes later the seven of us were on our way out to raft, six of us circling around Danny to make him feel safe. Soon we were on the raft, and everyone climbed up and ran over to the tower ladder. Danny said he was going to sit on the side of the raft for a while. We assumed this was because he needed a break from the stress of the swim out. The rest of us joined the small horde that was already scrambling up the tower ladder and jumping with abandon into the dark, green water of the lake.

Summer visits to Lake Taghkanic were a beloved ritual at St. Joseph's Normal Institute. Our days were filled with prayer, study, and sports. In the summer, the study tapered off, and the sports increased. But the prayer remained constant. We were in the first phase of training to become teachers in Catholic schools and, perhaps, Catholic colleges.

For city boys, Barrytown was a paradise on the banks of the Hudson River. Besides being a working farm, there were hundreds of acres of green, a rarity in New York City. We even had our own pond where we learned to ice skate and play ice hockey. If the ice was perfectly solid and smooth, school would be closed for the day so that we could skate. Sometimes at night when the ice was right and the moon was full, we were permitted to skate around the pond, stopping only for the hot chocolate brought out to counter a chill that no one ever felt. It was magical.

The emphasis on academics and religion was balanced by daily, physical exercise. Hockey and basketball in the winter, football in the fall, baseball in the spring and summer, and, of course, swimming in the summer as well. Normally we swam in the Hudson River, which bordered the property. The Brothers had acquired a pontoon raft as army surplus after World War II and anchored it about twenty yards offshore. The river was quite shallow along the beach, so reaching the raft was no problem, even for those who could not swim very well. Lake Taghkanic, of course, was quite different.

The raft was the noisiest place in the entire park in which Lake Taghkanic was situated. Screaming, yelling, chasing, jumping, plunging, daring, doing, and not doing. I remember stopping for a moment to talk to Danny, who had remained seated on the side of the raft.

"I'm doing fine just sitting here," Danny told me in his gentle voice, difficult to hear amid all the noise. "I don't think I'm ready to jump back in yet." I climbed back up the tower ladder and jumped back in the lake. All was well. I hoped the day would never end.

The endless human loop of climbing, jumping, and swimming continued uninterrupted. As I was climbing back on to the raft later in the afternoon, somebody asked if I had seen Danny. "Yes," I replied, "but it was a while ago. He wasn't swimming. He was just sitting right over there on the side of the raft with his legs dangling in the water. Ask Mike Payne. He must know."

"Mike doesn't know where he is," somebody yelled.

Panic suddenly washed over us like a breaking wave. Everyone began to jump in the water and dive down, around and under the raft. It was impossible to see very far in the dark water of the lake. Several boys swam back to the beach to see if Danny had returned there on his own or with someone else. Danny was not on the beach. We continued to dive and search under the raft, but the dark waters, even in the bright sunshine, prevented us from seeing anything except what we could reach at arm's length and touch.

One of the Brothers arrived on the raft with several lifeguards, who proceeded to dive and search. Again nothing—a result both hopeful and discouraging at the same time. Maybe Danny had gone for a walk by himself or had taken out a rowboat, neither of which we were supposed to do alone. We returned to the beach, where the Brothers had organized a search of the woods behind the shoreline. The lifeguards summoned all the boats on the lake back to shore. Danny was nowhere to be found.

A heavy silence fell upon us like a gloomy night. At five in the afternoon, we were told to line up to board our buses back to Barrytown. The lifeguards and the police would continue the search and would, without doubt, find Danny, who had probably become lost on a long walk in the surrounding woods. He would be OK.

We boarded the buses in silence. I cannot remember ever being enveloped by such a silence, even during all the hours that we spent in the chapel in silent prayer. We were, individually and collectively, grappling with disbelief and unspeakable fear. Each of us stayed locked in his private, silent world, confronting the possibility of the impossible having happened.

Suppose Danny was still in the water somewhere, hanging on to something, scared to death, with none of us there to help him? Danny did not drown, I insisted to myself, as much for Danny's sake as to relieve my own guilt and shame for having encouraged him to swim to the raft and then forgotten him.

That night for the first time in the three years that had passed since the night of our arrival in Barrytown as freshmen, I heard others crying, some sobbing, most of us trying to stifle the sounds. It seemed to take forever to fall asleep on a night when the weariness of endless repetitions of climb, jump, and swim would have normally brought swift slumber. Nobody slept, and the morning bell rang at five. We dressed and went to the chapel for morning prayers.

Brother John, the director, stood up in front of the chapel. He told us that divers had been brought in to aid in the search, which had continued with floodlights during the night. Several hours before, he received a call from the police captain directing the operation. They had found Danny's body somewhere beneath the raft. He might have become trapped and panicked. They would know more after the autopsy.

No one spoke then or for hours after. Danny Dundin, that gentle guy from Rhode Island, was dead. That wasn't possible. Not Danny. Nobody died at age sixteen. Our friends didn't die. God is good. How could he let this happen? There must have been some mistake. It couldn't be true. Not Danny! Not Danny!

It was my fault. I had begged him to come out to the raft. I had promised him that he would be fine. But I started having fun and forgot him. He wouldn't be dead if it hadn't been for me. Danny, can you forgive me? Danny, I am sorry, so terribly sorry.

I was alone with my feelings, but we were all suffering together, especially the six of us who had begged Danny to come out to the raft, the six of us who had promised to take care of him and hadn't.

Danny was dressed in the black-and-white habit of the Christian Brothers for his wake, the habit he would have received a year later when, with the rest of us, he would have completed high school. Danny's parents came down from Rhode Island. Sad and accepting, they took him back home to his final resting place. As we watched their car pull away, trailing the hearse carrying Danny, we tried but were unable to imagine their unimaginable pain.

For several months before Danny's death, I had decided that I wanted to leave Barrytown and the religious life. Lacking the maturity, even after three years, to simply say that I wanted to leave, I managed, by acting out, to get myself thrown out. I left Barrytown, but Barrytown never left me.

I returned home, but the world was different. Leaving Barrytown was more like leaving my real home, because that was where my father and brothers lived. When I returned to my other home, it was a strange place, and not simply because my family had relocated to Washington Heights.

With the exception of the death of my grandmother when I was nine, one of my major memories of those early years is that of constant arguing, which substituted for discussion, sometimes even for hellos and good-byes. Complicating matters was the fact that Aunt Dolly was an epileptic. Medication to control epilepsy was not yet available in those days, so Dolly's seizures ("spells," we called them) were severe, frequent, initially frightening, but ultimately accepted as a fact of life, at least of our lives.

Uncle Tommy, who argued daily with Aunt Dolly, seemed otherwise relatively normal. For example, he had a real job at Con Edison, which was something Dolly couldn't do. But his grip on his job always seemed tenuous to me, even as a boy. He would later be fired when I was thirteen. This sad event would be followed by a sequence of menial jobs for the rest of his life. His failures at employment, however, in no way prevented him from having strong opinions on everything and even stronger criticisms of everyone, including my mother, Kitty (Catherine), whose work as a telephone operator supported the rest of us, including him.

Aunt Dolly, Uncle Tommy, and my mother all had nicknames—or rather, given all the arguing, noms de guerre. Aunt

Dolly had christened Uncle Tommy the Generalissimo, because he had been a PFC in the US Army during World War II. He never went overseas; in fact, he never left New York City, where he was assigned to the military post office. Despite that limitation, however, Dolly had no trouble quickly promoting him through the ranks to generalissimo.

Tommy, in turn, baptized Dolly as the Other One, a name he would use even when referring to her in her presence. Their exchanges and interactions could involve almost any subject. There was no issue that could not be argued. I particularly remember one discussion about the weather. The Generalissimo, sitting in the living room, said to no one in particular, "It looks like a nice day." The Other One immediately replied, "What are you now, a goddamned weatherman?"

The two of them, in turn, called my mother the Actress because of her dramatic, emotional reactions to their constant arguing. Whenever she couldn't stand anymore of their bickering, she would come into our tiny living room, where the debates usually took place, and pound her chest like Tarzan while screaming, "Stop! I can't take it anymore!"

That usually worked, but if it didn't, she would roll out her ultimate weapon: "If you don't stop, I am going to put my head in the oven!" Sometimes, she actually carried out this threat, but, as far as I know, never turned the gas on. In any case, the oven usually brought the arguments to a grumbling halt. All things considered, with or without the benefit of twenty-twenty hindsight, we were just one, big, unhappy family.

When my sister, Rosemary, was about thirteen, she followed the family tradition and gave Aunt Dolly another nickname. She had noticed—I noticed next to nothing—that Aunt Dolly never wore a brassiere, which, in the late 1940s, was considered extremely avant-garde and liberated. But Dolly was neither of these. She was just a forty-five-year-old woman who didn't wear a brassiere. With that image in mind, my sister's nom de guerre for Dolly required no additional explanation or background information. "Princess Hanging Ninnies" said it all.

Throughout our Washington Heights neighborhood, Aunt Dolly was known, with wary admiration and grudging appreciation, as a sort of impulsive crime stopper. By the 1950s, Dolly had availed herself of epilepsy medication, which enabled her to travel about more independently. As a result, she did a lot of the shopping and, in the process, discovered her crime-stopping skills. One day she was in a grocery store on Audubon Avenue, waiting in line to buy a container of milk. There were about six customers in the store at the time. A young man entered, pulled out a gun, ordered all of them to put their hands up, and told the owner to give him all the money in the cash register.

According to the eyewitnesses, the owner and the other customers, Dolly, without hesitation, ran behind the counter, stood in front of the owner, and began to berate the would-be stickup man.

"Why don't you get a job and earn your own money, you lazy son of a bitch? Get out of here and leave these people alone. You're no man. You're a punk and a coward."

The victims thought they would be shot as soon as the robber had dispatched Dolly. But Dolly continued, "Go on, get out of here. Get a job. Leave people alone."

Whatever plan the gunman had had, Dolly surely hadn't been part of it. He looked around nervously, seemingly confused. After a brief, silent hesitation, he suddenly shoved his gun back into his jacket and ran out the door. For a moment, everyone but Dolly remained silent with their hands still up in the air, while Dolly, who had never put her hands up during the attempted robbery, ran to the door, yelling "Stop, thief!" Dolly's daring deed won praise from the store owner, advice from the police, and a reputation for courageous madness throughout the neighborhood.

When I became a freshman at Manhattan College, my sister had already married and moved to her own apartment. Her departure might have made Dolly zero in on me a bit more. As a college freshman, I soon realized that I basically knew everything and would, from time to time, demonstrate my extensive knowledge by commenting on everything at home. Dolly, who had never given me a nickname (my sister and I had simply been known as "them"), responded by giving me a nickname based, apparently, on my newfound knowledge of everything. She began to call me the Big Bag of Shit.

Some evenings would find us all clustered around our black-and-white television set, the Actress, the Generalissimo, Princess Hanging Ninnies, and yours truly, the Big Bag of Shit. There was no agreement at all about what to watch. If I wanted to watch a baseball game, for example, Dolly would veto it because "It was a repeat. You saw it last night." Tommy always wanted to watch war movies. I assumed that was due to the lack of combat he had experienced in the post office. Kitty usually preferred to watch a program with a happy family in it, which, for me, was like science fiction.

Dolly liked sad movies. When I came home at night from my after-school job at St. Clare's Hospital, Dolly was usually watching a movie. I would always ask her what it was about, and she always responded with the same words: "It's sad. It's about life."

That was unforgettably sad.

I was holding the small cardboard box tightly with both hands as the train slowed to a halt at 242nd Street Van Cortland Park, the last stop on the IRT Number One subway line. The doors opened onto a sunlit platform. I exited the train and walked to the center of the open-air platform. Before opening the small, cardboard box, I asked a man passing by if he knew the time. He told me it was two twenty in the afternoon.

I thanked him and carefully opened the box. Inside the box was our blue, gray, and white homing pigeon, Duke, about to make his first solo flight. He hesitated briefly in the bright light and then flapped his wings and flew straight up into the blue. He circled slowly several times, high in the sky, surveying a part of New York City that he had never seen before. Suddenly he seemed to know exactly where he wanted to go. He banked left and darted south in a straight line. Duke was going home.

Home was the roof of an abandoned building on Columbus Avenue between Ninety-Eighth and Ninety-Ninth Streets. Sonny Dolan, Richie Norris, aka Crumb, and I owned about fifty pigeons, which we housed in a coop that we had bought for ten dollars. The pigeons were of various types, flights, baldies, owls, tipplets, teagers, and bronzes. Duke was our only homer and was named after Duke Snider, the center fielder for the Brooklyn Dodgers and a home-run hitter.

We had purchased Duke right after his birth. We had kept him in a separate, small coop while we trained him to return to the roof after late-afternoon flights. At six months of age, we felt he was ready for his first solo flight. That was how I wound up on the open-air platform at 242nd Street, seven and one-half miles away from Duke's home, a suitable distance, we believed, for his maiden voyage.

The station stop at Van Cortland Park also had the added advantage of allowing a passenger to take a return trip without paying another fare, since the station stop was the last on the Number One line. Following Duke, I boarded the next train south to Ninety-Sixth Street and Broadway, remembering that the man had told me it was two twenty just before I released Duke from the cardboard box.

Subways were for us kids like airlines. They took us from one world to another within minutes. New York City was a patchwork of neighborhoods and public spaces, which, although physically contiguous, were worlds apart socially, economically, and culturally. I was only eleven years old, but I could travel around these worlds endlessly, without a passport and for only a dime.

Six years later I was back on the subway platform at 242nd Street Van Cortland Park as a new freshman at Manhattan College.

For the next four years, I would ride the Number One train every morning from my home in Washington Heights. After my last class of the day, I would board the Number One train once again for a ride south to my after-school job at St. Clare's Hospital on Fifty-First Street between Ninth and Tenth Avenues.

Before long, I knew every station stop, every bend and curve along the route, and every apartment or factory building hugging the elevated tracks on either side. But sometimes the ride to work after school would be very different than the ride I had taken in the morning. Everything looked the same; the train accelerated, slowed, and lurched at the same places as it always did; yet everything seemed different.

On those days, I felt that I belonged to a world larger than the one I lived in, a world from which I had, in a sense, come and for which I was beginning to long, a world that I wanted to connect to but that remained too indefinite to describe. It was like a new and bigger home in which I had never been but one in which I knew that I would feel welcomed. It was a world called Europe, the Western civilization of which I was a member but hardly knew.

Manhattan College offered, at that time, a liberal arts program that chronologically mapped the evolution of Western civilization across the four years of our college life: from its ancient, classical, Greco-Roman roots in freshman year, through its medieval development in sophomore year, then across its post-Renaissance transformation into the modern world in junior year. The current state of Western culture, the contemporary world of the mid-twentieth century, concluded the program in senior year.

This evolution was traced via the disciplines of philosophy, history, literature, and fine arts during those four periods. In addition, courses in physics, chemistry, biology, psychology, mathematics, and foreign languages were required to complement and enhance our understanding of the evolution of Western civilization.

What had happened on those days when the world seemed different on the train ride to work after class? They were days of sudden awareness of my indebtedness. I had discovered that the world I knew, the world I took for granted, was born of an unblinking confrontation with life, a willingness to challenge and to be challenged, an openness to the disturbing loss of certainty.

I began to see the world as it had been before it became the world as I had always understood it. I came to realize that there was a time when the concepts of fate, destiny, tragic flaw, substance, and accident had yet to be distilled and harnessed by the Greeks out of the galloping confusion of human life. I could imagine the debate, as Parmenides stood on one bank gazing at the unchanging water, while Heraclitus waded across from the other side, never stepping in the same stream twice. I was there when the past was being forever transformed by the birth of new ideas.

Sometimes on the train ride to work, the world seemed different because I had learned something more immediate and personal, honest and true. Such as the day Dr. Mullaney, a philosophy professor, confessed his need to be best in something when he was in graduate school because he wasn't the best in his philosophy courses. As a result, he had the shiniest shoes in graduate school. Or the day Harry Blair, an English professor, held up a copy of *The Complete Works of Shakespeare* and said solemnly, "This, gentlemen, is my Bible, the complete exposition of the human condition."

One afternoon as the train rumbled south, I sat staring out the window, still spellbound by the words of Miroslav Turek, professor of contemporary history. He was a Czechoslovakian who had witnessed Hitler's triumphant entry into Prague months after the Western Allies had betrayed the Czechs in the Sudetenland. He transported us into the silent throngs that helplessly witnessed their defeat. He made us angry. He made us feel shame. He inspired us. He made us want to act, like the students in the opening section of Erich Remarque's *All Quiet on the Western Front*, but in defense of Czechoslovakia rather than the Fatherland.

William Reilly, a professor of medieval philosophy, and known affectionately, therefore, as William of Levittown, where he lived on Long Island, concluded a debate one day on the ethics of the atomic bombing of Japan and the end of World War II:

"I was an infantryman in General Patton's Third Army," William of Levittown said. "We had beaten Germany. I had survived without a scratch all the way from Normandy to the Elbe River. We were told we were going to be part of the coming invasion of Japan.

"Combined casualties were predicted to be over one million. I wasn't going to be so lucky a second time. Then we got the news. Atomic bombs had been dropped on Hiroshima and Nagasaki. Tens of thousands had been killed, and Japan had surrendered. I was happy that we had dropped those bombs. Let me know in our next class if I was I right or wrong and why. No more than two hundred and fifty words."

The factory and apartment buildings we passed on the ride to work seemed strangely fragile that afternoon in 1959. We were in the middle of the Cold War. New York could be Hiroshima or Nagasaki. Perhaps for the first time, I had the Japanese perspective on atomic bombs.

The best subway ride to work came in senior year after I was accused of plagiarizing a paper I had written on Flaubert, "The Living Death of Madame Bovary." Although accused of an academic crime, I was flattered and elated because I knew I had not plagiarized my paper. It was all mine. I was told by the professor that he was going to fail me because "No undergraduate could write such a paper" as the one I had written. That was quite an accolade. I smiled all the way to work. The world was truly different that day. Eventually the professor accepted the fact that the paper was mine, but that was almost anticlimactic.

After my last exam on the last day of my senior year in college, I stood on the platform overlooking Van Cortland Park. I thought of the subway rides to work after school during the previous four years and the way that the world would irreversibly change on some days. There was something painful about learning. It was a form of separation, taking leave of the known world for the unknown, discovering the new, and bidding good-bye to the old and sometimes, in subtle ways, even to family and friends.

I thought of our homing pigeon, Duke, who knew his way home from the spot where I was standing. But I was no longer sure where home was. I was only sure that this was not the last stop.

UNFINISHED WORK

Life's challenges often require a virtuous response. Skill is required, however, to know which virtue to summon to meet the challenge. The required virtue is not always a glorious one, like courage, commitment, or perseverance. At certain moments in one's life, in fact, the most important virtue might be one's ability to remain anonymous. Anonymity is like being invisible, even though you aren't. You are always present, never absent, but somehow you go unnoticed. This was, and probably still is, the most important survival skill in military training, particularly basic training.

I began my basic training in August 1961, at Fort Dix, New Jersey. It began the way I assume it always had, with a lot of screaming ("idiot" was a favorite), pushing, shoving, intimidating. It seemed to be a novel way of saying, "Welcome. Nice to have you here." As we stood in a huge mass, our names were called out alphabetically for assignment to one of four platoons in the training company, Company Q, Fourth Training Regiment.

Upon hearing our names called, we had been instructed to respond with a loud yell of "Here, Sergeant," while grabbing our big sack of new army uniforms and supplies and running over to join the formations of our still-forming platoons. Along the way, we were assisted by the pushes, shoves, and screams of a gauntlet of noncommissioned officers.

I was very attentive as the sergeant worked his way through the alphabet down to *K* and yelled, "Keefe!" I grabbed my bag and ran over to my new platoon. The next name was Keegan, belonging to a big redheaded guy from Boston. He, too, ran over with his large duffel bag to stand next to me.

The next name proved to be a problem for the sergeant, whose extended pause brought on a cascading silence across the entire drill field. Finally, he asked, "What kind of f**king name is this?" This was followed by "Kranaki." No response. "Kystraki." No response. "Kryfski." Again no response.

Finally, the increasingly angry sergeant yelled, "Kryftofski!" A hand went up slowly from the middle of the huddled mass still waiting for their names to be called. "Do you mean Krystoforski, Sergeant?" asked the shy, halting voice of the man attached to the raised arm.

The sergeant angrily threw his clipboard on the ground and with long, deliberate steps strode over to Krystoforski. Upon reaching him, he put his nose right up against the nose of the trembling trainee.

In a voice that could be heard throughout Fort Dix, the sergeant screamed, "With a f**king name like yours, you oughta answer 'here' to anything! From now on, you got a new f**king name. Alphabet. That's your name. Got it? What's your name?"

"Alphabet," answered Krystoforski.

"Can't hear you!" bellowed the sergeant.

"Alphabet," yelled Krystoforski.

"Get over there to your f**king platoon, Alphabet," ordered the sergeant.

Krystoforski grabbed his bag, ran over and lined up next to Keegan. He had become the first fatality in the army's war on anonymity. We were all secretly grateful to Krystoforski for taking the heat off the rest of us. At least for a while.

When the huddled mass finally disappeared into an empty patch of drill field, we were turned over to our platoon sergeants, who took us on a tour of our barracks. We learned that the red-painted butt cans were not for butts. They were to be filled daily with fresh, clean water so that they would always be ready for inspection, their real reason for being. We were assigned bunks and ordered, "Lights out in five minutes." The lights went out, and we gratefully climbed into our bunks. It was ten at night, the end of our first day in basic training.

Sleep was brief. Around midnight, the lights were turned on. "Downstairs, in uniform, in two minutes!" shouted our platoon sergeant, Sergeant Herbert. We dressed quickly and rushed down to join our platoons lined up in front of the barracks. Standing in the middle of the drill field were the commanding officer, Captain Naumann; the first sergeant, Sergeant Hansen; and the drill sergeant, Sergeant Colavita. The platoon sergeants took roll call and reported, "All present and accounted for," to the first sergeant, who smartly returned their salutes before addressing us in a serious and solemn tone.

"Listen up, you six-month sacks of shit." (Most of us were, in fact, reservists, on six months of active duty before returning to our national guard or army reserve units and civilian life.) "You a**holes thought you were going to play soldier for six months and then go home to your girlfriends, who, as I speak, are screwing your 4-F friends. Well, they are going to be screwing for a long time because you sacks of shit ain't going home for a long time, if ever.

"You know why you ain't going home for a long time? Because those f**king Russkies just built a big wall. And they didn't build it in Siberia. They built it in the middle of f**king Berlin. So you six-month sacks of shit are now in for the duration, however long it takes to send those f**king Russkies back to Moscow. Some of you won't have to stay too long, though, because those f**king Russkies are going to shoot your ass. Tomorrow morning I want every swinging dick in this company out here at reveille, begging to kill himself some Russkies. Company dismissed."

Not an auspicious beginning to basic training, I thought, as I sat on my bunk, unaware that there would be even more bad news in just a few weeks when, at mail call, I would join Krystoforski in the ranks of those unfortunate soldiers who had been stripped of their anonymity. Back in civilian life, which seemed to have been years before, I had been dating a fourth-grade schoolteacher named Patricia. She was a lovely woman, extremely thoughtful and caring. These virtues led her to instruct her students to write a brief note to a soldier in the army defending America, me. Which they did, all forty of them.

The mail-call ritual called for an NCO (noncommissioned officer) to distribute the mail in front of a company formation, with two hundred basic trainees standing at attention, hoping to hear their names called. To receive one letter was a blessing; two drew some attention; three or more on the same day turned the trainee into a bright, inextinguishable neon light.

For the first time since starting training, I heard my name called. I left ranks and marched smartly toward the sergeant. I approached him, saluted, took my letter, about-faced, and began to return to my platoon in the same manner. Before I could reach my squad, however, I heard "Keefe" once again. I about-faced, returned to the sergeant, saluted, and took my second letter.

As I about-faced once again and started to march away, I heard "Keefe" again. Once more, I about-faced to the sergeant, who then began reading the names on the next batch of letters, all of which were addressed to me. As I stood before the sergeant, saluting, he yelled to the assembled trainees, "This guy must be a movie star, like f**king Elvis. He gets more mail than President Kennedy."

Standing eyeball to eyeball with me, he screamed, "Are you one of them Hollywood movie stars? You must be. You got all this fan mail here," he yelled as he counted my letters. "Forty! Forty letters to Hollywood, our own f**king movie star! Get back in your platoon, Hollywood!"

The worst had happened. I had a new name, and everyone knew it. Now I was just like Alphabet, who would become my best friend in basic training because we were going to spend so much time together. Whenever something had to be cleaned, picked up, moved in, moved out, carried away, dug up, filled in, polished, swept, mopped, counted, loaded, or unloaded, the sergeants couldn't keep themselves from yelling, "Alphabet, Hollywood! Get the f**k over here!"

If the task to be done, however, required more than our combined skills, others were chosen, apparently at random, to assist us. After eight weeks of carrying out these details, as they were called, I saw a pattern. All those called upon to assist Alphabet and Hollywood had, by more than coincidence, monosyllabic names. In basic training, obviously the most dangerous name to have, next to an unpronounceable one, was a name that was too easy to pronounce.

As the end of basic training approached, we became eligible for a weekend pass. The last step before receiving the pass was a rifle inspection in dress uniform. I worked and worked on my rifle until every part of it was blindingly, shiningly clean. As I stood at attention, the drill sergeant took my rifle, examined it, and threw it back to me, saying, "Filthy, Hollywood. Filthy. Clean it, or you're going nowhere." Keegan was standing next to me and presented his rifle to the drill sergeant. He examined it and said, "Nice job, Keegan. You're good to go."

When we had returned to the barracks, I asked Keegan if I could borrow his rifle for my second inspection. He gave it to me, and I returned for a second inspection. Once again, I stood at attention as the drill sergeant took my, or rather Keegan's, already inspected and approved weapon, opened the bolt, looked down the barrel, and threw it back to me. "It's worse than it was the first time, Hollywood." Apparently I could make a clean rifle dirty just by holding it. No weekend pass for me.

In basic training, you are subject to random acts of authority, just as in war you are subject to random acts of the enemy. Maybe that's one of the lessons of basic training, learning to adapt to the random. You can lose a lot of things when you go into basic training, like your identity, your self-esteem, your sense of independence. But the worst thing to lose, I learned, was your anonymity. Once lost, it can never be found again.

That's probably why I managed not to become famous. I can't imagine any other reason.

Beneath the heart of New York City rumbles the shuttle subway train, as it journeys back and forth from Grand Central Station to Times Square. A subway ride with only one stop. A metaphor for indecision as it goes back and forth, back and forth, restlessly lurching from the East Side to the West Side, incapable of being still, satisfied only with coming and going, forever saying hello and good-bye, yes and no.

The shuttle is also a mobile theater whose audience changes every five minutes. No other stage in New York provides the possibility of so many shows a day to so many different audiences. No wonder the shuttle attracts so many performers, who because of the brevity of the ride, need only master a short act, sing one song, play one tune before asking for a talent-affirming handout from ever changing hands. Beneath midtown Manhattan, you can almost feel like you are playing on Broadway, just twenty feet overhead at the Times Square end of the line.

The chance to have a new audience every five minutes also attracts a myriad of individuals who want to give speeches—political activists, disgruntled employees, marginalized members of society, who, with the aid of drugs or alcohol, have become members of separate societies of one. Some are only interested in getting their five-minute audience to lend them their ears. Others want them to lend them their wallets. Some want both, while some want nothing other than to stare straight ahead in disinterested silence after they have said what they needed to say. Petie McDonnell, a high school friend whom I hadn't seen in years, was a member of this last group. I would find that out one day when our paths would cross on the shuttle.

After six months of active duty in the US Army, I immediately went to work for IBM, as a member of a class of forty new employees who would be trained in the ways of systems and sales. The System 360, not yet announced, was on the horizon, and IBM was gearing up for a sea change in the world of computing. The System 360 was a group of systems of different capacities, the first family of computers that would allow users to grow and expand their systems without reprogramming. The System 360 would revolutionize the industry and put IBM in the lead for decades to come. This "industry of the future" attracted a lot of talented people, many engineers, mathematicians, MBAs, among them a large number of Ivy League graduates. I was the only philosophy major.

Everyone had been born somewhere other than New York City, but almost everyone lived in Manhattan. I was the only native New Yorker. I, too, lived in Manhattan but in the non-Manhattan part of Manhattan, Washington Heights, near the George Washington Bridge. None of my classmates knew that Manhattan actually continued north of the Metropolitan Museum of Art. Almost all were single and had their own apartments on the Upper East Side or in Greenwich Village. As a consequence, I was invited to many dinners and parties, events that I couldn't host because I was living at home with my mother, uncle, and aunt.

Most of my coworkers lived on the Upper East Side, which was on the cusp of becoming the singles strip of the sixties and seventies. It was a whole new world to me, even though I was the native. What was most new to me was the art of living, which was completely different from the one to which I was accustomed. As a result, I became a master of the faux pas, asking innocent questions that betrayed the tight circumscription of my life experience. (I once asked, "What is that for?" referring to salad dressing, having grown up with mayonnaise as a salad's only option.)

European experiences were described and discussed with an air of "Of course, you have been there and are familiar." I was, in fact, dying to go to Europe, but I had never been able to afford it. Almost all my colleagues had been there more than once, including trips with their parents, who always seemed to include a father who was a CEO, CFO, COO, or some other important, corporate powerhouse. Not only was my father not a corporate big cheese, but I didn't even have a father.

Some months after beginning my training at IBM, a woman in my office invited me to her summer group home in Quogue, Long

Island, also known as the Hamptons. Quogue elevated my sense of alienated insecurity exponentially. Everyone played tennis, discussed the stock market, and read financial magazines and newspapers, periodically referring to articles written by professors who had taught them at Harvard, Yale, Wellesley, Barnard, or Dartmouth.

Nobody ever mentioned Aristotle, which would have given me a shot at making an intellectual contribution. I had to listen more than contribute to most conversations. I didn't quite know how to break into a group with which I was unable to make any connection. I felt like an actor in a play for which I should never have auditioned. My attempts to camouflage my growing isolation and diminishing sense of self-worth with humor were not always successful and were often followed by painfully long periods of questioning silence.

The IBM training program continued, in some form, for more than a year, alternating between months of class and months of real work with customers. I was much more comfortable working with customers or attending class, neither of which seemed to make the social demands that would make me pull down a mask and slip into silence. Work and school only required competence and commitment, virtues that transcend and escape the monopolizing clutches of any social class. It was easier to work with difficult customers or programming problems than it was to socialize in the Hamptons.

One spring day I attended a meeting with several IBM colleagues at a customer location near Times Square. After the meeting, we were to return to our IBM office on Park Avenue and Thirty-Ninth Street for a postmortem on the issues that had been discussed at the meeting. The fastest way back to the office was the shuttle train from Times Square to Grand Central Station, just three blocks from the IBM office.

The train was somewhat crowded but not at all like the cramped trains that squeezed passengers into unnatural postures during rush hours. As the doors were closing, I heard a voice, a familiar voice that I could not immediately identify. The voice was loudly chiding the passengers on the train for "Running like rats to those holes you call jobs. Go ahead. Be slaves. Sell yourselves for a few bucks. For what? You're like rats in a maze. You'll do anything for the little bit of cheese they pay you. You're not people. You're puppets."

The voice, I realized, belonged to Petie McDonnell, a friend with whom I had attended grammar school and most of high school. He had been a great athlete and a gentle soul with a great sense of humor. Petie and I had grown up together, studied together, and played sports together. He had been a gifted basketball player. We had lost touch in senior year of high school, when I had changed schools.

Petie had an uncanny ability to create the perfect nickname for fellow students and teachers. (Our double-chinned principal became Jack the Sack, and our fellow classman, J. J. Finnegan, who had a habit of pushing people out of his way, became Savage JJ.) I wondered what names were going through his mind for all us "rats" on the train, rushing around the city during our workday.

There he was, standing by a door, shouting at the other passengers as the train rolled toward Grand Central Station. I was with three IBM colleagues who acknowledged Petie's tirade by looking at each other with raised eyebrows, cynical smiles, and quiet nods in Petie's direction. That Hamptons feeling came over me, and I pulled down my mask. I was embarrassed. Not about salad dressing, Europe, or the stock market this time. I was embarrassed to know Petie, an old friend. Fearing that he might recognize me, I turned my back to him.

The train slowed to a crawl before finally stopping. Before the doors opened, I thought that I should go over to Petie, talk to him, try to help him out. I didn't know how to do that without letting my coworkers know that Petie and I came from the same place, the same world, from which, day after day, I had been moving away, the world of lower-class poor people who had no part in my new upper-middle-class world.

Though an outsider in that world, I was silently pledging allegiance to it by denying my care and friendship to an old friend in need. In my mind, I shuttled back and forth between helping and hiding, doing and avoiding, being courageous or being cowardly. Petie was trying to tear off my mask, and I was holding it on with both hands. I was embarrassed that my coworkers should ever know that I knew Petie, embarrassed to be the person I really was.

The doors opened. I got off the train with my coworkers and never looked back at Petie. I heard him welcome the new passengers aboard. "Run like rats to those holes you call jobs. Go ahead. Be slaves. Sell yourselves for a few bucks. For what? You're like rats in a maze. You'll do anything for the little bit of cheese they pay you. You're not people. You're puppets."

The doors to the train closed as we started to walk away toward the office. I turned and saw Petie standing near the door, seemingly talking to himself. The train disappeared into the tunnel, and Petie disappeared from my life. I never saw him again.

I felt like Petie's namesake, a man who more than once denied and failed his good friend.

It was about one o'clock in the morning. I was seated on the Pont de Sully, my back propped up against a streetlamp on the bridge. I had had a few glasses on wine, perhaps more than a few, to celebrate my arrival in Paris for the first time, late that afternoon. The full moon was flickering in the waters of the Seine, and Notre Dame was bathed in an enveloping amber light. It could have been a dream.

I had found a small, inexpensive hotel on the Rue des Saints Peres, near the Boulevard Saint-Germain, and spent the previous few hours strolling along the Seine and pausing at several cafes.

Now I was on the bridge that connects Île Saint Louis and Île de la Cité, the home of Notre Dame. It was a warm summer evening, and Paris did not seem to be overrun with tourists, probably because it was one in the morning. Maybe it was the wine, but everything seemed just perfect, just as I had imagined it many times during my young life.

I had spent much of the day on a leisurely drive up to Paris from a small pension in Burgundy. Paradoxically I was in no rush to get to Paris because I wanted to enjoy the anticipation of finally reaching a destination of which I had dreamed for years. I had studied French in school for four years and could survive reasonably well in the monolingual countryside. Cities were easier because many French spoke at least some English. Again, paradoxically, it was for that very reason that I preferred the countryside and small towns, because they presented me with the opportunity to exercise my French and hopefully improve it.

Pont de Sully is at the eastern end of Boulevard Saint-Germain. From there to Rue des Saint-Pères is a bit of a walk along Boulevard Saint-Germain. After passing the Cathedral of Notre Dame and crossing the Seine at the intersection of Boulevard Saint-Michel, the heart of the Quartier Latin and the Sorbonne, I turned right at Café Cluny and walked west along Boulevard Saint-Germain. By then it was about two, and Paris was quiet.

All the shops and restaurants were closed, although lights still flickered in some of them. I walked past cafes that I had heard or read about, left-bank venues for Sartre-centered political and philosophical debates, like the Brasserie Lipp, a stone's throw from Café Flore and Les Deux Magots. On a street just a few blocks from Rue des Saint-Pères, a small neon sign caught my eye. "Hôtel New York," it read. In Paris, I was neither thinking nor dreaming of New York the way, in New York, I would think and dream of Paris. It was almost an intrusive reminder of my real life, interrupting the dream I was living at that moment.

I turned right on Rue des Saints-Peres and walked toward the Faculty of Medicine, which was across the street from my hotel, Hôtel de l'Académie. Since I was still more excited than tired, I decided to continue past my hotel and down the street to the banks of the Seine at the end of the street. The little sign, Hôtel New York, was on my mind. It was like that sign I used to see, over twenty years before, from the roof of my kindergarten. The sign read *Hotel Paris* and was painted on the side of the building that stood on the corner of Ninety-Sixth Street and West End Avenue. I was four years old when I first saw it.

My sister, three years older than I, had been teaching me the alphabet and helping me learn to read small words. That's how I knew that "H-O-T-E-L-P-A-R-I-S" was "Hotel Paris." "Hotel" had been a word that I had heard many times, but "Paris" was new to me. My sister said it was a city in a country called France. The Americans were fighting there. That's why we had those air-raid drills, she explained.

I liked kindergarten, particularly when we played on the roof. I also liked the little band in which I played the tambourine. What I didn't like was being left-handed because that caused trouble with Miss Finnegan, one of the older teachers. One day I was eating tapioca pudding at lunch. Miss Finnegan lightly smacked my left hand and transferred the spoon I was using to my right hand. I began once again to eat the tapioca pudding, but lacking ambidexterity, I spilled the tapioca pudding on the table. Once again Miss Finnegan lightly smacked my hand, the right one this time. I remember looking at my hands and thinking that neither one was able to help me eat, so I stopped eating until Miss Finnegan finally allowed me to use my left hand several days later.

Except for that temporary problem of being forced to use my right hand, I really loved kindergarten, so much so that my sister, who picked me up after school, had to lie to get me to come home with her. She would tell the same lie every day, and I would believe it because I so much wanted it to be true. She would tell me that a new pair of sneakers was waiting for me at home, despite the fact that my mother wouldn't permit sneakers on my somewhat-flat feet. "This time it is really true, Marty," she would say, and I would believe her, only to find once again no sneakers at home.

I stood on the left bank of the Seine and watched the water rush by, pulled along by a strong current. Most of the lights of Paris were dimmed or extinguished. I felt I was straddling two worlds, the world of dream and the world of reality. As I watched the Seine stream by, those two worlds seemed to blend, indistinguishably mixed, one with the other. As excitement melted into weariness, I turned my back to the Seine and walked slowly down the Rue des Saints-Pères to Hôtel de l'Académie and my first night's sleep in the darkened City of Lights.

There is a first time for everything in Paris, which seems to make it possible to see Paris many times for the first time, as a word on a wall, as a magical moment on the banks of the Seine, or as an unforgettable evening of wandering and dreaming.

In the late 1960s, Lafayette Street in Greenwich Village was lined with small factories and businesses, most of which have long since gone as the area has become increasingly upscale. Nearby institutions like Cooper Union, NYU, and Astor Wines on the corner of Astor Place are still there, but most buildings have changed their identities. Former factories have become expensive residences and storefronts have been transformed into trendy restaurants at the northern end of NOHO, North of Houston, as the area is now sometimes called.

In 1969, I had moved to Third Street, just below NYU and Washington Square Park. I was quite busy in those days with work and graduate school, followed by more work to pay off gambling debts. I discovered that driving a taxi until dawn, after working all day and studying or attending class every evening, was an immediate and effective cure for my gambling habit.

I had been transformed into a gambler, ironically, by winning. I usually struggled with paying my tuition each semester. At the start of one fall semester, however, I found a way to earn money quickly and without working for it. That September I made a bet on a football game and won $400. Since I considered myself knowledgeable about football, I thought I had discovered an alternate source of income and tuition. So I bet again and won. And again a third time, with the same results. I considered this to be a sort of sports scholarship.

The rest of September and early October brought continued success. I was certain of my betting prowess. In fact, I was blinded by it. When I lost my first bet in mid-October, I considered it an anomaly and doubled up on my next bet to redress the wrong. Unfortunately another anomaly occurred, followed by yet another.

I found myself in the fantasy world of bets with long odds because they would pay more. The more desperate I became, the worse were the teams I chose. My teams were always in impossible situations, like third and long, third down with thirty-five yards to go for a first down. For me, however, that situation became more like third and longing, as I hopelessly and helplessly craved miracles that never came. Having used my winnings for tuition payments, I was forced to expend considerable time and energy assuring the bookie that the payment, though late, was guaranteed.

Finally the day came when my bets would no longer be accepted until I had paid my previous debts. Not only was this the gambler's version of the cold-turkey treatment, but gambling was my source of income for gambling debts. How could I pay off losses without a chance to win? It was made clear to me by the bookie that I needed to find an alternate source of income. Soon. That's when I applied for a hack license. Driving a cab was something I could do whenever I had time to do it, which turned out to be between late evening and dawn, as well as weekends.

Returning home after my midnight-to-dawn or weekend shifts, I was usually able to find a parking space on the street for my 1966 white Buick Opel. Although the Opel was manufactured in Germany, my particular car never exhibited any of the high-quality engineering found in other German cars, like Mercedes or even Volkswagen Beetles. Perhaps Buick had sent its own engineers over to Germany from Detroit. That was one possible explanation for the quality deficit.

In those days, customer care was a concept whose time had not yet come unless, of course, you purchased something extremely expensive. Today I receive customer care even when I buy a cup of coffee. The employees at Starbuck's are concerned about what I think and how I feel. Receiving care with your coffee, however, would have been regarded with suspicion back in 1969. Especially in New York, especially on Lafayette Street.

I was absolutely religious about washing my Opel once a year, especially since it was white. Getting to a car wash, however, was not a simple task for me, given my busy schedule. My opportunity came one late-fall afternoon when I was notified that my evening class had been canceled. The nearest, and only, car wash was Moe's Clean Cars on Lafayette Street. Whenever I drove or walked past Moe's, it was always busy, with cars lined up along Lafayette Street, awaiting their turn. The price might have helped, too. Moe only charged three dollars, plus, of course, a tip for the guys who dried the car off. No tip, no drying. That was the unwritten rule at Moe's.

I took my place at the end of the line of cars on Lafayette Street. As I waited, I scanned all the cars in front of me and wondered why they were waiting to be washed. They all looked quite shiny and clean to me. The line of cars inched along at a snail's pace. I should have brought along some homework, of which I had a lot. Finally I was the next car to enter Moe's magic car wash.

As I pulled in, there was a guy with a high-powered hose who sprayed each car as a preparatory step to the wash, a sort of pre-soak. He looked slowly back and forth at the Opel and then turned to me with a look that was a mix of squint, wince, and grimace. "You want this washed?" he asked. Feeling slightly indignant, I replied that I hadn't come to the car wash for an oil change. Moe and I had not gotten off to a good start.

I was told to get out of the car before it went through the car-wash machine. Moe said I could join the other people behind the glass barrier who were watching their cars going through the washing process. I joined them and anxiously awaited my Opel's transformation from dirty to sparkling white. The customers standing next to me were complimenting each other on how new and shiny their cars began to appear as they moved slowly through the soap-sudsing and water-spraying stations, before being driven off the line and over to the car dryers.

My white Opel finally emerged and was driven over to a swarming group of car dryers, blue towels in hand. There was so much drying going on that I couldn't see how clean my car was. One of the dryers held the tip can about two inches away from my face on the assumption, I believed, that anyone who owned my white Opel would be, at best, a poor tipper. Reflexively I threw in a dollar. They opened the door for me and thanked me. I thanked them in return and drove away.

I drove out onto Lafayette Street, made a left onto Great Jones Street, pulled over, and got out to examine the results of the annual car wash. I could not believe my eyes. As opposed to all those other bright and shiny cars, my white Opel looked like it still needed a bath. It was as dirty as ever and looked as if it had never been in the car wash. Once again I was indignant. I got back in the car, returned to Lafayette Street, and rejoined the end of the line waiting to enter Moe's Clean Cars.

After another long wait, I finally pulled into the car wash and stopped in front of Moe. He looked at me quizzically. "Weren't you just in here?" he asked.

"Yes, I was," I replied. I proceeded to tell him what I thought of a car wash that would turn out a car that looked like mine. He listened silently. I paused.

He looked me directly in the eye, and in a tone as solemn as one that usually accompanies advice for a lifetime, he counseled, "Listen, Jack, and remember this. You bring shit in; you get shit out. Your car couldn't be cleaned with nuclear radiation."

Speechless, I got back in my car, reversed out of the entrance, and drove off onto Lafayette Street. For the third time that day, I had become indignant. I drove toward the Lower East Side, over to the FDR Drive, and south toward the Battery, trying to dissipate my anger. Moe's comment was a variation on a common acronym in the computer world of those days: GIGO, garbage in, garbage out. GIGO meant that computers could only work with what they were given and were unable to perform miracles. One and one would always be two. Only humans could come up with three.

The more I drove, the more relaxed I felt. I soon found myself waiting in another line of cars, at the entrance to the Staten Island Ferry. A trip across the water, to and from Staten Island, a fresh breeze blowing in from the not-faraway Atlantic Ocean would be mind-clearing and car-wash forgetting. Standing at the front of the boat and watching the bow slice through the small waves, I felt a sense of timelessness, a sense that what was happening now had happened before and would happen again.

Looking at a passing ferry returning to the Battery from Staten Island, I thought of repetition, of sameness disguised as difference, of going and coming winding up in the same place. It was like gambling. Winning was losing. Expecting a year of dirt to be washed away from an old car in five-minute car wash was like trying to gamble my way into tuition payments. It was a belief in magic, a hope for a miracle, an attempt to make one and one equal three, more "third and longing," a feeling I often had when I bet on football games.

Several days later, while at work at the NYU computer center and going over some program results with one of the programmers, I asked her how she would describe the problem. She said to me, "Just another example of GIGO." I nodded in agreement. But in my mind, I saw Moe's face, and I heard him say quite distinctly, "You bring shit in; you get shit out."

Verona is a charming, old city in northeastern Italy, not too far from the transalpine route known as the Brenner Pass. I arrived in Verona late one summer afternoon, having driven down from Innsbruck, Austria. Since I had spent ten or twelve days in the very well-organized countries of Denmark, Germany, and Austria, I immediately knew that I had crossed the border into Italy when I exited the autoroute at Bolzano. At the stoplight, I saw two separate signs for Bolzano: one pointed to the left, and the other pointed to the right. "I'm in Italy," I said to myself.

I made a left and arrived in Bolzano, wondering what had happened to those who had made a right. Since it was well-past *mezzogiorno* and still a bit of a drive to Verona, I stopped in a caffè for a coffee and a snack. In this part of Italy, German is spoken as frequently as Italian. Except for the sign that made east and west the same direction, therefore, Bolzano and the surrounding countryside still had a Germanic Alpine quality. But the sun seemed slightly warmer. That impression might have been simply psychological, however, since I knew that I was now in Italy.

Verona, another two-hour drive from Bolzano but still in the land of lakes and Alps, would be my first overnight stop in Italy. Verona has a famous amphitheater called the Arena. Built in 30 AD, it still hosts performances of opera, music, and theater. I was looking forward to seeing some kind of performance there. Maybe even Shakespeare. After all three of his plays are set in Verona: *Two Gentlemen of Verona, The Taming of the Shrew*, and, of course, *Romeo and Juliet*. The city also boasted an established literary heritage. The Roman poet Catullus had been born there, and the great Dante had spent part of his exile from Florence in this ancient city.

After arriving in Verona, I drove around until I found the Arena. It looked like the Coliseum in Rome, which I had yet to see and only knew from pictures. I wanted to find a *pensione* near it. I saw a sign, Pensione del Brennero, and next to it, "*zimmer frei*" (rooms available). I knew that I had found my home for the next few days. There was a very pleasant young woman at a desk just beyond the entrance. She welcomed me in accented English, which disappointed me. I had been trying to be very ambiguously European on this, my first trip to Europe. Perhaps my clothes gave me away. Or maybe it was the general look of confusion on my face. Appearing to be what I wasn't, I suppose, didn't come naturally to me.

I showed her my passport and signed the register. She took me to my room, which was very charming and well-appointed. Not bad for about five dollars per night, as my guidebook had specified. My only disappointment was that I couldn't see the amphitheater from my window. No problem. I would be going there in the evening anyway. I asked Luciana (by now I knew her name) if she knew what was being performed in the Arena. She didn't but would find out and let me know when I came back to the lobby later.

After a shower, I returned to the lobby, where Luciana bade me, "*Buona sera.*" She told me—incredibly—that there would be a performance of Shakespeare's *Romeo and Juliet* that very evening in the Arena at eight. There was time for dinner and a leisurely *passegiata* over to the Arena. I found a small, outdoor restaurant called Da Giulio Cesare, named for the man who sometimes vacationed in Verona when he wasn't busy vanquishing another country. I had a dish of spaghetti, a salad, and the best bread in the world, all accompanied by two glasses of a tasty, local red wine. I was ready for the star-crossed lovers from the battling houses of the Montagues and Capulets.

It was a perfect night to be in the Arena. The darkening sky was a clear blue in the afterglow of day, and a full moon was starting to rise from behind the hills. I arrived early, before seven, and found a seat in the fifth or sixth row of the still-empty Arena. I pinched myself.

Here I was in this ancient amphitheater, beneath a rising full moon, about to see *Romeo and Juliet* in the very town in which the tragedy takes place. It wouldn't matter that the play would be performed in Italian. Like everyone else, I knew the play well enough, having both read and seen it a number of times. I would know what the actors were saying.

By eight all the seats had been taken. I looked up at the surrounding circle of stone galleries where the patrons of the ancient world would watch gladiators kill each other or watch lions and Christians wage a one-sided battle. Hard to believe that a culture that had left such a rich legacy enjoyed such awful killing. That type of entertainment seemed incongruous with the tenderness of *Romeo and Juliet*. Yet there is killing there as well, amid the tenderness. Not by the sword but by the incurably jealous and silly pride of two competing families.

A flourish of trumpets, and the chatter of the audience disappeared into a vast silence that filled all the empty space in the moonlit amphitheater.

"Two households both alike in dignity (in fair Verona where we lay our scene)," solemnly intoned a voice in Italian, and thus began this play in five acts.

Roughly an hour later, toward the end of the third act, Romeo and Juliet debate whether the bird they hear is a nightingale or a lark:

"Wilt thou be gone? It is not yet near day,
It was the nightingale and not the lark."

But it is the lark and Romeo must leave or risk being discovered and maybe even killed.

As Romeo and Juliet exchanged their tender farewells and the audience found itself transported to another time in Verona, the silence in the amphitheater, which enveloped the words of love on the stage, was suddenly and loudly interrupted by a man's voice, yelling from behind, "*Ecco gelati! Ecco gelati*!"

For a moment, the ice-cream vendor's voice was greeted with total silence. Then someone yelled, "*Al cioccolato, qui*!" It was followed by, "*Alla vaniglia, due*!"

I think there were more *cioccolatos* and *vaniglias* than the poor guy could handle. Perhaps the only people, in addition to myself, who were not ordering ice cream were Romeo and Juliet, who continued to soldier on with their lines despite the gelati outbreak.

I could not help asking myself, what if this had happened back home in New York? There would have been a riot and at least one mauled ice-cream vendor. Would that be because the tickets in New York were so much more expensive than they were in Verona? No. There was another reason. I had only been in Italy for about ten hours, but I had already learned something: the Italians don't let anything interfere with their daily life. Nothing is ever important enough to make you skip lunch or, in this case, gelati.

Soon the Prince was on the stage. Romeo had poisoned himself, and Juliet had stabbed herself. They and their doomed love affair had ended in tragedy, condemned by fate to carry the enmity of their families to its sad and inevitable conclusion:

"For never was there a story of more woe
Than this of Juliet and her Romeo."

The amphitheater began to empty out, but I wanted to linger awhile and absorb the new sense of time that wrapped itself around me: Shakespeare in an ancient theater, the Renaissance replanted in the Roman world, the ice-cream vendor inserting himself into the farewells of *Romeo and Juliet*, and in the distance, the quiet, swelling Alps born of a planetary heave before time had ever been told.

I finally rose from my seat, the last member of the audience to leave. I walked backward out of the arena because I wanted to remember that night and snapped and resnapped my mental picture of the Arena in the moonlight. I walked slowly away from the amphitheater toward my *pensione*. But it was only about ten thirty, and I wasn't in the mood to go back to my room. I would stop for a drink on the way.

On the corner across from my *pensione* was a crowded, noisy but upbeat caffè with an empty table in the corner. I went in and sat down. Eventually the waiter arrived and asked, "*Desidera*?" I had planned on having a glass of wine, *vino rosso*, but without thinking, I asked, "*Gelati*?"

"*Si, si.*"

"*Vaniglia e cioccolato, per favore.*"

"*Subito*," the waiter responded.

I listened to the colliding and competing Italian conversations around me and understood hardly a word. I was sorry that *Romeo and Juliet* had come and gone so quickly, but I was happy to be back in the middle of everyday life. Moments later a silver dish materialized on the small table before me. "*Ecco gelati*," the smiling waiter bellowed.

Before me, I saw scoops of chocolate and vanilla ice cream at opposite ends of the dish, in balanced separation, as different and alike as Romeo and Juliet, as the Montagues and the Capulets, as the past and the present. As different and alike as Shakespeare and the irrepressible, interrupting yet uninterruptible, Italian life that happily surrounded me. Saying good-bye to Verona would surely be touched with "such sweet sorrow."

Soon after exiting the Autostrada del Sole (the Highway of the Sun), I arrived one afternoon in Florence, Italy, at the wheel of a brand-new Karmann Ghia that did not belong to me. A friend had asked me to pick it up in Germany and drive it around Europe, before shipping it back to New York as a used car, which, in 1964, would reduce his import tax significantly. I was now two weeks into this happy task, with three more weeks to go.

The day had begun with strong coffee, yesterday's bread, and a heady sense of total freedom. I could jump in my car and go anywhere. I had no timetable and no reservations. In the passenger seat were several maps and a copy of *Europe on Five Dollars a Day.* As I sipped coffee that morning in Verona, I reminded myself that I was free to go in any direction, a twenty-five-year-old bird with wheels instead of wings. My only advance plans were plane reservations for a brief behind-the–Iron Curtain detour to Berlin and a flight from Rome to Athens.

I drove around looking for one of the *pensioni*—the Italian equivalent of an inexpensive B&B—recommended in *Europe on Five Dollars a Day.* I preferred one centrally located, with lots of street life. I soon found Pensione del Fiume, so baptized, I assumed, because it was near the Arno, the river that flows through Florence. From the window of my room, if I hung dangerously outside and twisted my neck to the point of pain, I could see the Ponte Veccchio and the Uffizi Palace. Not bad for four dollars a night.

While climbing the stairs to the second floor, my suitcase opened, spilling most of my clothes onto the stairway. The zipper had broken. Unfortunately the manager of the *pensione* was not to be found, so I went out to the street to find a shop where I could get it fixed.

Just a few doors from the *pensione* was the Caffe d'Arte, with a nod, no doubt, to Michelangelo, Dante, and all the other great artists and writers who had walked these streets. I sat at a table, and a very attractive, young woman came over, asking, "*Desidera?*" I ordered "*una birra*" in my best Italian. When she returned, I poured my Peroni into the glass, leaned back in the sunshine, sipped my beer, and reminded myself that I was actually sitting in a caffè in the middle of Florence. I felt as if I had just walked into one of my own dreams. I ordered another beer.

When Teresa (I overheard someone calling her name) returned to my table with a refill, I tried to explain in broken Italian that I had a "*valigia rotta.*" Did she know anyone who could fix my suitcase? Her English was not good but certainly better than my Italian. By word and gesture, she asked me to bring the suitcase to the caffè. I finished my beer, left a generous tip, and wandered out into the streets of Florence; I was anxious to see the city but even more anxious to come back and see Teresa.

The next morning I returned to the Caffe d'Arte with my suitcase. Teresa was busily waiting on several customers at the bar. She shouted, "*Buongiorno,*" to me and soon brought coffee to my table. As she looked at the suitcase, I tried not to look at her. Gradually I understood that she wanted me to leave it with her. She would talk to someone who could help. I thanked her, drank my coffee, and went off to see in the flesh or, more precisely, in the marble those works of art that I had only seen in pictures. My first stop would be the Galleria dell'Accademia, home to a number of Michelangelo's masterpieces, including the *David.*

For me, the *David* was so imposingly perfect that I couldn't conceive of it as having been made by human hands. It seemed to have been carved in another universe and parachuted into Florence. After staring emptily at the sculpture for minutes on end and beginning to feel guilty about my apparent lack of sensibility, I craved finding something with which I could connect, something of a more imperfectly human dimension that would enable me to understand what Michelangelo faced when creating.

Off to the side of the room that housed the *David,* was another room with more Michelangelo sculptures. I went in. Among those sculptures were some unfinished works. One appeared to be no more than a large block of unformed marble. I approached it and saw a bent leg with a large thigh, slowly emerging from the marble, as if rising from a grave, begging to come alive. Never before or since, have I felt so profoundly present during the process of creation. The *David* "was." But that leg was "becoming," and I was present at the birth.

My experience of Michelangelo's unfinished work at the Galleria blotted out other works of art that I saw that day and during the days that followed. After several hours, I usually became immune to the possibility of further appreciation, which was not fair to the artworks that I had yet to see. That threshold dissolved, however, when I stood before the unfinished works or later when I reflected on them during walks around the city and along the banks of the Arno.

Teresa found somebody to fix my suitcase, but it would take several days. I was glad. My suitcase was a continuing excuse for a conversation with her, however linguistically limited. I started drinking coffee four or five times a day, just to see her. And every time I saw her, it was as if she had once again magically materialized after having completely vanished. Teresa had that classic

Italian face that I had seen in so many paintings of the Madonna: chiseled features, light-olive skin, huge brown eyes, and a slight, innocent shyness thinly veiled by a warm, welcoming, understanding smile.

I was dying to ask Teresa for a date. I wasn't going to be in Florence that much longer, only two more days and nights. Due to my frequent visits to the cafe, "*Come sta*?" had evolved into the more familiar "*Come stai*?" I thought that might a good sign that I might not get turned down if I invited her to dinner. With time running out, I summoned the courage that evening to ask her.

"*Cena con me* (dinner with me)?" I asked timidly and inelegantly. Her response was somewhere between a smile and a soft laugh. I wasn't sure if she was reacting to my Italian or my request until she said, "*Si, si. Un piacere. Mercoledi sera*?"

"*Si, si. Va bene,*" I answered. Just in time, because I would be leaving the morning after, Thursday. I was so excited that, for a moment, I had completely forgotten about my suitcase. "*E la mia valigia*?" I asked.

"*Anche mercoledi sera. Alle sette,*" Teresa responded. My whole world would come together on Wednesday evening at seven o'clock.

Wednesday afternoon I returned to the Galleria to see that leg still struggling to climb out of the block of marble. I had never encountered a work of art—an almost work of art—like that. When I looked at it, I saw and understood something that I had never seen or understood before. The *David* was perfect, but this not fully formed thigh before me was reaching out, pleading to become more, yearning to be what it almost was, begging the artist to complete what he had begun.

For me, the problem with perfection, with the *David,* is that the yearning stops; the struggle is over. There is no unformed possibility waiting silently, desperately, for a hammer's blow and a chisel's chip to loosen the marble's imprisoning embrace. But the unfinished work is all about possibility. When I left the Galleria, I felt as if I were saying good-bye to an old friend who would never stop trying to materialize into a new form.

I arrived at Caffe d'Arte before seven that evening and waited for Teresa with hopeful anxiety. If I were Michelangelo, I would create the *Teresa* somewhere between the perfect and the possible. By herself, she seemed perfect. She was beautiful and gracious. She lacked nothing. But with me in her world, she entered the realm of possibility, like Michelangelo's unfinished work. Thinking about her became thinking about us. Several expectant minutes seemed endless.

She arrived a little past seven dressed in a simple yet elegant black skirt and white blouse. She was carrying my suitcase. She came to the table and sat down. "*Buona sera*," she greeted me with a smile.

"*Buona sera, Teresa.*"

"*Valigia rotta.* No zipper. Work not finished."

"*Non c'e' problema*," I said. I was so happy to see her that she could have told me that my suitcase had been stolen.

We left the café, and Teresa took me to a cozy little restaurant along the Arno called Da Beatrice. *How perfect*, I thought. Here in Florence, we were sitting in a restaurant named after the woman whose face had launched the more than fourteen thousand lines of poetry in Dante's *Divina Commedia.* The sun was sinking in the evening sky and the Arno was taking on new colors, pinks and purples. I wondered if Teresa looked like Beatrice. I knew she looked like the Madonna. During dinner, Teresa mentioned the little town of Fiesole, which is just outside Florence on top of a high hill overlooking the city and the river. She suggested going there if I had not seen it.

We drove up to Fiesole, a charming little town with a view that is itself a Renaissance painting. We walked around a small park that looked down on the city and held hands. I felt like Dante meeting Beatrice at the end of the *Purgatorio*, in the Garden of

Eden, on top of the mountain. We stopped walking, put our arms around each other, and, savoring anticipation, kissed, hesitantly at first and then fully. I believed I was kissing the great, great, great, great-granddaughter of a Renaissance Madonna.

For a moment, the whole world came together: Europe, Michelangelo, the Renaissance, the Italian language, Florence, art, a new world in the midst of the old, a new sense of life, so much larger than the life I had known before. Old possibilities were being newly realized. I felt so lucky and so happy with Teresa in my arms and Florence at our feet.

Several hours later I drove Teresa back to Caffe d'Arte. She insisted on walking home from there. I told her that I would come back to Florence one day. She smiled a smile that was grateful for the gesture but aware of the reality and asked that I stop by the Caffe d'Arte when I did. One day I did return to Florence, but it was many years and a marriage later. I would never see Teresa again.

The next morning I packed up the car, with my suitcase still broken, the work still unfinished. Sad and happy, I left the Renaissance world of Florence, returned to the Autostrada del Sole, and drove south to Rome, the Eternal City.

The Graduate Faculty of the New School for Social Research is located on Fourteenth Street and Fifth Avenue in New York City, just on the northern edge of Greenwich Village. In the late 1960s, I was a student there, working on my PhD in philosophy. (I was actually awarded an ABD, All But Dissertation.) I also had a day job at New York University, running one of their computer centers. That and monthly bills kept me grounded well beneath the philosophical ether. I sometimes wondered why I was studying philosophy. In retrospect, I think philosophy was my response, at that time, to the there-must-be-more-to-life feeling that slowly and steadily flowed in, like a tide, as my twenties flowed out.

To keep myself in shape and to reconnect with the concrete world that was threatened daily by philosophical abstractions, I joined a gym, the McBurney YMCA on Twenty-Third Street, just off Seventh Avenue. I threw myself into empty-headed, unthinking basketball, running, and swimming. It was a welcome release. After working out, there was nothing like a sauna and a steam bath, both of which maximized dehydration and provided perfect preparation for drinking beer.

The absolutely best place for drinking beer was at a restaurant called Steak and Brew, a chain that offered unlimited beer and salad with a steak dinner. Our particular Steak and Brew was located on Fifth Avenue and Eleventh Street, where on Tuesday nights they had a prime rib special for $2.50. My workout pal, Jim, and I would order prime rib, along with countless pitchers of beer and endless plates of salad. (The salad always made you feel you were on a mission to improve your health.) After a most enjoyable evening, the bill would be five dollars. Sports that we were, we generously left a 100 percent tip of five dollars.

Steak and Brew's business model must have failed to include people like us, hungry and dehydrated, who more than ate and drank their money's worth. As a result, Steak and Brew went bankrupt during the 1970s, an outcome for which I still experience periodic pangs of guilt, even though I know that I was just a single soldier in a large army of destructive consumers. Given the location of that particular Steak and Brew, it would be fair to say that "it takes a village" (in this case, Greenwich) to close down a business.

Within several months of joining, I became completely addicted to working out at the YMCA. No small part of that addiction was the postexercise ritual of dehydrating in the sauna and the steam room, each of which seemed to attract a different clientele. The dry heat and clear visibility of the sauna, for example, allowed readers to read their books and talkers to have eye-to-eye conversations. The wet heat and poor visibility of the steam room, on the other hand, precluded reading and compromised conversation because people were unable to see each other. As a result, readers and talkers gravitated to the sauna, while those who craved quiet and comfortable urban invisibility were the perennial inhabitants of the steam room. (People who also ate too much garlic the night before tended to furtively sweat it out in the steam room, an act little appreciated by others.)

I was primarily a sauna person, probably because I always needed to read something for my course work. I found a way to tune out the conversations so that I could concentrate on what I was reading. (Reading in the sauna also made me feel that I wasn't sacrificing my school work for the enjoyment of working out.) Sometimes, however, the ambient conversation would take hold of my consciousness and not permit me to tune it out. Sometimes I was even tempted to comment, but I always resisted the urge. And sometimes I resisted the urge because I was intimidated.

The most intimidating group in the sauna was a group of four or five older Jewish guys, all World War II veterans, a fact I picked up from their comments. They each had unshakeable opinions on everything and could agree on nothing. Every one of them spoke with absolute authority, in a tone that castigated any possible or actual disagreement as willful blindness or, worse, stupidity. They actually didn't debate anything because nobody paid any attention to the one who was speaking; they all waited only for him to take a breath so that a new speaker could jump in. Instead of a dialogue, they traded parallel monologues. They all seemed satisfied at the end of their daily "debates." I assumed that was the case because the only argument they each had heard was their own.

Whenever this group was holding forth in the sauna, I tried to read and pay no attention. But one day the urge to comment was irresistible, despite the fact that I was usually intimidated by their assertive self-assurance. That day they were trading comments on psychoanalysis, complexes, shrinks, patients, real men, wackos, wimps, and various others who couldn't handle the vicissitudes of life. I refrained from entering the fray until someone mentioned Nietzsche. My he's-a-philosopher-and-I-know-all-about-philosophy light went on. Feeling that they were invading my area of expertise, I felt brave enough, for the first time, to take on the gang that knew everything.

I leaned forward, and said, "Excuse me, may I say a word?" Projecting a self-assured voice of quiet, professorial authority, I continued, "I have to tell you that Nietzsche never said what you just said he said." *Too many "saids" in that sentence,* I thought, which may have weakened my authoritative posture. "Nietzsche never said anything like 'We are condemned to be free.' That was Sartre."

A totally enveloping silence rolled through the sauna like an invisible, noiseless avalanche. Ten penetrating eyeballs stared at me.

The silence seemed endless until one of the group, the unofficial captain of the debating team, leaned forward from his sauna perch in the second row, looked me in the eye, and proclaimed, "Let me tell you something, kid." Long pause. "Whatever you think, it's all in your head."

That statement brought slow, serious, silent nods of agreement from each of his debating partners. I felt as if they had just taken a vote on my execution and that they were unanimously in favor.

I, the condemned man, sheepishly echoed back their silence. Then slowly, one by one, they got up and exited the sauna. This was a first, a precedent. In my one year of membership at the YMCA, I had never observed this group being silent for longer than the time required to take a breath after delivering a lengthy opinion, during which, of course, someone else jumped in with an equally lengthy opinion.

I was alone in the sauna for the very first time since I had joined the Y. It took a while to get over my guilty isolation. I should have kept my mouth shut instead of pretending to be an expert. I was a long dissertation away from a PhD, so who was I to comment with such authority, even though I was, in fact, correct? That kind of behavior obviously did not lead to new friendships. My current isolation in the sauna proved the empirical truth of that thought.

But I had learned something here that sixty credits of graduate work in philosophy had not taught me. In eight words, the captain of the sauna debating team had, to my satisfaction, succinctly summed up the entire history of Western philosophy, which has always revolved around the question of internal phenomena versus external reality, the mind-body problem, or as Descartes puts it, "I think, therefore, I am," which roughly means "I'm here, but is anybody else?" I must have read eighty different books of or on Western philosophy. He had just deftly distilled them all into eight little words.

To improve my interpersonal-relationship skills, however, I abandoned the dry, cerebral sauna for the wet and sweaty steam room. Hidden in its concealing fog and unprovoked by its uninterrupted silence, I wouldn't say the wrong thing, even by saying the right thing. I learned that it was all in my head.

Van Cortland Park in the Bronx is home to many different sports and the venue for many cross-country racing events. Its many hills and huge fields make an especially ideal place to walk, run, or train for the New York City Marathon, which I did for a number of years. One of those years was 1977, the year of the infamous shootings and murders by an unknown killer who, based on his cryptic communications, became known as the Son of Sam.

What was most frightening about the Son of Sam was the irrationality of his actions. He wasn't robbing banks or mugging people. He espoused no known political or social cause. His targets were innocent people, usually couples parked on quiet streets or along lovers' lanes. That, of course, gave every psychologist, armchair or certified, the opportunity for extravagant Freudian analyses and hypotheses.

Son of Sam also created an enormous fear in the public. Where and why he would strike was an imponderable. He helped, however, the local media, which had effectively nonstop coverage that was more speculation than confirmed, factual news. Nothing sells like fear, and nothing stokes fear like speculation on the endless possibilities of his future behavior, his past life, or his likely identity.

Because he had been targeting couples, would that make you safe if you were alone? After all, if his actions were irrational, how could any rational analysis be reliably predictable? The irrational is, by definition, irrational. How can a rationally based prediction forecast the irrational?

One day the *New York Post* published a sketch of Son of Sam on its front page. The sketch had been the result of an interview with a survivor of a shooting of a couple in a parked car. It was a simple sketch, but given the climate of fear at the time, it was possible to find a match in one's mind for almost anyone you saw on the subway. Based on the sketch, Son of Sam was neither black nor Asian, but that still left millions of people in the Big Apple suspect.

Two days after seeing the sketch of Son of Sam in the *New York Post*, I was back in Van Cortland Park for an eleven-mile run in preparation for the New York City Marathon in late October. The trail began in the parking lot, looped through the woods, turned back along an unused stretch of railroad track, and ended back again in the parking lot. It was a warm, humid evening in late September. I had come directly from the office and began my run around six o'clock.

This was a run I had done many times, but it was actually the first time I had run it alone. Several friends were also training for the New York City Marathon, but none was available that evening for company. For many reasons, not the least of which is New York City paranoia, it is better not to run alone. There is always the possibility of an accident or a chance encounter with someone with evil intent. The odds of the latter seem to go up as the sun goes down in the western sky above the Hudson River.

It was a beautiful evening that still retained the hot, humid feel of summer even in late September. I started from the parking lot and made my way to the trail through the woods. I saw no one for the first few miles, after which I saw just one other runner, an older man who was making his way back to the parking lot. I reached Tibbetts Brook Park, about to begin the wide loop over to the railroad tracks that would eventually lead me back to the parking lot.

Sometimes when running, you start off tired and sluggish and you just keep feeling worse as the run goes on. Other times you start off the same way but begin to feel better and better the longer you run. That evening was one of the latter times. As I went along, I kept feeling stronger and stronger and gradually began to pick up the pace. There is such a feeling of freedom and, perhaps, invincibility, as weariness, contrary to the laws of nature, recedes the more you make demands on your body.

I began the wide loop and saw a few other runners and walkers mingled among a small parade of baby carriages. I was already soaked with sweat, but it felt good. Besides, I was already thinking of the little cooler in the back of my car with a couple of cold bottles of Beck's beer. They were like my gold medal for being out here that evening. I would earn this gold medal since I always came in first when I ran alone.

I exited Tibbetts Brook Park and ran for a few blocks past some private homes before reentering Van Cortland Park for the final three-mile stretch along the abandoned railroad tracks. A running path parallels the railroad tracks. The trees and bushes are set back, so it is possible to literally see for miles down the tracks. My sense of feeling good having become feeling better, I hoped that I would be feeling best as I approached the finish about two and one-half miles down the tracks.

Being able to see so far down the tracks enhanced my sense of being alone, which was, at first, a nice feeling, a sense of freedom, jogging through my own little universe and feeling in top form. This sense of well-being was suddenly interrupted, however, when in the distance, I thought I saw a solitary figure standing on the tracks. Either I had never paid attention—perhaps because my friends and I would talk a lot while running—or this was in fact the first time I had seen somebody just standing there, hanging out on the tracks. Not a big deal, I thought, just some innocent person walking along the tracks on a lovely late-summer evening.

At that moment, I was probably about a mile from the person I saw. Then suddenly he was gone. (I say "he" because I thought it highly unlikely that a woman would be walking along abandoned railroad tracks by herself.) I continued, picking up the pace since I had less than a mile to go. Then with about a half mile of railroad track between me and those sweating bottles of ice-cold Beck's beer, the figure emerged again from the bushes on the left side of the tracks.

As the half mile evolved into a quarter-mile, I could make out the fact that the figure was male. I wondered what he was doing on the tracks, jumping in and out of the bushes as I approached him. Soon I was less than a quarter of a mile away. I could see the figure clearly, or at least I thought I could. The face of the figure, still far away, began to take a shape, which I involuntarily ran through the photo file in my mind. Needless to say, the first picture in that file was the sketch I had seen the previous evening in the *New York Post*, the Son of Sam.

Maybe he had given up on couples because the police had his MO. Maybe he was embarking on a new set of targets, joggers, which would get him a lot of publicity in the run-up to the New York City Marathon. I began to argue with myself. *You are making this up*, I told myself. *This is unreasonable fear based on a sketch of a guy who is trying to kill couples, not joggers.* I was now within a couple of hundred yards of him, and he was walking toward me. I continued the argument with myself.

When I was approximately one hundred yards from him, I lost the argument. It must be Son of Sam. He was now targeting joggers.

What better place than this lonely stretch of railroad track? What better time than now, with the sun setting and the park almost empty? I began to feel a sense of desperation. It was Son of Sam or me.

I was about fifty yards away, and I instinctively ran right at him as fast as I could. I tried to run right over him before he could shoot me. As I reached him, he screamed and dived into the bushes. I ran faster than I ever had in my life, hoping to outrun the bullet that he was sure to fire as he made his way back out of the bushes. But the shot that I was trying to outrun never came.

For centuries, philosophers have argued about our ability to know "things in themselves," whether or not we can only know our sense perceptions of those things. It often seemed to me like a silly academic debate. After that day on the railroad tracks in Van Cortland Park, however, I have retained a newfound respect for the merit of their debate.

Just a week after my encounter in Van Cortland Park, the police did find the Son of Sam. He was living in Yonkers, just a couple of miles from Van Cortland Park. Could that have been him in the bushes along the tracks after all?

During the 1960s, there was a Chinese restaurant on First Avenue between Seventeenth and Eighteenth Streets. It was called Tom's Garden and, unsurprisingly, was owned by a Chinese man named Tom. He was a kind, pleasant guy who provided efficient service with a ready smile. More importantly he had the most succulent spare ribs and tastiest pork fried rice north of Chinatown. I seemed to gravitate to this menu whenever I was feeling blue, which was quite often in those days. Unlike my married friends, I seemed unable to have a meaningful, lasting relationship with a woman. Failure made me sad, and sadness made me one of Tom's best customers.

I had an apartment on the second floor of a brownstone on Seventeenth Street between First and Second Avenues. There was a tree outside the building, which could be used as a ladder into my apartment if I forgot my key. (The window lock was broken, but I never fixed it. It was too useful as an alternate front door.) In any case, I didn't have very much to steal. To say that my apartment was sparsely furnished would be quite an understatement: two old couches, a worn kitchen table, and a bed in the tiny bedroom. The only attraction in the apartment was its working fireplace, which added a touch of coziness to an otherwise-barren space.

There was, however, another attraction—if not to my apartment, to my street. Six brownstones away from me was the building in which Antonín Dvořák, the Bohemian/Czechoslovakian composer, had lived and composed his Symphony Number 9 in E Minor, famously known as the New World Symphony. Bringing up this fact with a new date usually gave a cultural veneer to my neighborhood and a level of undeserved cultivation to my otherwise-uncultivated apartment. Some people had new kitchens and bathrooms. I had a fireplace and Dvořák. That was something more than nothing.

I also had two other items: a small stereo and a black-and-white television set. They were the only possessions with some value, however minimal, not enough to attract a thief or to make it necessary to fix my unlockable window. Besides, directly across the street was the emergency room of Beth Israel Hospital. The traffic in and out of the ER would have been enough to scare away any would-be burglar. (On several occasions when I had forgotten my keys, I worried about being reported myself as I climbed the tree to the unlocked window.)

I had availed myself of the Beth Israel ER only once in the three years I had been living on Seventeenth Street. That visit, unfortunately, was sufficient to make me a bit of a persona non grata with one of the doctors on the staff. I had been skiing, slightly off the main trails, in Vermont with some friends and had fallen into a snowbank. Buried in the snowbank was a broken bottle that jammed itself into my knee. The nearest medical assistance was a doctor of osteopathy, who patched me up and told me to seek medical attention when I returned to New York. That I did, in the ER at Beth Israel Hospital.

After the mandatory three-hour wait in the ER, I was brought into a treatment room by one of the nurses. There sat a very attractive, redheaded, young female doctor, who spoke to me with what seemed to be a Russian accent. Perhaps that was the cultural divide that made my attempt at humor fail. After examining my knee, she asked if I had had a tetanus shot. Instead of simply responding in the negative, I clenched my teeth together, as if afflicted with lockjaw, and said, "No, did I need one?" She didn't think my attempt at humor was very funny. Fortunately I had never had any reason to return to the ER since that day. But I always found it comforting to know that the ER was waiting for me just across the street.

One summer weekend I was invited to a coworker's summer house in East Hampton. Returning home early Sunday evening after hours on the Long Island Expressway, I entered my building and reached into my pocket for my house keys. They weren't there. They were in the car. I went out and checked. They weren't in the car. I left my overnight bag in front of the apartment door and went back downstairs to use the alternate entrance, the tree. I climbed up the tree and saw that the window was open, just a few inches but open nonetheless. I always kept it closed.

I went into the apartment and saw pillows and some clothes strewn across the floor. Somebody had obviously been in the apartment. My apartment had been invaded! I couldn't believe it. I felt violated. I picked everything up and looked in the closets and drawers. Everything seemed to be there. Then I noticed the two empty spaces where the stereo and the television had been. They had taken the only valuable objects in the apartment.

I was getting angry. I picked up the phone and called the nearest police precinct to report the robbery. I was told that someone would be there within a half hour. I continued straightening out the apartment, which didn't take very long. There wasn't very much to move around and straighten out. Soon the doorbell rang, and I opened the door. There stood two policemen in uniform. They asked my name and if I was the person who reported the burglary.

I invited them in. In those days, cops actually came to your apartment for minor problems, the way doctors used to make house calls. (It might have also helped that my local precinct was next to the police academy, where, I assumed, there were lots of extra cops around to respond to complaints.) In any case, there they were, two cops looking about my apartment. They were becoming increasingly wide-eyed, I thought.

That was confirmed when one cop turned to other and, in a voice full of amazement, blurted out, "Holy shit, they got everything!"

The second cop looked around silently, nodding his head in agreement and finally commenting, "You've got some tax deduction here." At that point, he opened a closet door, saw nothing on the racks, and exclaimed, "They took all your suits."

I didn't have the heart to tell him that I had no suits. Then again given the tax implications, I thought I should keep that information confidential.

"How did they get in?" they asked.

"Through that window with the broken lock," I responded. "They probably climbed up the tree."

Everywhere the officers turned in the apartment, they found a reason to repeat their conclusion that "They got everything." One cop even opened the refrigerator, observed it was empty, and said in disgust, "What creeps. They took all your food, too."

Once again, I found silence to be golden.

Finally one of the officers wrote a number down on a blank sheet of paper and handed it to me. "This is your case number," he said. "Make a list of everything that was stolen from you and drop it off at the station house. We will send you an official confirmation that all the items were, in fact, stolen. You can file that statement with your income tax and, hopefully, recoup some of your loss."

I thanked the two police officers for their assistance. As they were walking toward the door, one of them turned to me with a compliment and some advice: "By the way, nice fireplace. Don't forget to fix the lock on the window; otherwise, you will be calling us again with the same problem."

They left, and I returned to feeling violated. I still had a hard time believing that strangers had broken into my apartment, into my life and that they had been in here walking around, in my home, as if it were theirs. I was becoming increasingly angry as the shock wore off.

They didn't get very much because there hadn't been very much to get. But that wasn't the point. They had come through that broken window into my life. Even if they had taken nothing, they would have taken something from me just by being in here. In return, they left a shopping list for me: one lock for the window, one small black-and-white television, and one small stereo phonograph. Hopefully those items would be financed by my big tax deduction.

It was now about nine at night, and I hadn't eaten since breakfast in the Hamptons. Even victims get hungry. Nothing like a quick fix from Tom's Garden. I called to order my usual duress dinner, spare ribs and pork fried rice. The ever-affable Tom told me that my order would be ready in fifteen minutes. I took my happily undiscovered spare key out of a cup in the cabinet. On my way to Tom's Garden, I bought some beer and a TV-replacing newspaper. When I returned, I sat at the kitchen table and opened the newspaper. As usual, there were violations everywhere in the city. In the country. In the world. I was not alone.

But I *was* alone. At least until I met Anna. I had been dating a number of women, but casual dates were the closest I could get to a relationship. I had had several relationships with wonderful women, but I ran away whenever commitment loomed. Maturity, at least in this regard, had been emerging in my life at glacial speed. Anna accelerated this process with a disarming combination of laser-beam insight and piercing, yet loving, wit.

I met Anna for the first time in 1969 at a dinner party in the apartment of a friend, Christine, in Greenwich Village. Christine was a gorgeous, tall, Swedish-American blonde, whom I had met through mutual friends in the mid-1960s. She was intelligent and magnetically gregarious, with a welcoming and engaging sense of humor. Christine and I would date periodically but we never had a serious relationship.

Anna had recently graduated from Fordham University with a Master's Degree in Social Work. She planned on becoming a clinical psychologist. Slender and vivacious, she had big brown eyes, long brown hair, and soft, olive skin. Anna was bright, quick, and very much a woman with her own strong and definite ideas. I liked her immediately, and later asked her for a date. She refused to say yes until she had spoken to Christine, a demonstration of openness and honesty that endeared her to me even more.

Anna and I were both struggling financially. She was working at Catholic Charities and I was working at a computer center at NYU. At the same time, I was driving a taxi to pay off my gambling debts, while preparing for my PhD comprehensive exams. I was a shaky candidate for a stable relationship, but we very much enjoyed each other's company.

Anna never forgot our first date. "All you talked about," she would say, "was John Steinbeck's book, *Travels with Charlie.* Really romantic, a man and his dog wandering around the United States." Then she would hug me, murmuring, "I should have realized how limited you were."

Anna always had a lot of good advice such as, "You can never go wrong by keeping your mouth shut." I tried that several times, however, and it didn't work, "Because," Anna said, "I know what you're thinking." As a matter of fact, she usually did know what I was thinking.

We both liked simple things. Anna would sometimes attend lectures with me at the New School. On weekends, we would ride bikes down to the Battery and take the ferry to Staten Island. Sometimes we would go fishing and Anna would cook the catch, if there was one. We both joined the YWHA on East Fourteenth Street so that we could swim together twice a week. And once a week we would watch the "Carol Burnett Show" on television while munching on a bucket of chicken wings from Chicken Delight.

It was all very simple. We laughed a lot.

In the summer of 1969, Anna went off to Greece with a girlfriend on a previously scheduled vacation. At the same time, I went off to Belmar, New Jersey, had too much to drink one night, and got myself arrested for arguing with a cop. It was an act of stupidity, which resulted in my spending a night in jail, where I had time to think back on my earlier and ever-failing career of crime. I could still feel the heel of my mother's high-heel shoe on the back of my head.

The following year brought a wave of marriages among our friends, which raised the obvious question and begged the obvious answer that I tried to keep dodging. I guess, on some level, I could not believe that anyone could really care about, or for, a confused, immature, self-destructive guy. I didn't think of myself in those terms. I just knew something was wrong, something I couldn't even articulate.

The idea of marriage and family meant loss of freedom to me. It meant the small, closed world I was running from, a world in which there was little happiness, a world full of tomorrows that would be indistinguishable from yesterdays.

Neither Anna nor I fit snuggly into our worlds, but we did fit together. Maybe it was the shared laughter that drew us closer to each other. Maybe it was our mutual love of books, of learning, of Europe. My respect and admiration for Anna were certainly a big part of the bond between us. She could do anything: cook, decorate, make her own clothes and unthreateningly discuss feelings -- none of which I could do.

Anna was a social worker. What people felt and thought were important. In her young life, she had cultivated a big, open, welcoming space inside, a space that had more than enough room for the problems of others. She kept some of that space available for me.

Anna made me feel that I wasn't condemned to being alone, that I could share someone else's life. I didn't undergo an overnight, miraculous conversion, but the conversion had started and it wouldn't stop for the rest of my life. Despite that, my shakiness as a marriage prospect must have been obvious. Years later, some friends revealed they had harbored the belief that Anna must have seen something in me that neither they nor anyone else could see.

Anna didn't need me. I needed her. But the *next-to-last* thing in the world that I wanted was *to need* anyone. I was afraid to need. I didn't trust being in need, a feeling so ingrained that it had the force of a wordless, unconscious vow that I might have taken long ago, at a time and place I couldn't recall. I only knew that I was committed to being uncommitted. Fortunately for me, however, the *last* thing in the world that I wanted was to lose Anna. I made the best decision of my life. Anna agreed and we were married on May 15, 1971 in the chapel at Manhattan College, nearly two years after we first met.

It takes time to accept need and to learn to trust. But finally, I was no longer, and would never again be, alone

THE PLAY'S THE THING

New York City is filled with celebrities, real and self-imagined. They can be found just about anywhere. Until the end of the twentieth century, some of the real ones could even be found at McBurney branch of the YMCA, which used to be just across the street from the Chelsea Hotel on West Twenty-Third Street.

The celebrities at the Y were hard to recognize because they were always incognito, dressed in the same uniform that everyone else was wearing: T-shirt, shorts, sweat socks and sneakers. (During a basketball game, I was even fouled once by Al Pacino. I didn't know who he was at the time. When I found out, however, I considered it to be the best play I had ever made.)

Once you came through the front door and passed beneath the inscription, "Enter here to be and to find a friend," you joined the indistinguishably classless society that was the McBurney YMCA. And your identity, especially on the basketball court, often became something like "Yo, blue shirt," which offered, to anyone who needed it, a comfortably concealing, urban anonymity.

I came at the celebrity problem, however, from the other direction. Unlike them, I was trying to get some attention, in pursuit of which I managed to become the unofficial master of ceremonies at the annual McBurney fundraising cocktail parties. In accordance with good fundraising practice, we tried to have a celebrity as our guest of honor each year. When the celebrity was a member of McBurney, our fundraising was especially effective. The guys with lockers near the celebrity were inspired to uncustomary levels of generosity when they learned, for example, that "Yo, blue shirt" was actually Jerry Ohrbach.

There were also celebrities who were known by reputation but who, unlike Al Pacino, would never be recognized. One such celebrity was the American playwright, Edward Albee, a member of the McBurney Y for many years. He was selected one year to be our fundraiser guest of honor, and I was given the task of introducing him.

Introductions can be very much like eulogies, the significant difference being, of course, that the person introduced is still living and listening intently to the introduction. In the days leading up to the cocktail party, I tried to find a way, in my introduction, to connect Edward Albee's professional life as a playwright with his extracurricular life as a long-time member of McBurney. What could connect the theater and the gym, the stage and the basketball court, the locker room and the dressing room? McBurney certainly had its own cast of characters, but they weren't quite like the characters that Albee brought to life in his plays.

I had been a member of the Catholic Big Brothers for a number of years. By incredible coincidence, my little brother, Joseph, was studying acting, and at that very moment, was preparing for a production of Albee's one-act play *Zoo Story*. I had seen some of Albee's plays. I found them riveting and, at times, painfully disturbing. I thought it would be a good idea to invite Joseph to the fundraiser so that he could meet Albee and discuss *Zoo Story*. That, I told him, would be a bit like discussing *Hamlet* with Shakespeare himself. No intermediaries. No scholars. No critics. Just the man himself. The basic, unadorned truth.

That's when the lightbulb went on. I had found the connection between the playwright and the gym. And I could sum it up in a single word.

It was a lovely September evening when we gathered together in the very expansive penthouse of one of our wealthier donors. The cocktail party began at six. At seven, I was to welcome the guests, encourage their financial support, and introduce our guest of honor, Edward Albee. During the cocktail hour, I introduced my little brother to Edward Albee and left them to discuss *Zoo Story* while I circulated among the guests and personally welcomed them. They were either members of McBurney, donors, or both. The hour passed quickly, and it was soon time to introduce our guest of honor. I was ready with my magic word.

I welcomed the attendees, thanked them for coming, and told them that I had taken an informal survey during the cocktail hour. My survey results were, I noted, a function of my listening in on conversations to determine which of Albee's plays seemed to be the most popular or at least the most discussed. The results were, of course, not scientific, but they were the best I could do.

"Based on my own personal survey during the past hour," I proclaimed, "The two plays by Edward Albee most discussed by you this evening were *Merchant of Venice* and *Death of a Salesman.*"

Fortunately, everyone, especially Albee, laughed, and I proceeded to the introduction.

"For a number of days," I confessed, "I had been struggling with a way to connect Edward Albee's professional life as a playwright with his life with us here at McBurney. Where, I asked myself time and again, do these seemingly parallel lifelines converge? And how would I describe this convergence?" Pause. "I found the answer in a single word." Longer pause. "That word is 'sincere.'"

Confused looks stared back at me, followed by muffled, inaudible remarks. Silent consternation rose like a wave from the audience and washed over me. "Let me explain," I hastened to add.

"The word 'sincere' is rooted in two Latin words: '*sine,*' meaning without, and '*cera,*' meaning wax. I know you must be thinking that 'sincere' was mystifying enough, what has 'without wax' got to do with anything?"

It was time to go on the offense. "The fact is," I explained, "'sincere' and 'without wax' have everything to do with Edward Albee. In the Greco-Roman theater of the ancient world, the actors wore masks. And the masks were made of wax. When the actors were without their masks, the audience could see who the actors were, the real people behind the wax masks. When you see a play by Edward Albee, you don't see any wax masks. His characters, however, do wear masks. Between the beginning and the end of his plays, Edward Albee subtly and skillfully removes these invisible masks.

The characters that emerge at the end of his plays are quite different than the characters that you met at the opening. Their waxless masks have been removed, and their true selves are on display."

Long pause.

"But what does all this have to do with the McBurney YMCA?" I asked. "Every time we enter McBurney, we, too, remove our masks. The circles we travel in are left at the door. The clothes we wear are left in the locker. We become who we are underneath all the trappings of our everyday lives. We get to meet each other as the people we truly are. That is why I chose to describe the convergence of Edward Albee as playwright and Edward Albee as member of McBurney as sincere. Unmasking is Edward Albee's specialty as a playwright and McBurney's specialty as an institution."

Long pause.

"So with that hopefully successful clarification of my use of the word 'sincere,' I now have the honor of introducing to you one of our most esteemed American playwrights and one of McBurney's most esteemed members, Mr. Edward Albee."

As Albee approached the front of the terrace where I was standing, I walked toward him and handed the microphone to him. He put his hand over the mic and asked. "Is that really true, about the word 'sincere,' I mean?"

"Well, yes," I answered. "If you check the dictionary for the etymology of the word, however, it may specify a different root. There's an ongoing debate. But this interpretation applies so perfectly in your case that it must be right or at least deserving of poetic license."

Albee thanked the guests for their continuing, generous support for the mission of McBurney and spoke briefly about his years of membership at the Y. He then invited us to attend that very evening a special performance of his latest play at that time, *Three Tall Women.*

After the fundraiser, we went to the theater, and for the next several hours, we watched Edward Albee remove waxless mask after waxless mask from his characters. Since these masks were invisible, I thought that it really didn't matter if they were *sine cera* or something else. What mattered was that they were removed.

Sincerely.

Except for Demerol, to which I became attached when I had a ruptured appendix, nothing has ever been more addictive than applause. I learned that when I was enrolled in a playwriting class at NYU in the late 1970s. The professor was Ed Bullins, an award-winning, black playwright, who had achieved significant success in the 1960s with plays such as *The Taking of Miss Janie* and dozens of others.

Like any other continuing-education class, the approximately twenty-five students brought varying levels of experience and accomplishment to the course. Unlike most of us, some of the students had already written plays and were hoping to present them in class. Instead, Ed Bullins wanted us to write a new scene, with a different center of gravity, for each class meeting. He would describe a situation with inherent conflict and ask us to write a scene that would deal dramatically with that conflict. Students would play the scenes' characters in staged readings.

He once challenged us to write a scene in which two people find something and then lay conflicting claims to what they find. Nothing came to mind for days, until I unexpectedly found my inspiration while walking through the subway station at Grand Central.

I saw three people sitting on a bench, an old man at each end and a middle-aged woman with several shopping bags in the middle. In those days, she would have been called a bag lady. The men would have probably been described as down and out or winos if they were drunk. The description, "homeless," had not yet come into common usage.

The three of them were sitting there silently, staring into the distance. In my mind, I could see an invisible curtain rising slowly to reveal the three of them on a stage, with the mosaic of subway-station, navy-blue tiles spelling out "Grand Central" on the wall behind their heads. I felt that I had found the dramatic setting for the next assignment. I had not yet imagined what they would discover or what the conflict would be and how it would play out. But I was certain that the scene had to be set on a subway bench.

I had become interested in playwriting during the previous semester when I was enrolled in a French conversation course. Our final assignment was to write a paper on something we had discussed in class. I chose Eugene Ionesco's play, *Tueur sans gages*, literally *Unpaid Killer*, a classic of the theater of the absurd. I wrote an analysis of the play and added a parody of it, entitled *Livre sans pages*, or *Book Without Pages*.

When she returned our papers the following week, the professor attached a note requesting that I come see her after class, which I did. She told me that she enjoyed my parody of *Tueur sans gages* and suggested that I send it to Ionesco. I was flattered but disbelieving.

"That's like writing to Shakespeare," I remember telling her.

She encouraged me not to be intimidated by Ionesco's fame. "Many people may think, like you, that he has neither the time nor the interest in what you have to say. That's a mistake. Send it, and I bet you that he will read it."

Not knowing Ionesco's Paris address, I called his publisher, Gallimard. They suggested that I send my manuscript to them and they would, in turn, forward it to Ionesco, thereby protecting his privacy. So I did, with an attached cover letter, which, I hoped, would mitigate what I still believed to be an extremely presumptuous act.

The professor was right. About a month after I sent my parody to Ionesco, I received a letter from Paris with Ionesco's own return address. In it, he thanked me for my comments on the play and said that he enjoyed my parody very much. I was torn between disbelief and jubilation. To this day, that letter hangs in a frame on my wall, silently reminding me of "nothing ventured, nothing gained" every time I walk by it.

For the next several days, I was obsessed with my mental image of the subway bench and its three occupants. Then I envisioned the bag lady standing up, picking up her shopping bags, and walking off. On the subway-station floor, between the two men, I saw an envelope that had perhaps fallen from one of her bags. I saw the man on the right slyly look down at the envelope, followed by the man on the left doing the same. After furtive glances at each other, they both suddenly reach down and grab for the envelope. The man on the right gets there first.

The conflict begins, as they both claim ownership of the envelope. The man on the left asks the man on the right to open the envelope. He insists that the letter will prove which one of them is the real owner because the writer is a good friend of his. The man on the right opens the letter and begins to read.

No sooner has he read, "Dear Charles," than the man on the left yells, "Yeah, that's me. Good ol' Charlie Boy! That proves it."

"No, it doesn't," counters the man on the right. "It's Charles, not Charlie Boy. Charles is my name, and this is my letter."

The letter itself becomes a third character, as the two men spontaneously and creatively engage in relating to the writer of the letter and to its contents.

Both men, in effect, begin to write their own stories as they fantasize relationships to the writer and to others mentioned in the letter. Gradually their separate scripts begin to clash. An argument erupts, and the man on the left tries to snatch the letter from the man on the right. As they are fighting over the letter and tearing it apart, the bag lady returns to take the seat in the middle once again. She puts down her bags, and the two men, suddenly silent, lean back into their original positions at each end of the bench. As they do, they each drop their outside hand over the end of the bench and let pieces of the now-shredded letter fall to the ground. Curtain.

I wrote this down and turned it into Ed Bullins at our next class. He assigned three students to read it. Curtain up. Scene read. Curtain down. Applause from the class and a standing ovation from Ed Bullins himself. I was ecstatic. I couldn't wait to get home to tell my wife Anna. Several weeks later when I put on a new navy pea coat and blue turtleneck, Anna asked why I had chosen what was, for me, a new look. She reminded me that I was wearing the exact outfit I had told her that Ed Bullins always wore. I acknowledged that fact. But, after all, wasn't I now a playwright, too?

I reworked that scene into a larger play called *Lost and Found* and shopped it around to any theater that had a mailing address. Every response that I received back was a form letter with "Dear (fill in the blank): Thanks but no thanks." It was painful and demoralizing. Then one day I received a letter from the Circle Repertory Theater in Greenwich Village, a theater I knew very well.

Circle Repertory was a top-tier, off-Broadway theater. I held the envelope in my hand. It was letter size, not the usual rejection-form postcard size, to which I had unfortunately become quite accustomed. Slowly I opened it. There was a full-page, single-spaced letter inside, which began with "Dear Mr. Keefe." I was flattered already and ambivalent about continuing to read; I enjoyed the hope while I feared yet another rejection, however well presented.

My glance fell to the bottom of the page, which was signed, "Milan Stitt, Dramaturge, Circle Repertory Theater." Milan Stitt! He was a well-established playwright whose play, *The Runner Stumbles*, made it to Broadway. Whatever he might have to say in the above paragraphs, the fact that he had taken the time to comment on my play was in itself, I believed, a great compliment.

The closing scene of the first act of *The Runner Stumbles* remains for me the absolutely best moment of silence that I have ever witnessed on the stage. When the two main characters, a priest and a nun, reach their hands out to each other as slowly as statues straining to move across space, they never quite touch and thus transform themselves into a human embodiment of the Sistine Chapel's *Last Judgment.* They seem to linger forever in that position until sudden theater darkness, curtain fall, bright lights, and intermission. Magic interrupted.

I read on. Milan Stitt, the great playwright, had enjoyed *Lost and Found*! That was his opening sentence. I continued reading. He thought, however, that some elements of the play needed reconsideration. The bag lady, for example, functioned more as a prop than a character. If I wanted to keep her, I would have to give her a reason for being, an identity, a life. Otherwise I should remove her from the play. The conflict between the men also needed a more developed resolution, perhaps with some kind of identification of the author of the found letter. He suggested that I rework my play.

These were, I thought, accurate and appropriate criticisms, which in no way diminished my sense of having attained some level of success in my attempt at playwriting. I immediately framed Milan Stitt's rejection letter (in a matching frame to Ionesco's) and hung it on the wall next to my letter from Eugene Ionesco.

I made several attempts to rewrite *Lost and Found* but never completed a successful rewrite and eventually abandoned my efforts. I still feel a gentle touch of pride, however, whenever I walk past those two letters from two great playwrights. But most of all, I still hear the applause of the playwriting class, particularly the loud clapping and standing ovation by Ed Bullins. I still carry that audience with me wherever I go, whatever I do. And I am still happily addicted to applause, without any hope whatsoever of rehabilitation.

The crowded, southbound Number Four Lexington Avenue Express train suddenly slowed down as it entered the Forty-Second

Street station and caused all the riders to lean forward into their fellow passengers before falling backward once again as the motorman accelerated slightly. The train stopped and the in and out shuffle of passengers began, like a change of casts on a stage. The train started to rumble forward.

Standing in the middle of the subway car, clutching the floor-to-ceiling pole, stood a middle-aged man and an attractive young woman in her early twenties. As the train picked up speed, commensurately with the noise level, I watched the young woman speak to the middle-aged man with great intensity. It was impossible to hear what she was saying. The middle-aged man just listened while the young woman continued to plead, it seemed, for the middle-aged man's understanding.

The train slowed as it approached the sharp curve at the Fourteenth Street station, and the rumbling noise faded. As it came to a stop, the middle-aged man, who had been listening ever since the doors had closed at Forty-Second Street, finally spoke.

Looking at the young lady with great seriousness, he asked, "Do you want my advice?"

Before she could reply, I blurted out "Go…" I caught myself and whispered inaudibly "Back to Bulgaria!"

A few passengers nearby gave me a mildly admonishing glance. I got off the train even though I was on my way to Wall Street.

This happens to me a lot. I tend to see the world as an enormous set for the movie *Casablanca*, where the same scenes are performed daily by unknown performers who have no idea that they are performing. The script for *Casablanca*, a copy of which a colleague once gave me as a Christmas gift, is a sort of filter on my mind, through which I absorb and interpret the everyday events of my life.

When I saw that young woman pleading with the middle-aged man, I imagined her saying, "Monsieur, you are a man. If someone loved you very much so that your happiness was the only thing in the world that she wanted and she did a bad thing to make certain of it, could you forgive her? That would be all right, wouldn't it?" There can be no other answer to that question than "Do you want my advice? Go back to Bulgaria!"

A friend once presented me with a problem and asked my advice on his proposed solution to that problem. If I had found the solution appropriate, with a reasonable chance of success, I would have supported and encouraged him to follow through. However, his proposed solution was such sheer fantasy that I felt compelled to quote Senor Ferrari, owner of the Blue Parrot and pleasantly scheming competitor with Rick's Café Americain. In response to Laszlo and Ilsa's decision to try to get a visa not just for her but also for him, Ferrari advises, "We might as well be frank, monsieur. It will take a miracle to get you out of Casablanca. And the Germans have outlawed miracles."

Saturday night was often movie night for Anna and me. Our favorite movies were *Dial M for Murder, Witness for the Prosecution, The French Connection*, and, of course, *Casablanca*. We owned these four films so that we could watch them whenever we wanted. I was also a fan of *Angels with Dirty Faces*, with Pat O'Brien as the priest and Jimmy Cagney as the crook, Rocky Sullivan.

Cagney winds up on death row with Pat O'Brien pleading with him to die as a coward so that he won't be a hero to the Depression-era kids in the neighborhood who worship Rocky as a brave tough guy. Cagney refuses but does die a coward. Because Pat O'Brien asked him or because he really was a coward? For me, that question has been a lifelong, internal debate, still unanswered. Even Pat O'Brien never knew for sure, and Cagney never told him.

Every time I hear an airplane propeller starting up, I hear the opening bars of "La Marseillaise" and Victor Lazlo's East European–accented voice say to Rick, "Welcome back to the fight. This time I know our side will win." Then I see Ilsa turn her tear-stained face to Rick and painfully whisper, "Good-bye, Rick. God bless you," before boarding the plane.

Another Wall Street–bound train pulls into the Fourteenth Street station. It is so crowded that it is impossible to observe anything. As I morph into a human pretzel, I realize that *Casablanca* has stopped playing in my head. All I can see in my mind's eye is "The End." I am left to ponder a question that I had never before asked myself. Which character in *Casablanca* do I most resemble?

I could not help admitting to myself that every time I had watched *Casablanca,* I had consciously or unconsciously identified with either Bogie or Victor Laszlo. Maybe that was because, either way, I would get the girl, Ilsa Lund. Or maybe it was because I wanted to be brave and noble, individual and strong, just like Victor Laszlo, who had been in and out of concentration camps, with the Nazis chasing him all over Europe. Rick's appeal, on the other hand, arose from his being a conflicted man of mystery, tolerant of corruption, and cynical yet betrayed by a past of good deeds.

Sometimes I would even identify with Captain Renault, particularly when Rick describes him as "just like any other man...only more so." Humorously cynical yet utterly unscrupulous, a man who identifies himself as "just a poor corrupt official who bends with the wind," Captain Renault appeals because he is brutally honest about his own dishonesty. Real men all three, full of contradictions and their own particular versions of honesty.

As the train accelerated, slowed, reaccelerated, and lurched its way toward the Brooklyn Bridge station, my inability to distract myself, with any other observation than my bent-pretzel, sandwiched-self, forced me into an honest assessment of my probable behavior should I have found myself in the world of *Casablanca.* The self-assessment was more painful to my morale than the crush of the subway passengers was to my body.

I discovered that I was really Jan, the boy in the man's world of *Casablanca.* He is trying to do the right thing for Annina, his fiancée, but is incapable of seeing the world as it is. Jan is decent, but he surrenders to the desperate, naïve hope of winning at roulette instead of taking decisive, courageous action, something Rick and Laszlo would do instinctively. His fiancée, Annina, the young woman whom Rick has told to go back to Bulgaria, is so much more mature and, in the end, is the one who does take the initiative and provokes the decisive action. Jan, the boy, is saved by the very woman he can't save because he is not man enough to do it.

That evening, after work, I stopped in a local pub. As I sat at the end of the bar drinking a beer and nursing my wounded, I-am-really-just-Jan-after-all ego, a very beautiful young woman, accompanied by a somewhat older, well-dressed man, walked through the door. In an instant, I forgot about identifying with Jan and became Bogie once again, saying to myself, "Of all the gin joints in all the towns in all the world, she walks into mine." I wanted to turn to Sam and command, "If she can stand it, I can. Play it," and I expected the barroom chatter to fade beneath the sound of "As Time Goes By."

But the music never came. I was left staring at myself in the mirror behind the bar, watching myself drink a beer. I recalled that nobody in *Casablanca* drank beer. They all drank champagne cocktails and Veuve Clicquot '26. I wondered if Jan ever grew up.

A number of years ago, the New School for Social Research in Greenwich Village offered a graduate course entitled The Writings of James Joyce, taught by a Professor Daniel from Princeton University. The course was also open to nonmatriculating students, of which I was one. I had read some, but certainly not all, of Joyce's writings. This course intended to cover most of what Joyce had written, with a concentration on his masterwork, *Ulysses.*

My impression of *Ulysses* was that it was more a rite of passage than a work of literature. Reading it from beginning to end was in itself not only an intellectual achievement but also an act of great perseverance. Understanding it was something else, a sort of certification as an intellectual. I had read *Ulysses* twice, proving my extreme perseverance but failing in certification as an intellectual because I didn't understand the book. Professor Daniel's class presented me with the opportunity to redeem myself and finally achieve that evasive intellectual certification.

The syllabus for the course was formidable. We would begin with *The Dubliners*, traditional short stories, meet Stephen Dedalus in *Portrait of the Artist*, read some of Joyce's poetry, move on to *Ulysses*, and, time permitting, conclude with *Finnegan's Wake.*

The Dubliners are wonderful short stories, and I liked Joyce's poem, *Ecce Puer. Portrait of the Artist* seemed like training camp for *Ulysses.* Students contemplating serious relationships might have also been scared away from marriage by one of the characters telling Stephen that "Reproduction is the beginning of death." And then came *Ulysses*, where we lingered.

As we spent weeks following Bloom's twenty-four-hour odyssey around Dublin, now and then bumping into Stephen Dedalus, Professor Daniel was often peppered with questions that were, in fact, not questions at all but rather barely disguised displays of prior learning: "Professor Daniel, Bloom is a man of experience in its most fundamental sense, a man who accepts the world as it is and life as it is. While Stephen casts his analytic net upon the world, seeking to capture and distill it in ideas, Bloom lets the everyday world wash over him in a free-flowing stream. Its sights, smells, and sounds, along with evoked memories and spontaneous thoughts, are multiplexed into a conscious whole, the conscious whole that powers *Ulysses*." To make this minidissertation a question, the student would add, on a rising inflective tone, "Isn't that so?"

Professor Daniel would only have time to reply monosyllabically before another student would orate in a basso profondo: "In *Ulysses*, the ties of language are loosened by puns such as the word 'will' bearing the triple meaning of desire, bequest, and Shakespeare's first name. Words are dislodged from their objects, just as lists of names of people we never meet are dislodged from the characters they name."

As Professor Daniel would wait in hope for the question yet to come, she would hear once again, "Isn't that so?" I wondered how many times these students had taken this course or how many times I would have to take this course before being able to ask such lengthy questions.

After six weeks with Bloom, we tiredly made our way back home to Molly. There was still another week to go, however, before the end of the semester, so Professor Daniel asked us to read *Finnegan's Wake* and write a report on it for our final class. She advised us that it would be difficult, which proved to be an understatement.

After slogging my way through the book and effectively understanding nothing, I came to the conclusion that Joyce wrote *Finnegan's Wake* the way he did in order to encourage readers to imagine their own stories and create their own books, since the one they were reading was essentially incomprehensible. I was intrigued by the fact that a book that nobody understood could provoke unending, opinionated discussion alongside that admission.

Maybe, as one of the students suggested, Joyce's words had become so separated from their meanings that *Finnegan's Wake* is just a book of meaningless words. If this were true, then I should be able to pick any page at random, remove it, and substitute a page that I had written in a similar style, without anyone noticing the difference. I decided to do this for my final assignment.

FINAL ASSIGNMENT

Dear Professor Daniel:

A friend of mine is a fireman in the South Bronx. Two weeks ago, a large chest was found and rescued from a burning warehouse near Bruckner Boulevard. Buried among the books and papers in the chest was an envelope on which was written, "First-draft, manuscript page for unpublished work. Do not discard. Extremely important and valuable. JJ."

Could "JJ." be James Joyce? When my fireman friend showed the manuscript to me, the style seemed like something that Joyce could have written, based on my limited exposure to Joyce's writings.

Needless to say, this tantalizing discovery provoked much interest among scholars and writers. My fireman friend is himself a lifelong friend of Professor Rick O'Shea of Fordham University, a well-known scholar of Joyce, who bounces back and forth between Fordham and Oxford. His preliminary review of the manuscript has led him to believe, pending further review, that the manuscript page enclosed is the original, first-draft, manuscript page for what is now page 127 in the Penguin edition of *Finnegan's Wake*, published in 1990.

I would very much appreciate your review of the attached page and your opinion on its validity and provenance.

Thank you.

First Draft of Page 127, 1990 Penguin Edition of *Finnegan's Wake*

"Ignotus rose to pose a question. Rose? A thorny one. Flourish the thought. You should hoe better. I dew. The dawn breaks for Robert Burns the thawn bricks and the thorn pricks.

"That's right, go to your left. Winsome she is but loses more. Caught a hot coal gets bitter with cold heat. Gets better with colonic or caloric don't know but fa caldo ist kalt. For peat's sake, a fire if you can befeuer I catch cold. Rake the ashes and slake the infernal thirst of a roll of paradice with beetrysts. Thanks, Man of Mantua, tu a man? Hold on and hold off comes the end of the line. Hear the meter? See the meter. Oje, mira! Cervantes unzipped his Spanish fly. Insecticide that was. Does he have a lach on his keep or a keyp for the lach? Answer if you no. Yes? Know! Lovely Roman hand guiding me. Could be verse worse verse. Jambo habari pombe tatu baridi sana tafadali s'il vous plait. Now try to fix the wave that broke for shore for shore. Calm jibs for sale under her merry orchards. Utter shudder Silas should have. No. Enough to suck the sand into a dreary dirge to purge the urge what a scourge.

"Possapickleplumputterpuppetplump. That's what I said. Possapickleplumpputterpuppetplump. Plumper this time. Caesar never looked back when he was affronted. That's how they got him. Next venit Livia. O rage, O desespoir, O vieillesse ennemi! Grab my bandolier, Baudelaire. If it gets hotter goes into the nineties fan de siecle. Need a good cleansing. Sing the Oratorio and go to Purgatorio. Ask Ali-Ghieri the Saracen who saw Sarah sin. Oremus and out. Furwhat Livia does know but true art on the corner of mossclad walls smiling in rainbow colors. You'd think all the dancing would stop but the music is instrumental in all that after all. Trumpet the sax and strumpet the sex. Smacked in the head with a tambourine HCE (He Can't Exist He Can't Explain He Could Exist Hic Cogitat Evidenter.) made note of it.

"Sharp pain he fell flat lost track of time last movement no phony sin but that was Moe's Art if you haven't heard. Didn't you see her heading for the hedge holding her head high hopping hopefully? Enough to make you cry for Phlegm and Pflaunt and that's a laugh. Ran rings around her finger they did. Livia was livid but living and lively. Pfutoosh! What?

"You heard me. Cough it up, Phlegm, you impostoring penile pest. Beat your drum with symbolic cymbals and cymbalic semaphores they're symbiotic you know. Wrahhhrockagoffidrillinga! Shows sympathy to pathetic Pflaunt looking gaunt in his new haunt. Is his haunt a house and Ireland an aisle like a Phew! in church? Think not knotty thoughts, you sinister bastard, HCE. I'm right that you are all that's left for Livia en rose."

One of the most appealing features of auditing a course is that you can't fail, which, I found, gave me the freedom to voice opinions that I would have normally been too timid to advance. Who was I to forge a page of *Finnegan's Wake*? I would never have tried that with Shakespeare. Discussing something about which you know nothing, with others who are similarly handicapped, is very liberating. It is even more liberating when there is nothing to be known about the subject about which you know nothing. That discussion is open to limitless creativity.

Maybe that was Joyce's mission after all. Maybe *Finnegans Wake* could be called *Portrait of the Reader As An Artist,* because in *Finnegan's Wake,* there is no Finnegan and there is no wake. In fact, there might have been no book at all, if Joyce had tried to publish it with a nom de plume other than his own.

Professor Daniel asked me for permission to use my "manuscript page" the next time she taught the course. Flattered, I responded, "Of course." I should take the course again. I felt that I was evolving into one of those students who asked all those isn't-it-so questions. Was I finally on the verge of being certified as an intellectual? Joyce would probably say, "Yes, but I don't No."

TOGETHER

"The next person who pushes into me is going to get hit in the head and the heart," yelled the heavyset black woman I was pushing against on the overcrowded elevator at the Westchester Medical Center. I had just been discharged after three weeks in the hospital, following open-heart surgery and multiple complications. What I dreaded most was not making it to the front door and out of the hospital. If that woman were to punch me in the chest, I might be back in intensive care. I begged her to relax, explaining that I was being pushed into pushing her.

We made it to the main floor without a punch. Anna and I hurried out the front door and into the parking lot. I just wanted to get away. I felt like an escaping prisoner. I had to get into the car and be gone before "they" came to get me and foiled my escape. I thought I was going mad. All I could think about was being free from the clutches of the Westchester Medical Center. Anna helped me into the passenger seat, and we drove away. I felt better as I contemplated the very real possibility of being home, being safe, and being alive.

It was a Saturday afternoon in early June, sunny and pleasant. I was exhausted, as much from physical debilitation as from the stress of the escape. I lay down on the couch, and Anna brought me a cup of tea. But I was nervous and found it difficult to relax. Anna said that it was probably the lingering effects of the anesthesia.

I'd had three major surgeries during my first five days in the hospital: open-heart surgery, then that same night, another open-heart operation to stop uncontrollable bleeding, followed four days later by surgery for an intestinal blockage, the cause of which was unknown. All required a lot of anesthesia. I was jumpy and on edge, particularly when I recalled the punch-prone woman in the elevator. I finally fell asleep.

Anna was at home for the remainder of the weekend but had to return to her office on Monday morning. Before leaving, she put out all my medicines along with a written schedule for taking them. I tried not to appear needy or nervous, but I was frightened to be alone, which I suddenly was when Anna closed the door behind her.

What-ifs ran through my mind. I tried to calm myself. Nothing worked until I recalled the irony of my being afraid to be alone. For years, I had been afraid of being together. Being together, being married, had been for me the most frightening possibility in the world. That fear had even continued into the early months of our marriage. The fear of being alone that I experienced when Anna left for her office after my open-heart surgery was the precise opposite of the fear of being together. In both cases, a heart problem, real or imagined, was at the center of those fears.

When we were first married and before Anna returned to graduate school for her PhD in clinical psychology, she had been a social worker with a relatively normal schedule. Anna would prepare dinner most nights at seven, which was a schedule that I had not been used to as a bachelor. I was adapting to a world of togetherness, which, for a number of unknown, buried reasons, was difficult for me.

One evening after we had been married for about two months, while we were having dinner in our Greenwich Village apartment, I felt a pain in my chest. I abruptly rose from the table, told Anna I would be right back, and left the apartment to go to St. Vincent's Hospital, about fifteen blocks away. Not surprisingly Anna was stunned and confused by my abrupt exit and had no idea where I had gone.

I arrived at the emergency room of St. Vincent's Hospital and told the nurse I was having chest pains, which is something they take very seriously in emergency rooms. A doctor came in and examined me with his stethoscope. They took down my medical history and my family's medical history. The doctor asked a lot of questions about the frequency of my pain, diet, exercise, marital status, and general health issues. They did an EKG. Finally he asked me to describe the circumstances preceding the onset of the chest pains.

I explained that Anna and I were newlyweds and had just sat down to dinner when the pains began. He asked what I had eaten.

"Hardly anything, when the pains began," I replied.

"You are thirty-two years old," he noted. "Is this your first marriage?"

"Yes," I answered.

"I suppose at thirty-two you are adapting to a new routine," he volunteered.

"Yes, I agreed. It's different, more structured, more organized. I'm adapting to togetherness."

"Well, we can't find anything wrong with you physically. Maybe you're under some stress in your adaptation to married life. What do you do for a living?"

"I run a computer center at NYU, and I am in a doctoral program in philosophy," I replied.

"Stressful?" he asked.

"Not really."

"I think you should just go back home and relax. I will give you a prescription for a mild sedative. By the way, how did you get over here, to the emergency room?"

"I jogged over from Third Street," I answered.

His eyes widened, and his eyebrows climbed up higher on his forehead. He looked at me as if I had just confessed to him that I was a serial killer. "You jogged over? You thought you might be having a heart attack, and you jogged over?"

"Well, I wanted to get here as quickly as I could," I explained.

He handed me the prescription, wished me good luck, and suggested I try something like yoga or meditation in order to relax myself.

I left the emergency room and walked home. Anna was waiting nervously. When I explained what happened, her fear turned to anger.

"Why didn't you tell me?" she said. "I didn't know what happened or why you suddenly got up from dinner and left without explaining why."

I had no answer except to admit that I had been feeling these pains ever since we returned from our honeymoon.

"But you go running every day. Do you really think there's a heart problem?"

Then I confessed that I had jogged over to St. Vincent's Hospital. The same expression of confusion and disbelief that I had seen on the doctor's face now came over Anna's face.

After thirty years of happily married life, the fear of a heart problem had returned, only now it was caused by the fear of being alone, not the fear of being together. But was it the same fear? Thirty years before, I was afraid of sharing my life with another person. Thirty years after I had begun to share, however, I was afraid of being without her, even for a few hours. Different fears, same symptoms. What I found in sharing was trust, something I learned from Anna. That was the difference in my fears.

In the afternoon, Chris, a neighbor, came by to say hello. Anna had asked her to look in on me. Chris asked me if I would like to go for a walk with her. She knew that I exercised regularly and thought it would be good for me. It was my first time out for a walk in weeks. At first I was nervous and unsteady, but soon walking became increasingly affirming. We walked about three miles, and I felt so much better. The walk restored my faith in myself, my sense of independence. My fear evaporated. I had survived being alone for the day by trusting another.

One month later we returned to Westchester Medical Center for a routine follow-up visit with the cardiologist. After the visit, we went to the fourth floor, where I had spent most of my hospital stay, in order to thank the nurses who had taken care of me. Anna had brought along a big box of cookies for them. When we later got on the elevator to leave the hospital, I looked about anxiously for the woman who was once going to punch me. She wasn't there. I stopped being afraid.

As we drove away from the Westchester Medical Center, I turned on the radio. A song from the 1970s by Linda Rondstadt was playing. It was called "Desperado." "Your prison is walking all alone through this world," she sang.

It is hard to escape from a prison you don't know you are in. Open-heart surgery had left me with a scar. But many years before, Anna had made that first incision, which had sent me running over to St. Vincent's Hospital, frightened by the pain in a heart that was, for the first time, beginning to open.

Aunt Dolly unexpectedly surfaced one night. Anna and I had been invited to dinner at the home of Anna's colleague Joan, who lived with her husband, John, in an apartment in Washington Heights, near Columbia Presbyterian Hospital. John was a resident there in internal medicine. Their apartment wasn't far from my family's apartment in Washington Heights, where my mother lived with my Aunt Dolly, christened Princess Hanging Ninnies by my sister, and my Uncle Tommy, named the Generalissimo by Dolly. They, in turn, called my mother the Actress because of her dramatic responses to their constant arguing.

As we were sharing a drink and getting to know each other, John recounted a "crazy experience" at the local A&P. I immediately suspected that my Aunt Dolly might be involved, because that was where she shopped. When John continued with "there was this madwoman," I knew without a doubt that it had been Aunt Dolly. But I was too embarrassed to admit to new acquaintances that "this madwoman" was, in all probability, my aunt.

As John continued with his account of his crazy experience with the madwoman in the local A&P, I tried to bury my embarrassment beneath attentive interest in his account of the event. "She was waiting on the checkout line. A short woman, with straight gray hair." Poker-faced, I quietly and internally confirmed Dolly's identity.

"Exactly what happened, I am not sure, but she apparently thought a Spanish couple in the checkout line—I could hear them talking in Spanish as I waited on a nearby checkout line—had cut in front of her. Well, she went crazy."

"'Go back home, you foreign bastards. You don't belong here. This is America, and it's for Americans. You're probably on welfare and don't even work for a living,'" John quoted her as saying. I recognized Dolly's MO—anyone who crossed her was typically accused of being unemployed, ironically something she never said of herself, even though she hadn't had a job since she was about sixteen years old.

I remained silent, looking for an opportunity to change the subject, which eventually came. Later that evening on the way home, I told Anna that I was quite certain that the woman in the A&P of whom John had spoken had without a doubt been my aunt Dolly. I confessed that I had been too embarrassed to say anything. Anna said she hadn't thought of Dolly, but knowing Dolly, she would not be surprised. It took years for me to admit the truth to Joan and John.

I had moved out of Washington Heights soon after being discharged from the army and beginning work at IBM. I continued to regularly visit the Actress, the Princess, and the Generalissimo, who were still living in the old apartment. Dolly dropped my nom de guerre and actually began to call me by my name, which confirmed what I had always suspected. The path to peace ran right through and out the front door of that apartment.

I sometimes imagine that Princess Hanging Ninnies and the Generalissimo were, along with the Actress, characters in a play on an invisible stage. They were given a copy of a script, and they read their lines as they were written, unable to rewrite them for themselves, as if they had no choice. Maybe that is why I still can't bring down the curtain on their play. I wish I could.

At eleven minutes before eleven in the morning, on the eleventh day of the eleventh month in 1975, all work stopped at the IBM office in Frankfurt, Germany, as waiters in white jackets arrived with trays of champagne. Under any circumstances, this would have been an incredible but welcome surprise. Having come to Germany from IBM USA, however, where prohibition had yet to be repealed (at IBM, that is), this was borderline fantasy. I overcame both my surprise and my prohibition inhibition and quickly joined my German colleagues in toasting Armistice Day 1918, fifty-seven years in the unforgotten past and the day that brought the end of the Great War.

I had been on assignment in Frankfurt for several weeks and had been staying at the Hotel Intercontinental, a quite elegant hotel not far from the IBM office. The project that I had been working on was taking longer than expected, and the project manager asked me to stay on for several more weeks. That would have been fine, except for the fact that Anna and I had been planning a vacation scheduled to begin the following week. "No problem," said the project manager as he opened a drawer filled with unused airline tickets. "Your wife will be our guest, and then you can have your vacation in Europe."

Arrangements were made for Anna to arrive in a few days. Gyms were not yet common in hotels, but the Intercontinental had a big, beautiful sauna, which I used almost every evening after returning from the office. Incredibly almost every evening it was empty. Only once while I was in the sauna did I see another person, an elderly gentleman reading a book. I assumed the women's sauna would be equally empty, if not more so, considering that the hotel catered to business travelers who, in those days, were mostly men.

Several days later Anna arrived, and I picked her up at the airport. Although she was tired, she wanted to have lunch and do some sight-seeing. We drove to Heidelberg for lunch at a charming little restaurant and later returned to the Intercontinental. She went up to our room to sleep, and I returned to the office. I suggested that she might like to take a sauna later. I was sure that the women's sauna would be at least as pleasant as the men's sauna was.

When I returned to the hotel around seven that evening, several hours earlier than I usually did, Anna was awake and looking forward to a sauna. Since we didn't know the location of the women's sauna, she would inquire at the concierge desk. We agreed to meet back in the room in about forty-five minutes after my trip to the men's sauna. Anna left, and about fifteen minutes later, I followed. I was looking forward to a really hot, empty sauna.

The door to the sauna had a small glass window through which, to my surprise, I could see a crowd of people, something I had not seen before during the weeks of my nightly visits. In the middle of the crowd, I spotted Anna wrapped in a towel and surrounded by naked men. Surprise turned to shock until Anna peered back at me, smiled, and beckoned me to enter. As I did, I noticed a group of naked young women sitting on the top row. I later found out they were Lufthansa stewardesses staying at the hotel. I sat down next to Anna in the front row. She was the only person in the sauna not completely naked.

Anna grabbed my hand and remarked, "You look surprised, Mr. Continental."

I was speechless. I had used this sauna more than twenty times, and it was almost always empty. More importantly I had had no idea that it was coed. I was still having trouble coming to terms with that fact. While I struggled with this new reality, a very muscular man climbed down from an upper row and began to do exercises near the stove. Anna was impressed.

"Look at the build on that guy," she said as "that guy" continued to do his Mr. Universe warm-ups.

I responded, "What's the big deal?"

"What's the big deal?" Anna asked. "I have never seen such a perfect build. Look at those muscles. Even his legs…they're beautiful."

At this point, the muscleman picked up what looked to me like a tree branch and began flagellating himself on the back, while periodically pouring eucalyptus on the fire. I could have sworn I heard Anna sigh, "Wow." I was now moving from annoyed to competitive.

He began doing push-ups and then sit-ups. More eucalyptus. More flagellation. Countless knee bends. Anna seemed hypnotized, unable to contain her admiration for this incredible specimen of masculinity and muscle. I was determined to find a way to compete with this guy when Anna suddenly said, "It's getting too hot in here. Let's go outside."

As we stood up to leave, so did Mr. Universe. In fact, he jumped in front of us and opened the door. We followed him out. I could tell that Anna's eyes were glued to him as he strutted off with slow, slightly swaggering steps, a white towel draped around his neck. I was happy to see him walk away. Unfortunately he stopped.

For a few moments, he stood still before a small, four-foot-square pool of water that I had not noticed before. He dropped his towel to the floor. We, too, had stopped walking. His hands were on his hips, and he began to take deep breaths, deeper and deeper, while bending down at the waist, then back up, and then back down again. He started flapping his arms back and forth like a big bird. I heard another almost inaudible "wow." Suddenly he stopped, stood straight, let out a great roar, and jumped into the pool of water.

He disappeared for some seconds and then emerged from the water with a great leap back onto the marble floor, all in a single motion. Anna's previously inaudible "wow" turned into "Oh my God, did you see that?"

I responded, "See what? No big deal."

"No big deal?" she asked in disbelief. "You can't do that."

"Oh, no?" I bragged. "Watch me."

I wasn't quite sure what I was going to do, but I had to do something. Since his routine had so impressed Anna, I decided I would do the same thing. It didn't seem that hard, and a "wow" from Anna would restore my threatened masculinity. At this point, being naked seemed normal, so I swaggered off to the four-foot-square pool with the hope of reclaiming my esteemed position in Anna's universe.

I stood at the side of the little pool and began to take deep breaths. I didn't know why I was taking deep breaths. But Mr. Universe had taken deep breaths, so it must be the right thing to do. I might have taken one-too-many deep breaths, however, because I started to get dizzy. I flapped my arms back and forth, just the way muscleman had done. I was ready. I roared as loud as I could and jumped in.

The water must have been thirty-three degrees, just warm enough for it not to turn to ice. Everything in my body stopped. I had no energy. I floated to the top like a dead man. I heard Anna shout, "Are you OK?"

But I couldn't answer since I was facedown in the water. Then I felt somebody pulling my arm. I turned my head and realized Anna was pulling me out of the little pool. She dragged me by the right arm and managed to get me onto the marble floor, where I lay facedown and naked, like a beached whale.

Anna rolled me over, and I saw a worried look on her face. "Are you OK?" she asked, her voice filled with concern.

"I'm OK," I murmured. "I just have to lie here for a bit. I didn't realize the water was so cold."

"Why did you have to do that?" she asked rhetorically, not really expecting to hear the answer she already knew.

Just then the group of Lufthansa stewardesses, having descended from the top row of the sauna, walked by. They were all giggling and chatting away in German. I didn't understand everything they were saying, but I did pick up the line that brought the biggest laugh. Nodding toward me, one of the stewardesses snickered, "Look at Herr Shrivel."

My war with Mr. Universe was over. I had agreed to an armistice even though he didn't know that we had been at war. Now where were those guys in the white jackets with the trays of champagne?

When Anna and I first began dating, she was living on the Upper West Side of Manhattan, my old neighborhood. One night I couldn't resist walking past the police station on One Hundredth Street, the scene of the great PAL heist, where my burgeoning criminal career had begun and ended in a single day. I thought of Sonny and Crumb. Long after I had lost touch with them, I heard that they had sadly ended up in prison for some unknown crime.

Anna was sharing an apartment on Ninety-Fourth Street between Columbus and Amsterdam Avenues with her friends, Bonnie and Christine. Their brownstone was not far from the brownstone where I had attended kindergarten on Ninety-Seventh Street. Looking west from Anna's building, I could see the high walls of the Hotel Paris. The words, "Hotel Paris," repainted many times, were still on the wall of the building.

The kindergarten, from the roof of which I had first read those words, was gone. Half the neighborhood had been torn down and rebuilt, and I, too, was long gone, living in Greenwich Village. Because of my kindergarten connection, whenever I found myself on the Upper West Side, I felt compelled to confirm that the Hotel Paris was still the Hotel Paris. Those words had been my introduction to another world, to Europe.

Anna and I visited Paris many times after we were married, on business or vacation or both. We stayed at many different hotels over the years, including several times at the newly upscale Hôtel de l'Académie, where I had stayed on my first visit to the City of Lights. We always found a hotel near the Boulevard Saint-Germain, straying no farther south than the Luxembourg Gardens or farther north than the Quai des Grands-Augustins. The narrow streets remained the same, while many cafes and restaurants changed names, old shops closed, and new shops opened.

In September 1983, I was on a business trip in Europe that would terminate in Paris. Anna and I decided to meet there. We would be arriving in Paris on different days, so we decided to meet at a café-restaurant that we had frequented several times. It was a pleasant, cozy, easy, and informal place, on the Boulevard Saint-Germain, just a few blocks from the Boulevard Saint-Michel. It was called Cour Saint-Germain, with tables outside and inside. I expected to come directly from the airport and would arrive around five o'clock in the afternoon, if my plane from Milan was on time and the traffic was forgiving.

Miraculously there were no serious delays and I arrived at Cour Saint-Germain around five fifteen. I saw Anna sitting at an outside table and decided to surprise her. I crossed Boulevard Saint-Germain so that I could walk by Cour Saint-Germain unnoticed and then crossed back again. I stealthily approached Anna, who was sipping a glass of white wine and puffing on a Gauloise. Anna had never smoked in her life. She had gone native, I thought. I came up behind her and said, "*Bonsoir, madame.*" Feigning no surprise, she responded, "*Bonsoir, monsieur.* Pull up a chair and order yourself a drink," which I did. And so began a perfect, late-summer evening in Paris.

As we chatted in the lingering sunlight, the waitress brought a dish to a woman seated alone at a nearby table. Anna thought the dish looked interesting and asked me to ask the woman what it was called. I turned to the woman inquiringly, "*Pardon, madame. Ce plat-la, comment s'appelle-t-il* (may I ask what the name of that dish is)?"

She told me, and I thanked her. As I turned to tell Anna, the woman touched my arm and asked, "*Et vous, monsieur, comment vous appelez-vous* (and what is your name, monsieur)?"

Ah, Paris, I thought, *what a city!*

After several drinks, we decided to have dinner at a small restaurant called Provence, between Boulevard Saint-Germain and the Seine. Anna and I had not seen each other in about ten days. There was so much to tell and so much to hear. After a very pleasant dinner, we walked leisurely down to, and along, the Seine before returning to Boulevard Saint-Germain and a café called La Rhumerie for an after-dinner drink.

The name, Rhumerie, always seemed ambiguous to me. It means "rum distillery," but if you sat in La Rhumerie for more than ten minutes, you might well wind up with a cold, "rhume," or at least a bad cough, because everyone in La Rhumerie, with the exception of the waiters and ourselves, was smoking nonstop. Finding *la toilette* in La Rhumerie was like making an instrument landing in a fog. But La Rhumerie did have a certain *je ne sais quoi*, as they say, and we would always stop there for a nightcap at the end of the evening.

The waiter came to our table. Anna ordered a cognac, and I ordered water. Anna was not much of a drinker, but that evening she really enjoyed the cognac. She ordered a second one, and I ordered another water. Later she ordered a third cognac, and I ordered another water. When the waiter returned with our drinks, I said to him, "Can you believe how much cognac she is drinking?" He replied, "Monsieur, I cannot believe how much water you are drinking."

No matter how many times you visit Paris, something always makes it seem like it's the first time.

Here I am on the Harlem River Drive in northern Manhattan, looking out on the sea of cars all around me. Late afternoon has become early evening. I look across the river at a still-dark Yankee Stadium. The Yankees must be out of town, or maybe it's just too early. I can feel the frustration rising, not only in me but all around me. Some car horns even honk, more a cry of impotence than effectiveness. I impatiently await the miraculous arrival of patience.

I thought I had found a cure for traffic jams, at least a self-pacifying, emotional cure. The cars would remain, but I would go away, somewhere. The soothing chant of the monks of Tamié, at the touch of a button, would drift from my speakers and carry me far away from the imprisoned cars on the FDR Drive or the Major Deegan or the New Jersey Turnpike. The result would be instantaneous out-of-here. No angry frustration. No impatience. Total acceptance. Peace.

I press that button now, here on the Harlem River Drive, surrounded by unhappy people in motionless cars. And soon peace seeps into my car like a soft, quiet fog, shapeless and pervasive. In fact, "peace" could be a translation for Tamié, if Tamié weren't, instead, a place, a small village in the French Alps. Tamié is not far from the beautiful old city of Annecy, with a town-center of flower-strewn canals flowing past strong, weather-worn, gray-stone buildings, a medieval center of tranquility from which all automotive traffic is happily banned. The center of Annecy is that rare place where time travel to the past is possible, even encouraged.

Anna and I had been staying in a farmhouse not far from Annecy and had no idea that a place called Tamié even existed. And we certainly had no knowledge of the monastery until we came upon it one afternoon, several days after our arrival, while out walking along a quiet country road. That evening, at the farmhouse, we asked the proprietress about it. She was only too happy to give us a detailed history. She was, by nature, a very friendly woman. But she became particularly warm when I innocently ingratiated myself by asking her if the woman working with her was her sister, since they both looked quite alike. As it happened, the other woman was not her sister but her daughter, which naturally made me *client numéro un* for the duration of our stay.

We returned to the monastery the next day and were welcomed inside by one of the monks. We were allowed to walk around the grounds as long as we did not disturb the monks at their work. We were also allowed into the church when the monks were not there, praying and chanting. We learned that the monastery had been opened in 1132 AD and had been in continuous operation ever since. The floors of the church attested to its age. The floor stones had been smoothed and polished by innumerable monks sliding their sandals along them every few hours of every day for nearly nine centuries. The floors themselves undulated like small, suspended waves on a sea of stone awaiting yet another irresistible push forward from the depths of the earth beneath the church.

This was a place of peace. I wanted to take some of it home with us. Near a side entrance to the church, the monks had set up a small shop, where they sold, among other items, tapes of their daily chants. We purchased several, which all began with the sounds of dawn at Tamié: chirping birds, followed by tolling church bells and the sound of monks' sandals sliding across the stone floors as they entered the church to chant the hours of the monastic day. These sounds are the peace I have carried about in my car ever since, driving the monks of Tamié along every highway in and around New York City, inviting them to miraculously dispel traffic jams and frustration with the simple beauty of Gregorian chant.

As we left the monastery, however, some passing cars reminded us that it was no longer the twelfth century but the late twentieth, even in Tamié. It was almost time to think about dinner. Arriving back at the farmhouse, we asked Madame if she could recommend a restaurant in the area. She sent us to a beautiful, little village called Talloires, which sits on the shores of Lac d'Annecy, a clear, sky-blue Alpine lake embraced by the deep-green arms of countless pines that mass, like a silent army, between the shores of the lake and the sides of the distant mountains. Talloires itself is a pretty, charming little village that attracts all sorts of people with, as far as we could tell, one thing in common: quite a bit of money.

There being an exception to every rule, however, we, too, were in Talloires.

This sole financial criterion resulted in a population of movie stars and crooked politicians, like Baby Doc Duvalier, who came to Talloires with all the money he had stolen from Haiti. The restaurant recommended by Madame back at the farmhouse, Au Père Bise, sat on the water's edge, surrounded by pines swaying slightly in the soft, Alpine breeze. An outdoor terrace, filled with patrons who, unlike us, seemed quite accustomed to dining amid such splendor, looked out on a world that brought to our eyes the same serenity that Tamié had brought to our ears. If only the monks could sing for our supper…

While sipping our aperitifs, we scanned the menus that the maître d' had given us. Patrons, we were to learn, ordered their dinners while relaxing on the terrace, and when all was prepared, including the decanted wine, they would be invited to dine inside. Having decided what to order, I picked up the wine list. Anna and I preferred a dry red wine on most occasions. I started reading the large, one-page wine list in the upper left hand corner, where the first bottle of wine was listed as costing about $3,000 American dollars. I quickly dropped my glance to the lower right-hand corner of the wine list, where I found a bottle of wine for only thirty-five dollars. I immediately felt much more comfortable wandering around this section of the wine list.

As I was busily searching for an affordable bottle of wine, the maître d', an affable, somewhat portly Frenchman in his late fifties, approached a German couple who had arrived before us. When they answered, "*Ja,*" to "*Vous avez choisi* (have you decided)?" the maître d' took their dinner order. His next question was, "*Et les vins, monsieur*?"

Although I was still lingering in the lower right-hand corner of the wine list, I was curious to hear what the German man's wine order would be. He first ordered a bottle of white wine, which I immediately found on the wine list and which cost approximately $600, followed by a bottle of red that cost about $800. Smiling broadly, the maître d' reached for the wine list and, looking the German directly in the eye, exclaimed, "*Excellent, monsieur, excellent.*"

Those words generated a sudden jolt in the pit of my stomach, which immediately compelled me to move farther north on the wine list. I was now considering a bottle in the fifty-dollar range, although that was still such a far cry from the $1,400 that had earned the German two "*excellents.*" Clearly I wasn't even yet in range of just a single "*excellent.*"

The moment of truth was approaching, as was the maître d'. "*Bonsoir, monsieur-dame. Vous avez choisi?*"

While Anna ordered, I gradually moved up on the wine list to a fifty-five-dollar bottle of Saint-Estèphe, just in time, as the maître d' was awaiting my dinner order.

The dreaded question followed. "*Et les vins, monsieur?*"

Intimidated, I ordered my fifty-five-dollar bottle of Saint-Estèphe with all the false authority I could muster.

At that, the maître d' reached for the wine list and, looking me directly in the eye, intoned, "*Excellent, monsieur, excellent!*"

In my head, I heard myself say, "*Professionel, professionel!*"

With full stomachs and that happy feeling that only a fifty-five-dollar bottle of wine can bring, Anna and I left the restaurant and strolled along the lake on our way to the parking lot, which looked like a traffic jam of Rolls-Royces, Mercedes, Porches, and the occasional Ferrari, all aglow in the light of the full moon over Lac d'Annecy. It wasn't easy to find our VW Beetle, sandwiched in, as it was, between a Rolls-Royce XL (Extra Large) and a Mercedes L (Large), but we did find it. It was a lovely night for a drive along the quiet, empty country road that wrapped about the lake like a necklace.

It was a relatively short distance back to the farmhouse, where Madame was awaiting our arrival and our verdict on Au Père Bise. In response to her question and with a bow to the maître d', we said in unison, "*Excellent, madame, excellent.*" We would be on our way the next morning after having discovered this very beautiful, simple yet complex, old yet new world in the French countryside, in the shadow of the French Alps.

A discordant symphony of blaring horns brings me back suddenly to the Harlem River Drive. Cars have started moving up ahead, exiting up the ramp to the George Washington Bridge. I will go straight ahead, to the end of the Harlem River Drive, north to the Spuyten Duyvil Bridge, and on into the Bronx. But the traffic going that way hasn't started to move yet. So there is still time to listen to more of the chanting by the monks of Tamié, as I look across the river at a Yankee Stadium, which is now as bright with light as the Lac d'Annecy beneath a full moon. There will be a night game after all.

Yankee Stadium is home to the best of the best of professional baseball, just as Au Père Bise is probably the home of the best maître d', at least the most professional one I have ever met. And I have met more maître d's than Yankees. Here inside my unmoving car, the monks of Tamié continue to soothe me with their chant, draining current circumstances of any real significance. This moment, right now, in this traffic jam is better than a good bottle of wine at any price. What words, I ask myself, could possibly describe this moment, right now, in this traffic jam, with this music, these memories, this feeling?

That is just when I swear I hear the monks chant, "*Excellent, monsieur, excellent.*"

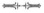

I was still groggy from the anesthesia when the surgeon came in to see me. He told me that the operation on my knee had been a success but my running days were over. To me that seemed like a contradiction, but I was too confused to argue. I couldn't believe—or, more precisely, I didn't want to believe—that I had run my last marathon. When I left the hospital several days later, I was given a pair of crutches to support me while my knee healed. The doctor told me that I would need them for the next ten days.

I had a business trip to Europe scheduled for the following week. Before the surgery, I had planned to reschedule this trip, but now going on the trip seemed like a good idea. It would be a denial-supporting distraction which would help me avoid the slow-falling wave of depression that was beginning to break over me. Three days later I was on my way to Kennedy Airport for a flight to London. From there, I would go on to Vienna, Paris, and back again to London for a final meeting before flying home.

After three days of meetings in London, I found myself once again at Heathrow Airport. Because I was on crutches, I arrived at the airport quite early for my flight to Vienna. With assistance from airport personnel, as at JFK, I checked in, hoping to find a place where I could quietly relax and read my book. Heathrow, like every airport in the world, it seems, is always crowded and noisy, with a PA system that never takes a break.

Sandwiched in between flight announcements was the constant reminder, "Your attention, please...If you see any unattended luggage or parcels, please report them immediately to airport personnel...Repeat. If you see..." In 1982, there was already a great fear of terrorists in London, but it was the IRA that the British feared, not Islamic terrorists.

I looked around and saw a pub. Unlike the pubs in London with their rather high-sounding names like the King's Arms or the Duke's Dagger, the sign outside just read, quite humbly and, therefore, quite atypically British, "Bar." Perhaps because it was only eleven in the morning, the place was empty. I was the first and only patron.

I leaned my crutches against the wood-paneled wall, slipped off my shoulder bag, and sat down at one of the tables. The bartender, doubling as the waiter, came and took my order for a pint of Courage ale. I opened the book I was currently reading, leaned back in my chair, and enjoyed that complacently relaxed feeling that arises after a plenty-of-time-to-spare check-in at an airport.

I still had several hours to wait before my flight. I sipped my beer and turned the page.

I remained the sole patron in the bar for the next hour or, in book time, for the next two chapters, during which the PA system droned on constantly. Then a well-dressed businessman with a large suitcase entered the bar, looked about searchingly, and sat at a table near mine. The bartender came to his table and took his order. I continued to read.

Perhaps fifteen minutes passed before I heard a voice from a nearby table say, with a very British accent, "Excuse me, please." By this time, a number of other patrons had entered the bar. It was close to lunchtime. I turned in the direction of the voice to find the businessman who had arrived minutes earlier, wanting my attention.

"Yes, can I help you?" I answered.

"Yes, please. Sorry to disturb you. Would you mind terribly watching my bag? I'll be back straightaway."

"Certainly not," I replied automatically. "Take your time. I have a long wait for my flight."

"Thank you very much." He got up from the table, sidestepped his way past his large suitcase, and exited the bar. I returned to my book and heard, "Your attention, please...If you see any unattended luggage or parcels, please report them immediately to airport personnel...Repeat. If you see..."

I felt a sudden jolt of anxiety as I looked over at his suitcase. His unattended suitcase. Not true. I was attending to his suitcase. But I don't know anything about that suitcase. I didn't even know who that guy is—or was, if he didn't come back. Am I attending to unattended luggage? I glanced over to my crutches. Could he be that diabolical? He found a guy who couldn't run for help to attend to his unattended luggage.

I wanted to yell to the other patrons in the bar that I might be minding a bomb. But that was just hysteria! He looked like a solid citizen, not a terrorist. Besides, he had a perfectly British accent, not an Irish brogue. But people aren't always what they seem to be, particularly if they want to blow other people up. I was awash in a flood of trite insights. What better disguise could he have than to appear to be exactly what he wasn't? And the accent. Practiced, perhaps. Or real. Maybe he was just an Englishman mad at other Englishmen. Maybe he had got fired this morning. Maybe I was going crazy.

"If you see any unattended luggage or parcels, please report them immediately to airport personnel...Repeat. If you see..."

I looked at my crutches, thinking of a getaway. I looked at the luggage and thought that maybe everybody had only seconds to live. I squeezed the arms of the chair in a complete panic. If I screamed, would I be a complete fool or a hero? I didn't want to die. Who cared what anybody thought? We all want to live. That guy was probably gone from the airport by now, waiting for a news bulletin. No, no, he wasn't. He'd be back. I had to get a grip on myself like the grip I had on my chair.

Son of Sam popped into my mind, along with that day in Van Cortland Park, when fear became suspicion and suspicion became conviction. I have often wondered about the guy who jumped back in the bushes. How many times must he have regaled his friends with the story of some mad runner on the railroad tracks in Van Cortland Park, a madman who charged at him like a wild bull, for absolutely no reason? I even wonder if he thought that I might have been Son of Sam.

"Thank you so much," snapped me out of my near panic. He was back. Nothing had blown up. He wasn't a terrorist, and his luggage was just luggage. I felt silly and relieved but more relieved than silly. He offered to buy me a pint, but I declined. He finished his drink, got up from the table, grabbed his luggage, wished me a safe journey, and left the bar. I signaled the waiter for another pint of Courage. I closed the book I wasn't reading. When the pint arrived, I stopped sipping and drank it down. It was time to hobble my way to the gate for the plane to Vienna.

I can't remember the flight to Vienna. My experience in the bar had temporarily suspended my ability to remember anything that wasn't seriously threatening. After four days of meetings at the Hotel Intercontinental, I found myself back at Vienna International Airport. But this time without crutches. Nine days after surgery, I felt comfortable enough to walk without assistance. With great joy, I had left my crutches in the hotel room. I never felt so good walking, however slowly, through an airport.

My joy was short-lived. We boarded the plane for Paris. It soon backed away from the gate and taxied toward the active runway. Suddenly it stopped. The PA system again. The pilot: "Your attention, please...We have a problem and must return to the gate. We will check it out and depart as soon as possible. Thank you for your patience." That was not good news, but it was certainly better than attending to unattended luggage.

We returned to the gate and were told over the PA system that there would be an announcement within the hour, which there was. The problem could not be fixed quickly, we were told. They needed a spare part that had to be flown in. They were going to bring in another plane to take us to Paris. "This will take time," announced the PA system. "Just relax. We will keep you informed."

Five hours later the PA system told us that the backup plane was arriving. We would be given boarding passes that would be either blue or green. Passengers with a blue pass would be seated in the front half of the plane and were to enter through the front door of the aircraft, while those with a green pass would be seated in the back half of the plane and were to enter through the back door. Thirty minutes later we were back on the tarmac, climbing two different stairways onto the plane. There was a slight problem, however. The blue seats were actually in the back half of the plane, and the green seats were in the front half of the plane. As a result, two long rows of people would have to pass each other, going in opposite directions, along the narrow center aisle of the plane.

On this flight, I was traveling with several IBM colleagues from the United Kingdom who were also attending the same meeting in Paris. While we, the blue passengers, slowly made our way past the green passengers, one of my British colleagues was talking to me. As I was squeezing past a rather substantial woman, she, hearing my colleague speaking to me, assumed that I, too, was English, and said to me in a very British accent, "You would think that the Micks were running this airline, wouldn't you?"

Under normal circumstances, this remark would have provoked a definite response from me, an Irish American whose ancestors had come to America during the British-induced Irish Famine in the nineteenth century. But I said nothing. Soon we were in the air on our way to Paris.

Why had I remained silent? Diplomacy, perhaps. It is more likely, however, that I was still grateful to the British businessman at Heathrow Airport for not blowing us up after all.

Paris, the penultimate leg of my business trip, was our next stop. I love Paris. Even though I would only be there briefly, I was grateful for the opportunity to just walk the streets whenever possible. There were two days of meetings ahead of me, but I would find some time to stroll along the Seine, have a drink or two in a café or two, and shop in a few of the bookstores near the Sorbonne. Then like every other time I have visited Paris, I would suddenly be back at Charles de Gaulle Airport, seemingly leaving Paris almost before I had even arrived.

Our British Airways flight was called for boarding. My English colleagues had already returned to the United Kingdom. There was, however, no lack of Englishmen on this flight, since English was the only language and British the only accent that I had heard while boarding. I took my seat next to a tweed-attired, older Englishman deeply engaged in his newspaper, the *Daily Telegraph*. He was reading the first page, seemingly fixated on the headline. Over the PA system we heard one of the stewardesses, "Ladies and gentlemen, please fasten your seat belts. We are about to push back from the gate. Thank you."

Our seat belts fastened, our plane rumbled down the taxiway toward the active runway for takeoff. The first officer, the copilot, announced that there would be no waiting since we were magically number one for takeoff. At the end of the runway, the pilot slowed down, made one left turn and then another, rotating the plane 180 degrees. We came to a stop and awaited clearance for takeoff. Thirty seconds later the engines started to roar, the wheels started to roll, and we were all pushed back into our seats as we quickly picked up speed and streamed down the runway.

If you fly often enough, you can sense when the wings are about to rise and angle back, lifting the still-spinning wheels off the disappearing runway. We were at that precise moment in the takeoff when the pilot suddenly applied the brakes. The plane went hurtling toward the end of the runway and finally skidded off onto the interior island of grass that separates the runways. We bumped and rolled our way to a stop; the plane half-turned around, as the engines died down. There wasn't a sound. Into this sea of silence dived the cheery, British-accented voice of our captain over the PA system. "Captain Smathers here. I say, bit of a red light on that one. We'll check it out straightaway."

Again total silence and then the roar of the engines, which Captain Smathers seemed to be testing, because we weren't moving. The engines continued to roar for several minutes and then gradually fell into near silence.

Once more the PA system, "Hello, Captain Smathers again. We can't seem to raise that red light again when we throttle up the engines. What do you say we give it another go?"

With that, Captain Smathers executed two more quick left turns for another 180-degree rotation and proceeded back to the other end of the runway, where we had begun our previous takeoff attempt.

At the end of the runway, Captain Smathers made yet another U-turn and without stopping—he must have already had clearance—charged full speed back down the runway, engines roaring as before. Total silence blanketed the cabin. Most of the passengers, I believe, wanted to yell, "Wait, let me off!" but were in a sort of catatonic shock and couldn't speak.

I willed myself back into the sauna at the McBurney YMCA, where I once again heard the comforting words, "Let me tell you something, kid. Whatever you think, it's all in your head." Then, seemingly miraculously, we were in the air. Quiet murmurs of indistinguishable words began to trickle softly through the cabin, as we dared to believe that Captain Smathers might actually get us to London.

I looked over at the tweed-attired, older Englishman sitting next to me. He was still staring at the headline on the first page of the *Daily Telegraph.*

Just before landing, we heard one of the stewardesses announce, "Your attention, please. On behalf of Captain Smathers and the entire crew, I would like to thank you for your patience and understanding. Welcome to London and enjoy your stay." Captain Smathers himself made it a point to shake hands with just about every passenger as we disembarked. "Cheers," said Captain Smathers as I shook his hand and thanked him for our excitingly safe journey.

Two days, three pubs, and one very long meeting later, I returned to Heathrow Airport for the flight back to New York City, my home, IBM office, and the headquarters of Dr. Norman Scott, orthopedic surgeon. Medicine has become so specialized that I think some of these orthopedic surgeons only work on knees. Perhaps some of the real specialists may only operate on right knees.

My follow-up appointment with Dr. Scott had been scheduled for the day after my return from Europe. I arrived promptly for my appointment at four o'clock. Dr. Scott was a highly respected surgeon but—and perhaps this was an occupational hazard—he was very direct and concrete in his interactions with patients. That style may be a critical quality in surgery, but it made conversation difficult and made his comments sometimes seem brusque and insensitive.

His conversational limitations became particularly obvious when we discussed my desire to do more running. "Forget it," he advised. "Your right knee is bone on bone. No cartilage between them. I drilled some holes in the bones to generate some cartilage growth, but that will only ease the pain. It won't change anything. Count your blessings. Your left knee is still good. For now, anyway."

"You mean my left knee will be a problem, too?"

"Osteoarthritis will probably show up there as well. And maybe even in your hips. That's the way it goes...How old are you?

"Forty-two."

"Forty-two. Well, look at the bright side. You'll probably be able to walk until you are about fifty-five. That's thirteen years. That's pretty good."

"Fifty-five?" I repeated in disbelief.

Dr. Scott leaned back in his chair and started laughing heartily. Then he leaned forward, slapped his knee and said, "Look at this way. You may not live to be fifty-five. So it may not be a problem." He slapped his knee once more and laughed. A conversation with Dr. Scott was, I thought, much more pleasant under anesthesia.

I have always gravitated toward water when feeling down, blue, or a bit overwhelmed. Fifteen minutes later I was standing on the bank of the East River, which is not far from Dr. Scott's office on the Upper East Side of Manhattan. There was a strong current pushing the river south and eventually into the ocean. Above the river, planes were lined up one after the other, waiting to land at La Guardia Airport.

I began to replay my recent trip in my mind. I had decided to go and not postpone it precisely in order to forget what was bothering me now. I was glad that I had gone. I had met a British businessman who had absolutely no idea how happy I was that he didn't blow us up. I had also discovered that some of the English believe that my Irish ancestors wouldn't know how to run an airline. And I had met the intrepid Captain Smathers, who would not be bullied by "a bit of a red light" in the cockpit.

"Your attention, please," I heard myself say. "Everything's possible. What do you say we give it another go?"

Here I am in a karaoke bar, watching my IBM colleagues sing. Although resigned to the impending humiliation, I still dread my turn to perform. I won't be able to decline when it comes. That would be considered impolite, particularly here in Tokyo, where it is possible to do something impolite every ten minutes without even being aware that you are doing something wrong. In Japan, there are innumerable, unwritten rules, which can only be learned by living at length among the Japanese people.

I never sing—not because I don't want to sing but because I am afraid to sing. I am afraid to sing because I have a voice that can turn heads completely around during the national anthem in Yankee Stadium or during "Auld Lang Syne" in Times Square on New Year's Eve. There has never been a large enough crowd within which to bury my voice and its total inability to intone the proper note. I can't even sing "Happy Birthday" in a large group without the person in front of me turning around and looking at me in critical disbelief.

While waiting to perform, I am, for the first time in my life, praying to hear somebody command, "Nonsingers, please leave the room," the way Brother Benjamin Benedict did back in Barrytown, New York. But that doesn't happen. I'm up next. When my Japanese colleague finishes his song, he turns to our table and yells, "Now, Marty!" The group at our table breaks into applause. I break into a sweat. I see Brother Benjamin Benedict standing before me. "Move your lips," I hear. "Don't sing." I can't refuse.

I get up from the table and take the mic from my colleague. I start to sing, my voice and courage powered by an evening of drinking. I will myself into a sort of schizophrenic state so that I won't even be able to remember the song I am singing. Somebody else is singing while I imagine myself somewhere else. Then it is over. All my IBM colleagues are on their feet applauding and yelling for an encore.

Could it be? I think to myself. *Maybe my voice has changed. Maybe I can't sing in New York, but I can sing in Tokyo.* The applause goes on, as do the demands for an encore. For the first time in years, my thoughts of Brother Benjamin Benedict are accompanied by a joyous sense of final and complete vindication. He was wrong after all. I have found my voice. I can sing. I agree to an encore.

I remember the second song, "I Left My Heart in San Francisco." This time I refrained from a schizophrenic escape and put myself totally into the song. Once again my IBM colleagues erupted into applause when I finished. For the first time in my life, I felt I had been able to sing and to sing really well. The proof was provided by my colleagues from IBM Japan.

After a final celebratory drink, we left the karaoke bar. As I approached the door, the manager of the bar rushed over to me and gave me a videotape of my performance. He said that I did a great job and that I would enjoy seeing myself perform. I thanked him, and we departed. After returning to New York, I put the tape away in a closet and forgot about it.

Months later while my wife and daughter were out shopping, I was looking through my closet for something and came across the tape from Tokyo. I had never watched it and was suddenly excited to see it. I turned on the television, slipped in the tape, and sat down to watch.

What I saw and heard was the most awful attempt at singing. The first song wasn't too bad because I looked as if I didn't want to be there and my singing explained why. The second song, "I Left My Heart in San Francisco," however, was particularly atrocious. I had a look on my face that said, "You know, I can really sing." To prove that point, every once in a while I looked as if I wanted to murmur, a la Sinatra, "Do-be-do-be-do," as my eyelids slowly slinked halfway down over my eyes, accompanied by what I must have thought was a slyly seductive smile. The only one I had seduced was myself.

Even though I watched alone, this was the most embarrassing moment of my life. My performance was so painfully delusional that I might just as well have said, "Can I sing? Are you kidding? Is the earth flat or what?" I sat there, blushing. I could feel the fire in my cheeks. I was completely humiliated. I had made a complete fool of myself. It hadn't been the first time, but it had definitely been the worst time. My short-lived vindication in my decades-old struggle with Brother Benjamin Benedict vanished. I never wanted to be reminded of this disaster again, nor did I ever want anyone in my life to know about it. I ejected the tape and walked quickly down the hall to the incinerator.

I had spent many years steeped in a quietly simmering anger at the weekly humiliations foisted upon us nonsingers by Brother Benjamin Benedict. Now I realized that I had sung my own way into my greatest humiliation. Perhaps Brother Benedict had actually spared me earlier humiliations. In any case, he had been absolutely right about my singing ability.

I am reminded of the time in arts and crafts class when my potato stamp kept crumbling. Brother Benedict pointed out what I was doing wrong, but I lacked the dexterity to do it right and became angry at him. Just before lunchtime, he told me I was "obnoxious," a word not yet part of my vocabulary. Over lunch, I looked the word up in my dictionary. When we returned to class after lunch, I immediately, yet belatedly, said to him, "No, I'm not."

Now years—not just a lunchtime—later I feel compelled once again to belatedly say something to Brother Benjamin Benedict. "You were absolutely right, Brother. I discovered that in a karaoke bar, a room in Tokyo nonsingers are never asked to leave. May you rest in peace."

Like every other evening before, in every other place in Ireland, we were able to find music that evening in a very large room in a hotel in Glengarriff, County Cork. Anna and I were making our first, and what would be our only, trip to Ireland, returning instead almost every year to Italy and France. The large room in the Park Hotel was packed with the local people from the town and surrounding area.

Two men stood on a small stage, one playing the fiddle, the other an accordion, quintessential Irish instruments. The music was obviously and recognizably Irish, but I had never heard any of the songs before. Though new to me, they were probably songs well-known throughout this part of Ireland, the Gaeltacht, where the Irish language is still spoken daily. The Gaeltacht might be considered the Irish, geographical equivalent of "*la France profonde.*"

A young boy approached our table and asked what we would like to drink. Anna and I both ordered a Guinness. When the young boy returned with our drinks, Anna asked him if it would be possible to request a song. The boy said he thought so but would check with the musicians. He soon returned and said the players would welcome any request for a song they could play. "How about 'Danny Boy'?" Anna asked. The boy said he would give the request to the musicians.

I turned to Anna and asked, with exaggerated disbelief, "'Danny Boy'? Everyone here must be a local. Listen to the songs. They are as Irish as Irish gets. I never even heard one of them before. 'Danny Boy'?" I repeated. "We're going to stand out conspicuously like the tourists we are."

"So what?" Anna replied appropriately. "I want to hear 'Danny Boy.'"

End of debate. I had heard "Danny Boy" thousands of times in my life and would happily listen to it thousands of times more. In truth, I wanted to hear "Danny Boy," too. I just lacked Anna's honesty, courage, and willingness to be an egregious tourist.

Perhaps a half hour passed, during which a half-dozen more Irish songs were played and sung by the duo. One of the two men then spoke into the microphone. "Ladies and gentlemen, we have a request. For 'Danny Boy.'"

I expected to hear some snickering laughter. Instead there was only expectant silence. The two men gently placed their instruments on the floor of the stage, looked at the audience, and then at each other and, after a silent count of three, began to sing "Danny Boy" a cappella.

There were three or four hundred people in that room, all listening attentively to a tale they all knew well. The brief, silent pauses in the song were immediately swept into the river of silence that flowed through the room. I had heard "Danny Boy" so many times, yet this time was so different, so hauntingly, piercingly perfect. When the final notes, bearing the words "Oh, Danny Boy, I love you so," floated out from the small stage and fell over us like a gently fading, summer mist, the river of silence flooded again into the room and remained.

Absolute silence. No applause, no yelling, no whistling. Unending, uninterrupted silence, like emotional connective tissue, transformed the audience of many in body into an audience of one in feeling. The only human voice to be heard was the one still resounding in our collective consciousness. Then as one, we all stood up together, yelling our approval and applauding until our hands hurt. I felt an elbow in my ribs. It was Anna, with raised eyebrows, reminding me, yet again, of how wrong I could be.

Listening to the silence in that room, I found myself being transported back to the Pocket Theater in New York City, which in 1969 was located at the northern edge of the now-gentrifying Bowery. There I had seen a play called *Ceremonies in Dark Old Men*, written by a black playwright named Lonne Elder. The Pocket Theater, as its name might suggest, was a small off-Broadway theater, perfect for the intimacy and proximity required, in my opinion, for the presentation of serious drama.

The entire play takes place in a barbershop on 125th Street in Harlem. The barbershop is a struggling, failing enterprise that functions more like a social club for neighborhood men than as a business. The owner, Mr. Parker, relies on his daughter to be the real breadwinner of the family. He also has two young sons, who, despite his best efforts, are drifting into a life of crime.

When tragedy finally strikes and a son is killed, Mr. Parker, a former tap dancer, is standing alone in his barbershop. As he thinks back on his past life and the present, tragic death of his son, he begins to dance and to cry at the same time. The audience is sitting in that barbershop with him, watching him try to deal with the pain and the loss. The happy, fulfilling time of his life, his tap-dancing career, is summoned out of a long-ago past to fight against the crushing force of the present.

As he cries and dances at the same time, we watch two people in one body struggle for supremacy, for life over death. Mr. Parker's tear-stained face sits atop an old and tired body, slowly doing dance steps that haven't been done in many years. We want to reach out and help him, hold him, support him. But before we can, the stage goes black, and the dance suddenly stops. The darkness submerges the theater into a deep silence that both blankets and binds the audience together. Silence floods its way through the

Pocket Theater in the same way that it would, many years hence, flood through that room in the Park Hotel in Glengarriff.

The lights go on in the Pocket Theater, but the silence and the stillness remain, until we, the audience, gradually realize that the barbershop world in which we have been living has been jarringly replaced by the ushers, seats, doors, and exit signs of the Pocket Theater. The actors return to the stage briefly for another bow and more applause. They now seem, however, like impersonators, because the real world of Harlem has disappeared and we are back in the strange world of the Bowery.

Down through the centuries, Christian monasteries have practiced what is called the *magnum silentium*, the great silence. The more obvious purpose of the practice has been not only to eliminate the idle chatter that distracts the practitioner and others, but also to hear what can only be heard in a receptive silence. What can be heard is more than words, communication beyond words, ineffable connection with the other, communion, quite literally. When communion has been attained, silence preserves it and only grudgingly will let it go.

Those two talented singing musicians in Glengarriff sang a song that everyone knew, yet it was, at the same time, a song that nobody had heard before. The silence was a way of hanging on to what had been heard for the first time, at least it was for Anna and for me. When we were leaving Ireland, Anna said that she would never forget the rendition of "Danny Boy" by those two singers in Glengarriff. In fact, she never did.

She often referred to their singing of "Danny Boy" as transcendent beauty, a beauty that lifts us out of our usual world and shows us the possibility of another. Anna imagined that, despite their talent, the singers probably had rather ordinary day jobs, possibly because they might never have had a break or perhaps because the sea of singing talent that is Ireland might have just washed over them, as it had washed over so many others.

Sometimes I imagine those two singers sitting in the barbershop in Harlem, waiting for haircuts that never come. When the bad news about Mr. Parker's son arrives, they want to let him know that they understand. So they start to sing "Danny Boy," to which Mr. Parker begins to slowly dance. The Irish singers take his hands and dance with him. Mr. Parker starts to sing along. The Pocket Theater becomes the Park Hotel, and Glengarriff becomes the Bowery. Song, dance, tears, silence. Tragedies merge. Silence explodes. We listen.

That night, in that hotel, in that small town, those two singers wrapped everyone who could hear in a silence I had never before heard—except in the Pocket Theater in 1969—and have not heard since.

While walking in the hills above Nice, not far from La Gaude, I found myself drawn into a galaxy of colors by a gravitational force that has always, and irresistibly, attracted not just hikers like me with walking sticks but also legitimate painters with their ready brushes.

As I ambled along, absorbed in the natural beauty of the South of France, Somerset Maugham came into my mind. He once had a beautifully situated house on the French Riviera, so beautifully situated that he put his writing desk in front of a large window, which allowed the intensely colored world outside to hang before his eyes like a painting.

Through that window poured a steady stream of soft light and bright colors, lavender fields wrapped in the embrace of green hills and, in the distance, a blue Mediterranean, itself streaked here and there with the white of a passing gull or a breaking wave.

One day, however, so the story goes, Maugham boarded up that window and took down that living painting. Apparently the beauty that the window brought in stymied the writing that he wanted to pour out. Once boarded up, the interior window apparently opened, and Maugham, now without distraction, followed his fluent pen as it slid its way across countless pages.

When I left the South of France and returned to New York, this possibly—or even probably—apocryphal story, like the landscape of southern France, receded from my mind and burrowed back into my unconscious. Some years would pass after that day in the hills above Nice before Maugham would once again come to mind.

On a cold and rainy February afternoon as I made my way along a puddled street in northern Vienna, I looked eagerly for a building with the address, Berggasse 19, the building in which Sigmund Freud had lived, practiced, and written for nearly half a century. Somewhere along that cobblestoned street of stately, if not particularly elegant, apartment buildings, I at last found Berggasse 19. There was nothing to herald the former, famous resident or the events within that building decades before, except for a small plaque on the wall from the World Federation for Mental Health in 1953, identifying the building as having once been Freud's residence.

The front door was unlocked. I entered and went into the entrance hall. Freud's apartment, number six, was on the second floor. A man carrying several bags of groceries entered and proceeded to walk up the stairs in front of me. He continued up another flight of stairs and entered an apartment on the next floor, directly above Freud's apartment.

I was struck by the fact that, in this place of recognition and remembrance, this memorial to a great thinker, the basic needs and simple activities of daily life were continuing, uninterrupted, just as they had when Freud himself and his patients had climbed up these same steps. Freud might have seen the continuance of such daily routines as a tribute to human resilience and renewal. I was, however, ambivalent about the propriety of such mundane activity in this very special place.

I had come to Vienna on business but was here at Berggasse 19 not only because of personal interest but also, and primarily, as a surrogate pilgrim for my wife Anna, a psychoanalyst and therapist who, at that time, was teaching a course on the interpretation of dreams, a Freudian specialty. I entered apartment six. Except for the custodian, there was nobody else I could see. Perhaps the other visitors were using Freud's discrete exit door, which allowed departing patients and waiting patients to avoid encountering each other.

There is absolutely nothing in the apartment. Instead, on the walls hang life-sized pictures of all the furniture, carpets, paintings, statuettes, and other furnishings as they were when Freud and his family, hounded by the Nazis after the German Anschluss of Austria, left for London in 1938. The apartment had been the family residence as well as Freud's office.

It is a spacious and pleasant apartment. The enlarged photographs on the walls are able to convey a sense of lived-in space, despite their obvious artificiality. I wandered from room to room, through most of the apartment, without seeing any other visitor. I savored the feeling of being alone in this Mecca of the unconscious. The apartment itself was interesting, but I had yet to experience that feeling of discovery and fulfillment that I associated with a pilgrim's arrival at his destination. That happened suddenly and totally when I entered Freud's office.

Freud's desk sat in front of a large window. Unlike Maugham's window, Freud's office window looked out onto the backs of surrounding buildings. Where Maugham saw sparkling sea and vivid colors, Freud saw gray, the leaden gray of the wintry Vienna sky and the gray stone of the surrounding buildings. There wasn't anything green or alive on the other side of the glass.

I looked at the picture of Freud's desk sitting before this window. I gazed at what he had seen. Gray stone. Blank walls. Nothing. If there was something to be seen, something to be found, it had to come from the inside. And it did. On this desk, in this room with this view, thoughts, ideas, insights, theories, and hypotheses streamed out of Freud like the light and color that streamed into Maugham's window in the South of France.

In this place, with nowhere to look but inside, Freud doggedly and honestly slipped under his own skin to discover and build a model of our human dynamics. Whether we agree with him or not, we cannot avoid the vision of ourselves that Freud has bequeathed to Western civilization, a vision that has become a sort of psychological filter of our life's experiences.

In this one room, I wanted the photograph of the desk to materialize into the dark mahogany of its subject. I wanted to sit in Freud's chair, put my hands on his desk, and look out through his office window, a window he had no need to board up since it was effectively boarded up by the gray mass of buildings behind it. I wondered what Freud would have done in the South of France.

Freud liked Italy, especially the antiquities to be found there. In his writings, Freud's metaphors often echo the world of the archaeologist, the difference being that his digs were in human consciousness, not in a buried city like Pompeii. Psychoanalysis is, after all, a careful unearthing of layers of experience and the reactions to those experiences.

Would Freud have boarded up his window in the South of France? Would Maugham have been a more productive writer sitting at a desk in cloudy, rainy Vienna? They both, in any case, wound up looking at the world from the inside out, through the glassless interior window that gazes unblinkingly on the truth of who we are. Opening that window is the work of art that materializes beneath the painter's brush, the writer's pen, or within the psychoanalyst's seeing ear.

Mortimer's is a bar-restaurant on Madison Avenue and Seventy-Fourth Street. Over the years, it has attracted important people like the Kennedys. It has an established-money feel to it, with a clientele that is either young and on-the-way-up preppy or established and staying-at-the-top Waspy. It is a comfortable, reserved place, where you can feel relaxed because nobody ever seems to talk about feelings. If customers ever did, they would do it, no doubt, with quiet dignity. Nothing angry or loud. There is also a pervasive air of ownership. The people in Mortimer's own things. "My" is a word frequently heard in the surrounding, muted conversations.

Mortimer's was where Anna, her friend Rosemary, and I would meet later that spring evening in 1984, after we had all dutifully and separately attended the award-giving, speech-making dinners to which we had been invited. We had all been scheduled to attend these dinners because they were in honor of people who were important in our professional lives. Attendance, therefore, was mandatory.

While Rosemary and Anna went down to the Roosevelt Hotel to attend an awards dinner given by the American Psychological Association, I went over to the Waldorf Astoria to attend a dinner honoring the vice chairman of AIG, my client at the time. Jake Randall, the vice chairman, was an interesting guy. The day he graduated from college in 1938, Jake had gone to work for AIG, a mammoth insurance company that had begun as a small agency in Shanghai. He oversaw all of AIG's overseas operations, which were extensive, since AIG did business in 138 countries,

Jake Randall had a reputation for being very rich and very frugal, virtues that were perhaps inextricably intertwined. Jake traveled a lot and was reputed to pack only wash and wear shirts, which he apparently hand-washed every night in his hotel room. I was seated with several colleagues and their wives at a table for which IBM had generously paid, with a view toward a mutually beneficial relationship with an important customer. The most important aspect of these dinners was showing up. Absence was much more likely to be archived than anything any of the three or four speakers would have to say.

IBM's strong turnout, so noted, would hopefully bear positive, future fruit. Toward that end, it was important to remind anyone with decision-making authority that we were enthusiastically present, which required us to make the rounds of the ballroom with "Hi, Bill," "Hi, Bob," and "Good evening, Mr. Greenberg." The latter was sometimes called Hank, but only by his close friends and associates. To Hank, a salesman could never be a close friend or associate because he was trying to sell something, which translated, in Hank's mind, into trying to get some of Hank's money, which did not appeal to Hank in any way.

Hank's real name was Maurice, but he called himself Hank because of his admiration for the baseball great, Hank Greenberg. He had an inclination to associate himself with the outstanding. Hank had a reputation for being smart, tough, and very attentive to detail. He applied the same analytical attention to office supplies as he did to acquiring multimillion-dollar companies. He could be quite intimidating. On the private elevator that went to the executive suite that Hank shared with the top AIG executives, it was always possible to tell which of the passengers was on his way to a meeting with Hank. He or she was usually the palest person on the elevator.

Hank expected his lieutenants to make decisions that he would have made in their place. This expectation to act as he would act led to a certain amount of imitative behavior on the part of his direct reports. At an IBM briefing on artificial intelligence, for example, Hank and his ten or eleven lieutenants were seated around an elaborate conference table at IBM corporate headquarters. My job was to make sure that nothing happened that might displease Hank.

As I paid close attention to the progress of the briefing, I noticed that Hank's changes in posture were quickly imitated by his lieutenants. If Hank leaned back in his chair, within five minutes, all the others would be leaning back in their chairs. I would also lean back in my chair. Ditto for forward.

Hank was not a Mortimer's guy, I thought to myself, as I began to think more about Mortimer's than Hank's remarks praising Jake Randall. Hank certainly owned a lot, but he was a little too direct to be a Mortimer's regular. The Mortimer's crowd exuded a genteel, relaxed air of having already won the game. Hank had won the game, too, but he was always training for the next one.

Hank was the final speaker. His speech, like those that preceded, was filled with words of praise for Jake. Hank, however, being as economical with words as he was with everything else, soon concluded his remarks about Jake, and we were released into the night on our own recognizance. It was still early, only ten, and a lovely evening for a walk. Anna and Rosemary did not expect to arrive at Mortimer's before ten thirty, so I began a leisurely stroll north to Seventy-Fourth Street and Madison Avenue. I had a feeling of mission accomplished: I came, I saw, and, most importantly, I was seen.

Mortimer's was crowded and buzzing, at least to the extent that the genteel can buzz. Anna and Rosemary had yet to arrive. There was only one empty seat at the end of the bar. I walked over to it and removed my light trench coat, revealing my formal, black-tie attire. I sat down and ordered a beer. There was a couple seated to my left. At least I thought they were a couple, until the woman who was seated next to me turned and said, "Coming from a party or going to a party?" I explained that I had just come from a dinner honoring an important customer of mine, which might explain my formal attire on a Thursday evening.

She smiled, introduced herself as Sally, and wondered why she had never seen me before in Mortimer's. I replied that this was probably only the second time I had come to Mortimer's. It was not exactly convenient since I lived downtown near the Flatiron Building.

"Oh, I like that area. Up and coming," enthused Sally. "Old factory buildings converted to lofts, right?"

"Yes, I replied. That's it exactly. By the way, my name is Marty."

Sally, blond and in her late thirties, hoisted her glass, drank down what remained, and pushed the glass toward the bartender, who had yet to arrive with my beer.

"Another Manhattan?" he asked, when he finally came over. Sally nodded in the affirmative. He soon returned with both drinks. I put a twenty-dollar bill on the bar. Feeling compelled to be genteel in genteel Mortimer's, I asked the bartender to put Sally's Manhattan on my tab. Sally thanked me and raised her glass in a toast.

"Here's to tuxedoes and dinners and Thursday nights."

We tapped glasses and drank.

Just then I heard a familiar voice behind me say, "Hey, Big Guy, what are you up too?"

Anna and Rosemary had arrived.

Sally, hearing Anna's greeting, turned to them and said, "Beat it, chicks. He's mine."

I had been aware of the air of ownership that floats about Mortimer's, but I was surprised to discover that Sally had acquired me. Anna, never at a loss for words, looked directly and smilingly at Sally and said with total aplomb, "Take him. He's yours. Good luck."

My feeling of being acquired or owned quickly gave way to a new ego-boosting feeling of being a sort of desirable prize, a momentary Mortimer's movie star. I was aglow as Anna smirked at me.

Not too creatively, I asked, "How about a drink?"

"Sure, Big Boy," answered Rosemary, who had yet to say anything. "I'll have a Manhattan."

"Me, too," said Anna.

"That's what I'm drinking, chicks. But the only Manhattan he comes with is mine," warned Sally.

As I reached into my wallet, I began to work on an escape plan and an explanation. My ego boost had dissipated. I should have lingered longer at the dinner or walked here more slowly or both.

I suggested to Anna and Rosemary that we drink up and get going.

"What's the rush?" asked Rosemary.

"Yes, Big Guy, did we break up your little party, so now you want to leave?" added Anna.

Sally, clearly becoming a little tipsy, impatiently ordered, "Forget them, Marty. Beat it, chicks. I told you he's mine."

As Sally reached for her drink, I put my arms around Anna and Rosemary and pushed them toward the front door. "Good night, Sally," I muttered apologetically. "I'm sorry for the confusion."

For years after that evening, whenever Anna and I would have a friendly marital spat, I would remind her that there were other women out there, attractive women like Sally, just waiting for me. Anna would reply once again that they could have me. Although it was invariably a jovial exchange, there was a little something more to it for me.

Sally had been real and, like Hank Greenberg at AIG, into acquisitions. Even if she had seen tuxedo-clad me only through the lens of her Manhattan glass, Sally had made me feel like one of the people whom I had chased around that entire evening just to tell them "Great to see you!" and "Really great to see you!" With Sally, I had been on the receiving end of solicitous attention, a rare blessing for a salesman.

From that night on, my every "Great to see you, Bob" brought an echo in my mind of "Beat it, chicks; he's mine." Mortimer's would forever be a safe haven for a weary salesman with depleted self-esteem.

It is a beautiful, spring evening in Greenwich Village. All the cafes and restaurants on Thompson, Sullivan, and MacDougal Streets have tables outside. If you walk south on Thompson Street from Third Street, where we live, you pass Grand Ticino, an Italian restaurant that Anna and I frequent almost every Friday evening. Taking the same stroll south on Sullivan Street, you pass the Sullivan Street Theater, which, for years on end, has hosted *The Fantasticks.*

And if you choose to walk south on MacDougal Street, you will find yourself standing in front of a small, charming French bistro called Chez Jacqueline, just north of Houston Street and directly across from the oldest Italian club in the United States, Tiro a Segno. Chez Jacqueline is a touch of Europe in the heart of Greenwich Village, a short walk to France from our apartment. There is also a real Jacqueline, a welcoming hostess and native of Nice, who presides, both affably and eagle-eyedly over the well-managed flow of food, drink, and clientele.

Today, May 15, 1981, is our tenth wedding anniversary and the second successful year that Chez Jacqueline has been in business, not a bad record of survival in a neighborhood that opens and closes new restaurants and cafes seemingly daily. Anna and I dine at Chez Jacqueline less frequently than at Grand Ticino, possibly because the latter is a shorter walk for us but probably because we never seem to tire of Italian food.

Anna and I plan to meet this evening at Chez Jacqueline after work, which means about seven. I arrive early. Jacqueline greets me, and I hand her a bouquet of flowers, which I tell her are a surprise for my wife, Anna, to celebrate our wedding anniversary. Jacqueline disappears into the back with the flowers. I sit at the small bar near the entrance, order a beer, and watch the early evening sun stream through the open doorway and big windows facing west onto MacDougal Street. Everyone at the bar, mostly friends of Jacqueline, is speaking French.

As I enjoy my cold beer, a waiter emerges from the back carrying an enormous, bulbous vase filled with Anna's peonies, those beautiful, perfume-scented, pink flowers that are only available for about six weeks a year, a period that happily includes our anniversary date of May 15. He places the big vase on the bar near the window in the corner. Jacqueline walks over and says, "Your wife should enjoy these during dinner. Your table is nearby. I will wrap them again for you later."

The six tables outside are occupied, but only a few diners are sitting at the inside tables. The refined sounds of the French language float on the soft spring breeze, mingling with the sweet scent of the peonies. The bartender reaches down and pushes a tape into the player behind the bar. To the sunlight, the scent of peonies, and the soft sounds of French is added the strong tenor voice of Pavarotti singing, fittingly, "O Sole Mio." Suddenly I'm in Europe, just blocks away from home and free of jet lag.

Like most wedding anniversaries, ours comes along when the world has forgotten winter's cold and looks forward to summer's warmth. I have tried each year to plan something different for our anniversary, not always successfully. Two years ago, I took Anna to a French restaurant in midtown Manhattan, called Le Mistral, another echo of southern France and the wind that blows north out of Africa. I had bought a bracelet for her and wanted to surprise her. Like this evening, I arrived early, which allowed me to conspire with the maître d' to place the bracelet under Anna's table napkin on the table at which he had planned to seat us.

Everything went wrong, however, when Anna decided that she preferred a different table. The maître d' tried gallantly to preserve the surprise, but Anna questioned why he had to replace the table napkin that she hadn't used. No surprise, therefore, but Anna was extremely pleased with her new bracelet and thanked the maître d' for his efforts.

As I sip my beer and await Anna's arrival, I reflect back on the foibles of my previous scheme and smugly compliment myself on the elegant simplicity of this year's plan. I drift back to the sounds of French conversation, the perfumed scents of fresh peonies carried on a soft breeze, and the lingering sunlight of this perfect spring evening. Sound, smell, and light combine to make Chez Jacqueline a magical island, full of soothingly stimulated sensations. There is no looking to the future or the past. Now is everywhere and everything.

I order another beer, and the bartender puts in a new tape. It's *Pagliacci* with the voice of Pavarotti. Anna arrives. I greet her, wish her a happy anniversary, and give her my seat at the bar. She orders a glass of wine, and we toast each other. As she speaks admiringly of the peonies, I once again gloat internally, happy in the realization of this year's successful surprise. Anna doesn't know that the peonies she is admiring are hers.

As always, Anna hands me a beautifully wrapped gift. Last year it was three beautiful ties. This year it is a wallet from Coach, to replace the aging wallet that I bought during my college days. (Anna has to explain the significance of Coach to me.)

Jacqueline comes to the bar to escort us to our table, in the corner near the window, next to the peonies. We decide to share a plate of *moules* before our dinner of *steak frites.* I order a red Bordeaux, and Anna and I toast each other once again.

She asks jokingly, "How long exactly have we been married?"

I answer, "Ten years, of course."

Anna replies, "Ten years? It seems like a hundred!"

She grabs me by the neck and kisses me. Jacqueline comes back to our table after dinner and insists on buying us a cognac to celebrate our anniversary. We gratefully accept.

When Jacqueline returns to our table with the cognac, I nod to her to bring the flowers to Anna. Jacqueline disappears into the back, as I anticipate a perfect surprise, particularly since Anna was admiring the peonies earlier in the evening. We continue sipping our cognac and toast each other yet again. Finally Jacqueline arrives back at our table with the flowers, but they are now wrapped in a pale-blue paper with the twelve pink bulbs peeking out over the top.

Jacqueline hands the flowers to Anna. "Happy Anniversary," she says.

Anna, surprised, asks, "For me?"

Jacqueline replies in the affirmative. Anna looks over to the corner of the bar where the peonies had been. "Oh," she sighs. "How beautiful! These are the flowers that were on the bar. My favorite flower! My favorite color!"

"Your husband and I thought you should be able to enjoy them during dinner. Why keep them hidden in the back? It's still a surprise, no?" Jacqueline smiles and leaves.

Anna gets up from her chair and comes around the table to kiss me. "Thank you, Big Guy. I love them. Happy Anniversary."

I pay the check. Anna and I make our way to the door where Jacqueline is waiting to say "*Bonsoir.*" She kisses Anna on both cheeks. Then it is my turn. As she kisses me, she whispers, "Monsieur, remember never to hide beautiful flowers."

What if Jacqueline had not put the peonies on the bar? They were needed to paint a singular moment, a stopped-clock still life, a final brush stroke on a small canvas that made the world near perfect, however briefly. As I glance over Jacqueline's shoulder at the empty space that was once the big, bulbous, vase filled with beautiful, pink peonies, I whisper, "I promise," back to Jacqueline. "You have made our anniversary part of something bigger. That made it even better."

We go home a different way, east along Houston Street and north on Thompson Street up to Third Street. Along the way, we pass our favorite Italian restaurant, Grand Ticino. As usual, it is crowded and cheerful. Good food, certainly. But I see no peonies. I feel no magic. We turn right on Third Street and arrive home to begin our eleventh year together, just a short walk away from Europe.

Several weeks later when we return to Chez Jacqueline, we see, sitting on the bar near the corner, a big, bulbous vase filled with pink peonies.

I came out of the changing room at Moe Ginsberg's and stepped up onto the platform where the tailor would measure my new slacks for alterations. As he measured, I looked into the mirror and noticed that the slacks had pleats. I never liked pleats. I turned to Anna, who was observing this process, and said, "The pants have pleats."

"So?" Anna answered.

"So? I don't like pleats."

Harry, the salesman, was an old Jewish guy who looked like he had been around since knickers and had answered every objection ever posed by a customer. Sensing that the transaction might be in jeopardy, Harry looked me in the eye and asked what I did for a living.

"I'm a brain surgeon," I replied.

"All the brain surgeons are wearing pleats," Harry noted without missing a beat. "Haven't you noticed?"

At that point, the only surgeon I had ever known didn't wear pleated pants. Rudy Bono, MD, was a general surgeon at St. Vincent's Hospital in Greenwich Village, where I found myself with a ruptured appendix in the autumn of 1973. Some hours before my surgery, Rudy came into my room and introduced himself as the surgeon.

He examined me and explained in somewhat-technical terms what he would do when he performed the appendectomy. I was in a lot of pain and didn't pay very close attention until he was leaving the room. What attracted my interest was a departure that was anything but surgically precise.

After shaking my hand, he backed away from my bed. He told me he would see me in the OR in a few hours. He then tripped over the visitor's chair near my bed and fell down on the floor before he could reach the door. As he lay on the floor, he laughed loudly, repeating between gusts of laughter, the question, "And would you believe I'm your surgeon?" I couldn't help laughing myself, even though it pained me terribly. Later on the operating table, I couldn't help worrying about Rudy's question.

After an injection to relax me, I was taken to the OR. As they wheeled me in, I saw eight or ten people, nurses and interns, with eager eyes and green masks, awaiting my arrival. Their eyes had that intense look of a player walking to the plate for his first at bat in the major leagues. I wondered if they were hoping to pinch hit for Rudy. That made me more nervous.

They put me on the operating table, and the anesthesiologist administered a spinal injection. Very quickly my legs became numb and immobile. I felt paralyzed. It was a frightening feeling. Then Rudy's face appeared directly over mine.

"We've begun," he said.

"We?" I said. "What are you doing up here when my appendix is down there?"

He laughed and assured me everything was under control.

He asked how I was feeling. I told him about the numbness from my waist down.

"That's how it's supposed to be," he said.

"I am also feeling a little numb up here," I said, pointing to my chest.

Rudy's eyes widened. "You are not supposed to be feeling numb up there," he insisted.

Now I was really scared. "Please knock me out," I begged. "I can't take being awake." Somebody then put something into my IV.

Later I woke up in my room in great pain and terribly nauseated. I remained in the hospital for another ten days, sometimes comforted by the magic powers of Demerol, a potent painkiller given to me every morning at ten, right after the delivery of the *New York Times.* Because of the timing of these two daily events, I was never able to read much of the newspaper.

After the nurse administered the Demerol, the pain receded almost immediately, followed by a feeling of warmth and well-being, a sense of invulnerability. I stopped perceiving the world as something to which I had to adapt, such as stepping out of the way of an oncoming truck. I was suddenly impervious to such threats. My feeling of well-being removed all threats from the world.

Once I had entered this invulnerable state, I was never able to get beyond the headline on the first page of the *New York Times.* Pain-free, I was soon blissfully asleep for hours. On the sixth day of postoperative care, however, I was forced to reenter the world of the vulnerable. At ten that morning, the *New York Times* arrived, but the Demerol didn't. I was no longer in great pain, so it should not have been a problem. But it was. I rang for the nurse.

The nurse entered my room and asked what the problem was. I told her that she had forgotten my Demerol. She said that she hadn't forgotten. My doctor stopped prescribing it.

"But I have tremendous pain," I lied, with the sincerity of an addict.

"I'll bring you some Tylenol," she responded and left the room. I began cold-turkey withdrawal from a five-day addiction.

Demerol and I parted company for another twenty-five years, until I went to my doctor's office one day for a procedure that required an anesthetic. After resting for an hour following the procedure, I was supposed to be accompanied home by someone. Demerol, I found, challenged my relationship with the truth. "My wife is waiting outside," I lied and left the office in the care of myself and Demerol.

I emerged into the sunshine of a beautiful fall day. I realized that I was not far from my favorite men's clothing store, Moe Ginsberg's, on Fifth Avenue and Twentieth Street. I had been planning to buy a new suit. It was a lovely day, and I had no further commitments. For the first time in my life, traffic seemed friendly, not dangerous or threatening. I reminded myself to be careful and waited for a green light before crossing Third Avenue and Twenty-Eighth Street.

Walking slowly with both exhilaration and deliberation, I arrived at Moe Ginsberg's store on Fifth Avenue. I took the elevator to the sixth floor and emerged from it into a sea of suits. A young salesman was waiting to greet me. Harry must have retired long ago.

"Good afternoon. My name is Jason. How can I help you today?"

"Hi, Jason. I'm Marty. I want to buy a suit."

"Sure thing, Mel. Let me measure you." Definitely not Harry. Harry never forgot a name.

Jason took my measurements and escorted me to the appropriate racks, well stocked with suits my size. I marveled at the selection. Jason plucked out a navy blue suit and said, "What do you think, Mel?"

"It's Marty, Jason. I like it."

"Try it on," said Jason. "Then you will know for sure."

I went into the changing room and put on the suit. As I stepped out, Jason gushed, "You look like a million. Fits like a glove. Perfect. You should get more than one."

Jason started pulling suits off the racks, one after the other. I liked them all. Jason reminded me that they would all fit like the first suit I tried on, like a glove. Jason continued to select suits while Demerol and I nodded in agreement. In no time at all, Jason had lined up seven suits for me. "Winter is coming," he said. "You could use a really good, fashionable overcoat. I got just the thing for you."

Jason disappeared for a few minutes and returned with an overcoat. I tried it on. It looked fine to me. I couldn't say no to anything. "I'll take it," I said to Jason, whose smile now knew no bounds.

"Do you want us to do the alterations?" he asked.

"No, I have a tailor near home."

"I'll get everything together for you then," Jason offered and walked off.

A smiling Jason accompanied me to the cashier, who took my credit card and wrapped up my purchases. Once again I was back on the elevator and then suddenly outside in the sunshine on Fifth Avenue. The world did not seem as welcoming as it had when I entered the building. The Demerol was wearing off. Laden down with eight boxes of purchases, I took the subway to Grand Central Terminal and the train to Bronxville. I was anxious to show them to Anna and get her agreement on my good taste.

I hung up all my suits and overcoat in my closet in preparation for modeling them for Anna. When she came home that evening from her office, I told her that I had something to show her. I poured her a glass of wine and told her to relax. I disappeared for a few moments and put on my first suit. I slowly entered the living room and awaited Anna's acclaim. It never came.

"You like that suit?" she asked in obvious disbelief. I left the room to put on suit number two.

I returned to the living room with the second suit, which generated no more interest than the first suit. After modeling seven suits, the only one Anna liked was the last suit, the navy blue one, the type of suit that I always wore. I hoped to salvage at least a second purchase when I returned to the living room with the last item, my new overcoat. As I turned around in the living room for her to see the overcoat from every angle, I asked, "What do you think?"

"It looks like you are wearing a circus tent," Anna replied with her usual directness.

The next morning I was back at Moe Ginsberg's store with seven boxes. When smiling Jason saw me, he was suddenly crestfallen. I felt for him. "I'm sorry, Jason, but my wife didn't like almost everything I bought. You must know how important it is to have your wife's agreement." Jason nodded slowly and sadly. Then I had a sudden inspiration that could lift Jason's spirits.

"I just remembered, Jason. I could use two new pairs of slacks. One with pleats. You know, the kind the brain surgeons used to wear."

Les and I had just gone for a workout at the Y on Twenty-Third Street and were strolling along Sixth Avenue looking at used books. A warm, sunny Sunday afternoon always brings out a lot of street vendors, who line both sides of the avenue with their tables of items for sale, many of which are books. Les and Peggy were visiting from Connecticut and staying with Anna and me at our apartment on Twenty-Second Street near the Flatiron Building.

At the corner of Twenty-Fifth Street, a bookseller was displaying a large book that caught my eye. It was lying on a table by itself, its well-kept cover bearing a beautiful photo of a European cathedral with its spires rising into a clear-blue sky. I couldn't immediately identify the cathedral from a distance, but as we approached the table, I could see that it was Chartres Cathedral, which I had visited several times. It would make a lovely coffee-table book, easily accessible on a daily basis, a book I would find quietly and refreshingly inspirational in the middle of rushed and manic New York City.

I realized that I had seen this same book once before, many years before, lying on a coffee table in Franklin Borchardt's apartment on Morningside Heights near Columbia University.

The photograph on the cover of the bookseller's book, a view of the west facade of Chartres Cathedral, was the same photograph I had seen on the cover of the book on the coffee table. The only difference was the spelling of the word "cathedral." In Franklin's home, "cathedral" had been spelled "kathedrale." Images of that visit poured through my mind like light through Chartres Cathedral's stained-glass windows.

I loved the differences in spelling and sound of foreign words. I remembered Franklin's Sunday missal, printed in both Latin and German. I was dazzled by the fact that it was incomprehensible to me yet perfectly understood by Franklin. Years later I reminded Franklin, who had become chair of the German Department at Duke University, about how impressed I was with his missal. His response was, "I guess I was pretentious even back then."

The same book that had been on Franklin's coffee table was now on the table in front of me on the corner of Twenty-Fifth Street and Sixth Avenue. What was radically different now, however, was the fact that I had visited Chartres Cathedral several times since I had last seen this book at Franklin's apartment. Having visited Chartres, I had, in a sense, walked into this book and become an invisible presence in its photographs. I could almost see myself seeing Chartres Cathedral.

Whenever I have visited Chartres, I have been unable to resist rubbing my hands on the walls or the columns and wondering what other hands had touched them long ago. As the artisans of the past live on in its stones and windows, so does the Latin language continue to thrive in Chartres Cathedral's dedication to the Latin liturgy, where Gregorian chant, along with the soft smoke of burning incense, continues to rise up within its walls, as it has for centuries.

The picture on the cover showed the west facade's round rose window, flanked by the cathedral's two very different spires, opposite the altar at the far eastern end of the building. As I turned the pages, I saw the two other rose windows, on the north and south facades, which, with the west window, create a triangle of painted light in the middle of the church. I saw myself standing in that pool of light, where I had, in fact, stood several times over the years.

"Can I help you?" said the voice of the man selling books.

"Yes, how much?" I asked him, pointing to the book I had been perusing.

"Five dollars," he replied.

Five dollars was a great price, I thought. My friend, Les, however, leaned over to me and whispered in my ear, "You never pay the price they ask. Offer him something less and he'll take it."

I should not have listened to Les. Against my better judgment, I asked "How about three dollars?"

The bookseller tilted his head quizzically to the right, looked at me in disbelief and repeated "How about three dollars? Really? Well, how about seven dollars?"

Contrary to plan, my bargaining had increased the price. I knew I had made a mistake, but a combination of pride and embarrassment would not allow me to offer to pay the original price of five dollars. Instead we walked on to look at other books on other tables. I was mad at myself and mad at Les. I had thrown away something I valued very much for two dollars.

That book, for which I have since searched in vain many times along Sixth Avenue, opened a door to the past like no other in my life. It not only presented one of the high points of Western civilization but also represented my first exposure to the new world of the Borchardts, which, ironically, was a vestige of that old world of Chartres Cathedral that they had left behind.

For that reason, Chartres Cathedral will always be Chartres Kathedrale for me, a living monument which, like the original cathedral, has been rebuilt with the stones of childhood memories and the later experiences of touching its walls and standing in its streaming, stained-glass light, where I still stand today, child-man, unseen in those photographs in the book I can no longer find.

Anna's fortieth birthday was approaching. During the years since our marriage, she had accomplished so much. Anna, by now a seasoned psychotherapist, had opened a private practice in Manhattan, received her PhD in clinical psychology and had become one of the Directors of the Training Institute for Mental Health, also in Manhattan. I wanted to do something special. She liked jewelry, which was fortunate since it was the only item I felt comfortable buying for her. Lately she had been admiring several pearl necklaces that she had seen. After some inquiries with friends and at work, I was referred to a small company on Madison Avenue, not far from my office. They sold only pearls. I went there one afternoon and sat for a lengthy lecture by the proprietor on the life of a pearl, how it begins, evolves, and becomes—or doesn't become—beautiful.

It was more information than I could completely process, but it was interesting. The proprietor then presented me with a dozen strings of pearls, some of them freshwater pearls. They were all quite lovely, which made it extremely difficult for me to decide. I was eventually able to reduce the dozen possibilities to three. But I finally gave up and told him that I could not make up my mind about which of the three strands of pearls Anna would prefer. I thought it might be the strand with the largest pearls because they had a beautiful, soft, rosy-pink glow to them. But I wasn't at all certain.

"No problem," he said. "Take all three to your wife and let her decide. Bring back the other two and pay me for the one you want to keep. That will be fine." I told him that her birthday was still two weeks away. Again I heard "no problem" and left his office with the three strands of pearls. I took the subway home with the three strands of pearls buried in my briefcase, with my two arms wrapped tightly around it.

My next big decision was where to have the birthday dinner. I wanted to invite some of Anna's girlfriends who lived in or near the city. I decided to host the dinner at El Quijote, a Spanish restaurant on the ground floor of the famous and infamous Chelsea Hotel on West Twenty-Third Street. It had been a favorite of ours for a number of years. El Quijote is a happy place, full of soft lights and cheerful people. Opened in 1930, it has been staffed by generations of Spanish immigrants from the Galicia region of Spain, home of its founder.

Among the many attributes of El Quijote was its location on Twenty-Third Street. We lived on Twenty-Second Street, and the YMCA, where I had been a member for many years, was directly across the street from the restaurant. The two locations had a certain symbiotic relationship. El Quijote was a pleasant place to have a beer after a workout, and the YMCA was a good place to sweat out the garlic from El Quijote's tastiest dishes.

One morning, when I was scheduled to drive to Princeton, New Jersey, to make a presentation, Anna yelled, "Oh my God! How much garlic did you eat last night? You can't talk to anyone this morning. They'll run away."

I decided to go over to the Y and solve the problem in the steam room. Armed with a package of Certs, I entered the steam room at about six thirty. Fortunately it was empty. I began chewing on some Certs as the steam started to work its magic on my pores.

After about ten minutes, I heard the door to the steam room open. Without my eyeglasses, I couldn't see anything through the haze. Then I heard, "Oh my God! Is there a dead body in here?"

That outburst was followed by the door slamming shut. I was alone again. This happened several more times that morning until, after consuming all the Certs, I left the steam room, feeling the way you must feel after a detox treatment. Garlic and the steam room, poison and its antidote.

"Your table is ready," said the maître d' at El Quijote when he approached us at the bar the evening of Anna's birthday. I had invited four of Anna's girlfriends and asked the maître d' to give us a table that could easily be converted to handle six people after these surprise guests arrived.

Unfortunately Anna told the maître d' that she wanted to sit in a booth, which was where we usually sat in El Quijote. Tonight, however, a booth would be a problem. Not only could six people not fit into a booth, but I had also arranged for a mariachi band to come and play after dinner. While they played, they circled the table, something they couldn't do if we were sitting in a booth.

The maître d' told Anna that a table would be a better choice and began to show us to the table. Anna turned to me and asked, "Who is he to tell us where to sit if we prefer a booth? We always sit in a booth. I want to sit in a booth."

I tried to convince her that a table would be fine, without giving away the surprise visit of her girlfriends. That did not work. She insisted on a booth. Finally the maître d' looked at me in exasperation and raised his hands and eyebrows in surrender. He took us to a booth.

A few moments after we were seated, the maître d' arrived back at the table with a large vase filled with the two-dozen roses that I had bought for Anna. I had forgotten about the roses, which added another layer of difficulty to sitting in a booth. The roses took up so much space that I couldn't see Anna across the table. With both hands, I spread open a passage in the middle of the roses so that I could see Anna and asked, "Can you now see why the maître d' wanted to put us at a table?" Anna smiled, thanked me for being thoughtful in bringing roses, and apologized for the fuss.

Anna's girlfriends Maureen, Rosemary, Peggy, and Joan, arrived at El Quijote soon after we had been seated. While Anna adapted to this pleasant surprise, the maître d' brought over another table so that we six now had a large table off to the side of the main dining room. Several bottles of wine arrived shortly thereafter. We toasted Anna's fortieth birthday, and the waiter took our order. I skipped the *pollo ajillo,* which had driven me into the steam room several months before and ordered the *paella valenciana.*

After dinner, while we were having dessert and coffee, the maître d', to whom I had confided the three sets of pearls, brought them over to the table. "These are for you," he said. Anna was speechless. I explained that since I had been unable to decide which of the three necklaces she would prefer, the jeweler told me to show them all to her. "It is your decision," I said. "I will bring back the two that you don't want."

Rosemary immediately suggested that Anna keep all three necklaces. This suggestion was seconded unanimously and in unison by the other three women. I said nothing, quietly recalling the old proverb, "No good deed goes unpunished." While Anna was apparently debating, the maître d' arrived with a complimentary after-dinner drink for us. As soon as he put the drinks on the table, as if on cue, the mariachi band burst through the front door, playing and singing as they approached our table. They circled the table and sang a beautiful Spanish love song to Anna. Several more songs followed as they continued to circle our table, first in one direction and then the other. Finally they serenaded Anna with "Happy Birthday" and danced and played their way back out the front door to thunderous applause from everyone in the restaurant.

Anna had not, in fact, been debating about which necklace to choose. She said she immediately knew which necklace she preferred. What was delaying her announcement was the fact that she did not want to say good-bye to the other two necklaces and acknowledged how appealing Rosemary's suggestion to keep all three had been. As I had predicted to myself, Anna chose the necklace with the large pearls with the rosy-pink hue. Anna leaned over to me and gave me a big kiss.

Despite the fact that every attempt I had made at surprising Anna was, though well intentioned, somehow flawed, I tried one more time to surprise her. On a business trip to the Far East, I bought several pieces of jewelry for her in Hong Kong: a matching ruby and sapphire ring, bracelet, and necklace. I was returning home around Valentine's Day. The ring would be the first gift. Then in May, the bracelet for our anniversary. Finally in August, I would present Anna with the necklace for her birthday. No more surprises in restaurants.

When I returned from Tokyo, I took Anna out to dinner and gave her the ring. She loved it. I was happy. Three months later we again went out for dinner, and I gave her the bracelet for our anniversary. She loved that, too, but asked how I was able to find a match for the ring I had given her three months earlier. I told her that I had bought both in Hong Kong.

"You mean you have been hiding this for the past three months? Right in our apartment? And you didn't give it to me?"

I confessed that I had also squirreled away a matching necklace for her birthday. Anna smiled and called me a sneak, while her big brown eyes told me that I would be incapable of being either a thief or a spy. Anna never used words to say the most important things. That came as no surprise.

Returning home from work one evening about three months after we were married, I stopped in the incinerator room on my way down the hall to our apartment. As I was discarding some papers, I noticed in the corner of the room, behind some cardboard boxes, a large canvas, the front of which was facing the wall. I could not resist turning it around. I recognized it immediately. It was mine.

I had decided to attempt to paint after being struck by Marcel Duchamp's canvas, *Nude Descending a Staircase.* The figure moves from step to step while yet remaining on all the steps it has already descended. The painting is like a movie in which the innumerable still photos, of which the film is composed, appear on the screen simultaneously, instead of replacing one another in a sequence that simulates motion and reflects passing time. In Duchamp's painting, the past and the present coexist, the latter never disappearing into the former.

Anna and I became engaged to be married around the time that I began to write my never-to-be-finished doctoral dissertation on the French philosopher Henri Bergson. His work is concerned, in a major way, with the concept of time, differentiating between the homogeneous time of science and the heterogeneous time of consciousness. In the former, every moment is the same. In the latter, every moment is different because it includes all previous moments. Duchamp seemed to me to have captured this distinction pictorially and became my inspiration to try my own hand at painting.

I had never picked up a paintbrush in my life, except to paint a wall. Attempting to create a painting was, therefore, the height of presumption. Not knowing what I was doing did not seem to me to be an impediment. Rather ignorance gave me free rein to express myself, unconstrained by basic rules, techniques, and the formal elements of painting. I was a self-declared, de facto expressionist, without having any idea of what expressionism really was.

Ignorance and pomposity can be soul mates. I went out and bought a canvas—not a small canvas but a big canvas, a five-foot-square canvas—along with an easel, gesso, a palette, and eight different colors of paint. The only thing I did not buy was a smock. I was a member of the sweatshirt school, something more authentic. I was soon ready to begin.

I told Anna that I was working on a painting. She was surprised. She didn't know that I painted. "I didn't, either," I confessed. I told her that I took up painting because it relieved a lot of the stress of working on my dissertation. Standing before my big canvas was like getting out of prison. I felt free and happy. Best of all, whatever I put on the canvas usually looked pretty good to me.

Months passed. Anna was anxious to see my artwork. I kept telling her that it wasn't quite ready for viewing, even though I was working as fast as I possibly could. That was the trouble with being an expressionist. You never knew when you had fully expressed yourself. It always seemed to need more work. But the truth was that I was afraid that Anna would be her always honest and direct self in her criticism, a noble but, to the recipient, painful virtue.

Seeing my painting in the incinerator room was a blow to my ego, but it was not the first downsizing Anna had undertaken since our marriage six months before. I couldn't object to her discarding other possessions that she had thought were no longer needed, such as clothes and shoes that I never wore. She was right. I had a hard time throwing anything away. I needed her decisiveness to get rid of things. But this was different. Throwing my painting away was like throwing away one of my books, something I was never able to do. Even more, the painting was a reflection of my inner self, something not easily cast off.

As I dragged the canvas down the hall and back into the apartment, I thought of the day when I had finally worked up the courage to show Anna my first and last painting, my contribution to expressionism. I had invited her to dinner at my apartment on Seventeenth Street. The painting was sitting on the easel in the middle of the living room, bathed in bright light and covered with a sheet. Anna arrived, and I offered her a glass of wine. She looked at the shrouded easel and said she really could not wait to see my painting. I insisted that she drink her glass of wine first while I gave her some background on my *Opus Number One.*

I confessed to her that I felt nervous because I was putting my deep, inner self on display for the first time. She told me not to worry. She admired my attempt to paint as well as my courage to display what I had painted. Anna admired most honest attempts to accomplish something new. Feeling more encouraged, I finished my glass of wine. I walked over to the easel and, with a slightly dramatic flourish, pulled the sheet off *Opus Number One.*

Perhaps it was Anna's presence that was the cause, but for the first time, I looked unemotionally and objectively at my creation.

I saw a huge, blue, oceanic background enveloping at its center a steep mountain, which was rising out of the deeper-blue depths. There was white, foamy turbulence on every side of the rising peak. The mountain itself was capped in menacing, fiery reds and yellows as it pushed its way out of the sea and into the lighter but gradually darkening pale-blue sky.

I didn't feel as confident as I usually did when I viewed the painting by myself. Sheepishly I turned to Anna and asked what she thought of it.

"What do you plan to call it?" she asked.

"I really don't know," I lied, even though I had been leaning toward *Opus Number One*. "Do you have any suggestions?" I asked timidly.

Anna, who was embarking on a career in clinical psychology, remained silent for a while and then asked, "How about *Penis over Miami*?"

It was my turn to be silent before we both laughed out loud. She had a point, I thought. We smiled at each other. As I considered Anna's suggestion, the canvas did begin to resemble a Freudian conflict transposed into lines and colors. Perhaps my great work was no more than a five-foot-square Rorschach test.

I refilled our wine glasses as we both laughed again about the giant stride I had made for Irish expressionism.

"You ought to translate your painting into words. I think you might have an interesting story to tell," Anna suggested. Psychotherapy, which would become Anna's lifelong profession, is known as the talking cure, which, like art, seeks to access and liberate those ineffable feelings we struggle to articulate. *Penis over Miami* didn't exactly tap into the ineffable, but it did reveal a presumption that was quickly cured by good humor.

About one year before we were married, I found an apartment in Greenwich Village. It wasn't a big apartment, but I was able to make room for everything including *Penis over Miami* by squirreling it away against the back wall of a clothes closet. There it would remain—safely, I mistakenly thought—until the evening I discovered it in the incinerator room.

When I confronted Anna that evening about my painting, she asked me how often I looked at it. "Never," was my response.

"It's not something either of us wants to see hanging on a wall in this apartment, is it?" Anna asked.

I answered with affirming silence. It was the separating, more than the abandoned painting itself, that was the problem for me. I just had a hard time saying good-bye to anyone or anything.

Several years later we built a weekend house in Pennsylvania. We did all the painting and furnishing ourselves. More specifically I did the heavy lifting, and Anna did the decorating. We had a fireplace in the living room, above which was a large empty space begging for my creative intervention. I told Anna that I had some ideas on what to put there. That was fine with her as long as I showed her what I had in mind before I started banging holes in the wall.

Anna loved to sew. She made many of her own clothes, as well as curtains and pillow covers. She always had bolts of fabric lying somewhere around the house or buried in closets. Looking at some of these fabrics one afternoon, I was inspired to, you might say, fabricate a painting. I decided to build a four-foot-square frame and attach pieces of her fabrics to it.

I worked in secret until the fabricated painting was completed. It was a beautiful mix of blues and greens with a hint of light in the distance, like a just-rising or a just-setting sun. One afternoon while Anna was away shopping, I stapled the fabric to the frame I had made and hung the frame above the fireplace. I thought it looked great.

When Anna returned later that afternoon, I pointed to my creation. "What do you think?" I asked.

Anna gazed at it for a few moments and said, "You know I like it. I really like it."

I was aglow with newfound validation. I sat down on the couch and looked up at my new masterpiece above the fireplace.

It was just like looking out to sea from Miami, but without the penis.

One afternoon as I passed by a small shop in Greenwich Village, I saw in the window a reproduction of Edward Hopper's *Night Hawk.* In the brightly lit *Night Hawk* diner, there is no companionship in its etymological sense, no breaking bread together. *Night Hawk* overwhelms with a loneliness that cannot be undone by physical proximity.

In this diner, physical proximity instead exacerbates the loneliness. People are physically together yet so painfully apart, each one locked in a separate, seemingly inaccessible world, inches away from each other on the canvas, but as distant, as unreachable, and as surrounded by space as a star in the night sky.

Night Hawk brought me back to Forty-Second Street and that long-ago day after a funeral, when my uncle was eating franks and beans off an old metal plate in a shabby diner. I remembered feeling sad as I watched him, and I never knew why. Seeing some people eat alone still saddens me, especially those who, like my uncle, seem disconnected, as impervious to the world as a metal plate.

No matter how many stars I see in the sky, it is the dark, empty, unbridgeable space between them that strikes me, more than their pinpoints of light. Food and eating are to be shared. Otherwise, aloneness dominates and sadness seeps through.

On an extended field exercise in the army in the early 1960s, I was reminded of that shabby diner in Hell's Kitchen, when we were fed C rations from World War II. By luck of the draw one night, I wound up with a can of C rations marked "Franks and Beans, 1942." If I hadn't been so hungry, I would have discarded it. Instead, like everyone else that night, I heated my C rations over a

Sterno stove and ate franks and beans that had been canned years before my uncle ate his franks and beans off that old metal plate, a sort of mess kit without a handle.

As Tommy declined over the years, I often volunteered to take him to his many doctor appointments. During a visit to the VA Hospital on Twenty-Third Street and First Avenue, the doctors discovered that he had suffered at least one silent heart attack while also suffering from metastasizing prostate cancer. When he was released from the hospital, he was more angry and suspicious than ever, and he even alienated Anna, a practicing clinical psychologist, by telling her that her profession was nothing more than manipulation.

While visiting my mother and uncle one evening weeks later, I found him slumped in a chair, half sleeping. Barely audibly he murmured that he wanted to go to bed. He could no longer walk on his own. He was too heavy for my mother to help him into bed. I lifted him up and half carried, half dragged him into his bedroom. I laid him down on his bed.

As he lay there, I sat on the edge of the bed. We then had what was perhaps our first conversation. He told me how much he had liked the army and how much he wished that I had liked it, too. He spoke about the army maneuvers that he had participated in down South in 1940. "The army gave me a wonderful chance to be with a lot of good guys, to see places I had never seen, to lead a completely different life."

I nodded in agreement and told him that it had been a fine opportunity for him. I didn't ask why he had given up something he loved so much or why he had lost his commission in the national guard.

Before closing his eyes for what might be his final sleep, he looked at me and whispered, "Too bad you never liked the army. I loved the army. It was a great life as an army officer."

As opposed to his endless suspicions about the government and large corporations, particularly Con Edison, that statement was the most open, honest feeling Tommy had ever shared with me in the many years that had passed since our lives came together after my father's death.

As he lay in his bed and stared up at the ceiling, I saw a man for whom I had always felt sorry, a man alone, a terribly lonely man, a failed man, a man who had no idea how sad it was to watch him eat franks and beans off an old metal plate in a shabby diner in Hell's Kitchen.

The morning after I had carried him into bed, Tommy was readmitted to the hospital. I went to visit him the next day. While I sat by his bed and tried to make conversation, he was mostly silent. He had an air of resignation that seemed to me to be a blend of acceptance and courage. His lifelong, angry suspicion had dissipated. His eyes no longer projected blame everywhere but on himself.

Tommy finally spoke. He said that he had to go to the bathroom. I rang for the nurse to help me put him in his wheelchair. As we lifted him from his bed, we noticed that he had already relieved himself in his bed. The nurse was annoyed. Tommy said that he still had to go to the bathroom. We put him in the wheelchair and took him to the toilet, where we sat him down and closed the door. I went back to his bed and sat in the visitor's chair.

As I looked at the empty bed, I began a silent conversation with the invisible man in it. I told him that I was sorry for his illness and his suffering. I told the empty pillow that I wished we could have had a real relationship, like a father and his son, even though he was just an uncle. I had become so used to my father being dead for so long that I was unaware of how much I truly missed having a father. It wasn't fair to expect Tommy to be a father, but I never forgave him for not trying harder to be one.

While I waited for him, I heard Tommy huffing and puffing behind me as I rode my bike in Central Park. I saw the sweat on his brow when we stopped to let him rest. I saw him trying hard to help me, even though he would have been happier back in Kelly's saloon. I was grateful. For that one hour in Central Park, he had been the father I had lost. But that hour would never be repeated. I looked at his empty hospital bed and saw the presence that Tommy had been in my life.

He died in the hospital a few hours after I left him. Following his funeral, he was buried in a plot allocated to him and his two sisters, my mother and my aunt, his lifelong companions.

After the funeral, I drove home alone, but no more alone than I had ever been with Uncle Tommy.

The spacious open-air restaurant in the small seaside town of Santa Margherita in Liguria is called La Cambusa. The sea, which provides most of the menu's offerings, slaps gently against the rocks that define the outer edges of the restaurant. The early moon is rising in the dusk-colored sky as we sip our aperitifs at a table directly across from the small building that houses the kitchen and a bar.

Three low steps lead up to the kitchen entrance through which waiters stream in and out with steaming plates of *zuppa di pesci*, linguine, clams, mussels, branzino, and calamari. The dexterity of the waiters, as they carry huge trays laden with overflowing dishes, is matched only by the grace with which they climb and descend the steps leading to the entrance and exit doors of the kitchen. It is a choreographed flow of white shirts and black ties slipping noiselessly in and out of the kitchen and back again to the tables.

Our waiter arrives with our appetizers, two small bowls of *zuppa di pesci*, as a prelude to our favorite dish, *linguine alla Cambusa*. This eponymous specialty is an overflowing dish of *linguine aigli'olio* buried beneath a small mountain of clams, mussels, and shrimp, the whole sprinkled with generous splashes of fresh parsley and chopped tomato. We learned not to ask for formaggio, because the first time we ordered *linguine alla Cambusa*, we had asked the waiter for some cheese. With a slight look of shock on his face, he politely refused, explaining that "*Pesce e formaggio non vanno insieme*" (fish and cheese do not go together).

As we begin to sample our *zuppa di pesci*, Anna suggests that I turn around and look behind me at the entrance to the kitchen. I turn and see a small, white dog that has decided to rest on the top step, right in front of the entrance and exit doors to the kitchen. The waiters continue to flow gracefully in and out. Nobody says a word to the little dog, which has rolled over on his side and is resting his head on the top step.

By now the moon is bright white and high in the sky. The wind has picked up slightly, creating a soft, refreshing breeze across the little peninsula jutting into the sea, holding La Cambusa in the palm of an earthen hand. The slap of the waves against the rocks is just a bit louder than when we arrived. The scent of the steaming *zuppa di pesci* mixes with that of the sea, distilling the air in La Cambusa into a salty perfume. Anna reminds me of the *burrasca* that once came in from the sea when we were here having dinner. (A *burrasca* is a sudden storm that is not uncommon on the Tyrhennian Sea, on which Santa Margherita is situated.)

Tonight the sky is clear, and the wind is soft. There will be no storm to disturb the little white dog, now sleeping before the entrance to the kitchen. Nor will he be disturbed by any of the waiters, who continue to dance around him as they rush in and out with their trays, accepting his arrival and presence as something as natural as the rising and the shining of the moon or the fresh breeze or the waves slapping against the rocks. They all belong here in La Cambusa.

Anna and I had come back to Santa Margherita almost every year since we first inadvertently drove into it in 1977. We had been driving along the coast to visit the beautiful, wine-producing Cinque Terrre and the small town of Portofino (which turned out to be as disappointingly artificial as a movie set). Driving a mere five kilometers beyond Portofino, however, we had come upon the charming town of Santa Margherita in Liguria.

In contrast to Portofino, Santa Margherita is a real, working, lived-in town, where many people still fish for a living. It is a bustling town of shops, bakeries, fresh seafood, and fresh produce vendors. Along the waterfront, there are hotels, cafes, restaurants, and a large fish market. We always stayed at the small, three-story Hotel Laurin, where each room has a large balcony overlooking the sea, about ten yards away. It is a short walk to the beach, which we visited almost daily during our late-summer sojourns, usually in early September.

Because we came to Santa Margherita most years at roughly the same time, we saw many of the same people again and again. There was Signorina Alessandra, an attractive and apparently very popular, twenty-year-old blonde, who received a phone call every five minutes. In that pre-cell-phone world, phone calls to the beach were announced over the PA system. "*Signorina Alessandra, tele'fono*!" would boom the voice of the PA system. No sooner had Signorina Alessandra returned to her blanket, however, than the PA system would call out once again, "*Signorina Alessandra, tele'fono*!"

But the main event on the beach, as Anna pointed out to me one day, occurred around two every afternoon. At that time, a German couple in their late forties would execute the oil ritual. The woman, who was topless, would lie back on her blanket while the man dutifully and meticulously rubbed oil all over her body. At that moment, Anna would usually ask me to stand up so that she could take a picture of me or, rather, pretend to take a picture of me.

As I stood before our blanket, I could see Anna gradually move the camera in the direction of the Germans for that year's snapshot. The Italians, and Europeans generally, are very casual about being topless. But when the two o'clock oiling began, everyone quietly and very discretely took notice. Being topless is one thing, but an oil massage is clearly another, even for Italians.

Our typical day in the sun would end around five, and we would return to our hotel for showers and a drink on our balcony. We would watch the sun begin to dip in a cloudless, blue sky while we listened to the clanging of boat bells as the boats in their slips rose and fell on an endless stream of gentle waves. Then we would return to La Cambusa for another fine dinner.

As I watched the waiters that evening silently and physically acknowledge the little dog's presence by taking extra steps along the well-worn path into and out of the kitchen, I thought of visits that we had made to the ancient city of Pompeii many years before. Rome may be the Eternal City, but Pompeii is the Eternal Dig, with home after home being unearthed from their sudden burial in volcanic ash two millennia ago.

As in many other homes in the ancient Roman world, the floor of the entranceway to the House of the Tragic Poet in Pompeii is decorated with a mosaic of a dog, not a lovable dog but a threatening dog, warning anyone with evil intentions that he is in danger of being attacked by the master's fierce and faithful companion.

"*Cave canem*," the Romans used to say, "Beware of the dog." That warning is echoed in many houses throughout Pompeii, the city that died a death so sudden that people and animals have been preserved in the very positions in which they drew their last breaths. Here in Santa Margherita, however, as I observe the reclining, little, white dog and the sidestepping waiters, "Beware of the dog" transforms into "Take care of the dog."

Would the ancient Pompeiians, for whom, it seems, the sole purpose of a dog was to protect its master and his family, have found the behavior of the waiters in La Cambusa that evening incomprehensible, a world turned upside down and standing on its head? Would they say there should be no tolerance for an animal that inconveniences human life?

It was impossible to wonder about Pompeii without wandering a few hours north in my mind to Rome. Years before on my first visit there, I had found myself alone one night in the Coliseum under a full moon. The more than several glasses of wine that I had drunk with dinner came to the aid of my imagination. The Coliseum was empty, but my mind saw it filled with the life of the ancient world. I sat on a hard stone bench that was nearly two thousand years old. I heard the voice of Professor Woods, our fine arts professor in freshman year, describe the Coliseum. "Monumental, majestic, standing like a Roman legion, fastened to the earth, unmovable, invincible, as lasting as human history."

A pigeon landed on the bench in front of me, perhaps expecting s little snack. I had nothing to offer him. He looked a bit like Duke, the homing pigeon of my childhood, blue and gray. I wondered if the Coliseum was that pigeon's home the way the roof on Columbus Avenue between Ninety-Eighth and Ninety-Ninth Streets had been Duke's home, a home to which he would unfailingly return. For the first time in years, I recalled that Duke had arrived back on the roof at 2:32 p.m., having flown seven and one-half miles in exactly twelve minutes on his maiden solo flight.

Unlike Duke, however, I was changing homes. The old and new had traded places. The old was the new for me. I had found a new home, the dwelling place of the larger family to which I belonged. Sitting in the moonlit Coliseum, I felt I was back on the subway going to work after class on one of those days when I had learned or discovered something that made the world forever different. For me, the last stop on the Number One subway line would prove not to be 242nd Street Van Cortland Park, but rather a place like the Coliseum or Santa Margherita, where the old became the new in my life.

While Anna and I were having our dessert, one of the waiters brought out a small bowl of food and a dish of water for the little white dog, which appeared to quickly eat and drink everything before reclining once again. Another waiter, passing by, removed the bowl and the dish. The attentive service to the dog was so undifferentiated from the excellent service we received that I joked to Anna that the dog might have requested the check, as the waiter removed the bowl and dish.

Santa Margherita and its environs host a lot of wealthy people in gigantic yachts with uniformed crews. Observing this, it is quite possible to feel that care and concern do not reach much beyond care and concern for self, of which we, too, vacationing in Santa Margherita, were probably guilty from time to time. If Anna had not pointed out to me the care and attention that the staff was giving to the little dog, I might have missed it all, as I sometimes do. Since that evening, "*Cave canem*" has come to mean "Beware of being inattentive and not caring."

Learning is possible even in the often-mindless world of vacationing. Over the years, I learned much in the schoolhouse that is Santa Margherita, but I always needed Anna to escort me to the classroom for my lesson, which usually entailed learning to see what was right in front of me.

The foothills of the surrounding mountains hugged the shores of Lago Maggiore, as we boarded the small ferry in the early evening. The ferry connects the town of Stresa, Italy, to the Borromeo Islands that sit offshore in Lago Maggiore. One of those islands is called Isola dei Pescatori and was reputed to have a charming lakeside restaurant, our destination that evening.

A man, who called himself Walter of Stresa, was on the dock with an accordion and singing a song about Isola Bella, another of the Borromeo Islands. As the sun descended on the mountain peaks in the distance, the heat of the day began to fade. The sky and a rising moon were taking on new colors, pinks and purples. The ferry slipped away from the dock and into a refreshing breeze, with the muted sound of the engine deferring to the slapping of gentle waves along the bow of the boat.

A rising, swelling moon gradually replaced a sinking sun, and Stresa faded gracefully into a larger landscape of lake and mountains. Pinks and purples soon began to give way to the bright white of a full moon bouncing off the lake. The fading lights of Stresa glimmered reassuringly in the distance, reminding me of the lights from apartments along Central Park West, which had been our beacons home when, as kids, we had ventured into the park at night.

A big full moon, like the one rising over Lago Maggiore, would sometimes shine down on Central Park. One night in particular in Central Park, the most beautiful full moon I can remember rose in the sky. That night, twelve of us, six girls and six boys, sat in a corner of a large field next to the moonlit lake on 103rd Street.

We huddled together in a big circle around an empty bottle of Pepsi-Cola, under a moon that was not quite a harvest moon but much bigger than usual. The entire park was bathed in the moon's soft, white light, illuminating all the trees, benches, fields, and walkways around us as if it were day.

That same soft moonlight shimmered on the small waves as Anna, Maureen, and I stood at the railing near the front of the boat and watched Isola Bella slip by. Maureen, a dear friend and professional colleague of Anna, had been traveling around Italy by herself before meeting up with us in Stresa.

In a few more minutes, we would dock at Isola dei Pescatori, so named because it had long been home to the many fishermen who used to fish in the lake. When fishing was no longer a viable industry in Lago Maggiore, Isola dei Pescatori had become a tourist destination with several small, welcoming restaurants.

By the time we docked, the once-multicolored moon had turned bright white, moving slowly from the mountains in the east to the center of the lake. We had a short, pleasant walk from the dock to the restaurant, Casa del Persico, which was on a small, sandy beach. Little waves rhythmically lapped at the shore, just a few feet from our table.

It seemed natural to order the local favorite, perch, fresh from the lake and prepared *alla Borromea,* brushed with butter and pan fried with diced lemon, capers, and mushrooms. This delicious dish was served with a heaping, steaming plate of risotto, which we all shared along with a dry white local wine. Dining on perch, however, did seem a bit strange when I recalled the small perch that we used to catch in the lake on 103rd Street in Central Park. We always threw them back in the water and never thought of cooking them and eating them.

After dinner, we walked around Isola dei Pescatori and looked out on the islands of Isola Bella and Madre rising before us from the lake. Anna and Maureen compared notes on our separate European excursions. We returned to the ferry dock and boarded the next boat back to Stresa. There were only two other passengers on the boat, which allowed for a very quiet, almost contemplative, return trip.

On the beach in the moonlight was a circle of teenage boys and girls surrounding a small fire, the eternal appeal of shared light and heat in surrounding darkness. Their loud, then increasingly inaudible, exchanges as our boat moved away were invariably followed by louder group laughter, an affectionate laughter, I thought, that excluded no one, even if the joke had been at that person's expense.

Their laughter carried me to another beach by a lake. The sun is still shining on that beach. There is the sound of many voices and a lot of laughter. We are waiting to go back in the water after lunch. The dark, green lake beckons. Then I hear a gentle voice with a funny New England accent say, "I don't know if I want to swim out to the raft." We hear Danny, but we don't listen to him.

Anna, Maureen, and I drifted off into private reveries, each of us alone with the water, the moon, the distant mountains, the night, and the soft sound of the lake separating before the bow of the boat. I continued to listen to the fading sounds coming from the shrinking circle of teenagers around the fire on the beach. The expanding lake pushed Isola dei Pescatori into the night and into the past, taking its place alongside another night by another lake.

That other night by that other lake we were going to play spin the bottle, a kissing game. When the bottle finished spinning, with either end pointing to one boy and one girl, the two were required to kiss. There was a lot of nervous laughter as the game began. I was more than nervous and with good reason. I was fattest kid in the circle. Every girl's last choice, I thought. So I hoped for the best, which meant that the bottle would never point to me or that, if it did, the girl would be understanding.

One of the girls spun the bottle. Happily it did not stop at me. Again and again it was spun with the same positive result. The kissing became more competitive, with kisses of increasing intensity, lasting longer and longer.

As the game continued, I became more relaxed, almost convinced that the bottle would always bypass me and stop elsewhere. But I secretly envied the boys who got to kiss the girls, especially Patricia. I couldn't take my eyes off her. I was even annoyed and jealous when my friend Charlie kissed her and she seemed to enjoy it.

I was glad to be only a spectator but was still dying to kiss Patricia, torn between feeling happy to be safe yet still wanting not to be. The game went safely on until the sky finally fell. The bottle stopped spinning and pointed at Patricia and me.

She looked at the bottle and followed its line across the circle to me. She stared at me, at first with disbelief and then with disgust. She stood up. "I am not going to kiss that fat slob!" she yelled angrily. "I will not. Never!"

Some of the others tried to calm her. "It's just a game," someone said.

"It is not a game to me. Kissing him is not a game," she fumed.

Amid the booing and laughter, I got up off the grass, slipped quietly out of the chattering circle that was debating our ill-fated kiss, and left the park, seeking a sheltering darkness.

Home was not far away, but I did not want to go there. I wondered if I should keep on walking until I got skinny. I would walk through life and never eat again. I did not want to see my friends again. They would only laugh at me or, worse, pity me.

While the small ferry made its way back to Stresa, gently rolling over the lake's small waves, we three stood silently at the railing and watched the boat follow the path of white light that the moon had laid across the water. Approaching the now-deserted dock in Stresa, our boat reversed engines and glided to a stop. In my mind, I was watching the little boy I used to be walk home alone, like a perch dodging the moonlight, eventually slipping safely away into the darkness.

Maureen said she was tired from her journey up from Rome and wanted to return to the hotel. Anna and I walked back with her to our hotel. After an exchange of "*Buona notte*," Anna and I decided to take a short walk along the shore of the lake, not wanting to let the moon go away. We said hardly a word to each other but shared everything in our still-moonlit world in silence.

The moon began its slow, unwilling descent behind the mountains to the west, leaving behind a darker, emptier sky. We sat on a rock, dipped our feet in the lake, and watched the disappearing moon roll up its white-light carpet from the lake. Anna held my face in her two hands and kissed me.

I felt loved and wondered if anyone was kissing Patricia in the moonlight.

Uncle Charlie was quiet and reserved. Socially, he was physically present but emotionally absent. It was not that he was shy. It was as if his mind had been abducted and held captive somewhere else. His silence seemed to mask something that he was unable to share, perhaps even with himself. But I liked Uncle Charlie for his gentleness and appreciated the fact that he never raised his voice, a trait that was all-too-uncommon among other members of the family.

We hardly ever heard Uncle Charlie's voice at all. When we did, it was a soft murmur from a corner of the room. Everyone liked

Uncle Charlie because he neither agreed nor disagreed with anything that was said. He was more a part of the decor than he was a part of the conversation. He got along with everyone.

The only negative comment I ever heard about Uncle Charlie was that he had once tried to commit suicide.

My cousin David Dolan was a bright guy, an only child of my father's sister, Helen, and her husband, Uncle Charlie. They were the most affluent branch of the family, residents of a big private house in Dumont, New Jersey. Aunt Helen was very proper and pleasant, even when correcting my English grammar. Unfortunately she was also a terrible cook, which made dinner in Dumont hospitable and well-meaning but essentially unpalatable.

Aunt Helen and Uncle Charlie provided David with an excellent Jesuit education, first at Xavier High School in Manhattan and then at Fordham University in the Bronx, where he earned both bachelor's and master's degrees in philosophy and foreign languages. Perhaps it was something in our shared Irish DNA that led both David and me to follow the same academic path at different schools.

After graduation, David went off to Europe. He worked as a volunteer at a hospital in Hanover, Germany, and soon became fluent in German. When he returned to the United States, I helped him get a job at IBM, where I had been working since being discharged from the army. David had never been drafted or served in the military. I never knew why since it was mandatory in those days.

David, like his father, Uncle Charlie, had always been somewhat socially disconnected. I felt only part of him was present whenever we met, the rest of him somewhere else. I never felt he was hiding anything. I don't think he knew what it was he couldn't say, only that it was unsayable. But his emotional absence and his silence never seemed to me to be a harbinger of harm, either to himself or to anyone else.

"Your cousin David has died," Anna said to me, with some hesitation, soon after I walked in the door on that Friday evening in May 1988. "We received a call about half an hour ago from your cousin Maryellen."

David dead? He was not yet fifty years old. "What happened? How did he die?" I asked. Anna looked away and was silent for a moment.

"Maryellen said that he shot himself. His body was found in the hills near Albuquerque." Anna put her arms around me and hugged me, while I tried to understand what had happened. But the shock of the news made understanding impossible.

I was familiar with Albuquerque and the surrounding hills. We had gone hiking there some years before. It is a good place to be alone, nobody for miles, just the mountains in the distance. I remembered once seeing some round-armed desert bushes that looked like they were kneeling with their backs bent to the desert floor, staring at the heavens, as if silently imploring them to release the rain that never comes. While we walked along, we could hear above us the distant murmurs of passing jet planes, the twentieth century slipping by, silver wings crisscrossing in the blue sky, seeming to sketch an indifferent blessing on all below.

I tried to imagine what happened. David there in those hills, all alone, as he often was. Did he walk around, debating before deciding? My mind could hear the gunshot, the sharp crack, which, muffled in and mumbled back by those echoing hills, must have slid along the sides of those distant mountains and barked across the emptiness of the lonely valleys between them before tailing off to the west to become a whisper lost in the wind on the barren desert.

I could hear the bullet's dull thud, which, unheard and unfelt, must have rolled David's eyes back, making them white beneath the blue belly of the New Mexico sky, spinning them inward in failed pursuit of the world's last impression, as the bullet sailed along that path well-worn by torturing thoughts.

It was a sound that David never heard as he sat, maybe, with his back to a tree, staring ahead in the deserted wood, somewhere in those hills near Albuquerque. All nature's dark force had brought him there, and he must have struggled to understand why.

Suicide cannot be understood, because suicide always seems, after the fact, to have been preventable, if only the warning signs had been heeded. There had been warning signs with David—perhaps even pleas for help—but I did not see them as such or perhaps denied them because I didn't want to deal with them. I never imagined impending suicide. At worst, I thought David was simply stressed, obsessed, perhaps suffering from a passing bout of depression.

Why had David done this? I had not seen him often during the previous ten years, only when he had come to New York on business or, even more infrequently, when he had come to visit with his family. We had stayed in touch periodically, writing the occasional letter or Christmas card.

During the year before his death, however, his letters had become increasingly strange. His handwriting would change from paragraph to paragraph, sometimes from sentence to sentence. Even the color of the ink he used would change, reflecting, it seemed, not the number of times that he had started and stopped the letter but rather his suddenly changing mood.

When David died, he left behind his wife, Ana, and their three children, Frankie, Carla, and Charlie. David had met Ana in her native Argentina, where he had gone to work, initially for IBM and then for another company. Later he and Ana had returned to the United States when David had found a new job with yet another company, located in Albuquerque.

Even when surrounded by those we love, we all face death alone. Maybe in our last moments as we try to make sense of our lives, we find an understanding in the eyes of those who look back into ours with love. Those eyes were missing during David's final moments. He was alone, walled off from those who loved and cared for him, surrounded only by his own inaccessible solitude. He left this world, having neither understood nor been understood.

As in a dream, his consciousness, which had once crawled on all fours across the world that was the big house in Dumont, New Jersey, must have slipped down beneath the bent wall of the sky, like falling firelight to fading flame, David slumping, his back still against the tree, head bent forward, his bleeding wound his last exchange with the world around him.

I had ignored David's letters, attributing their bizarre quality and angry ranting to unreal demands driven by confused motives. But David did care about a cousin with whom I had had no contact in over thirty years. Cousin Walter, known as Wally Boy, was the son of my father's brother, Walter, a controlling, abusive man and failed father, who succeeded in transforming his son into a marginal, confused, and self-destructive young man. Wally Boy apparently had had a stroke, and his wife was suffering from emphysema. They had three teenage children.

David, sensitive and well intentioned, was concerned for their welfare and felt that some of his cousins should and could take them into their homes. He exempted us from this responsibility because, I assumed, we only had a one-bedroom apartment in Manhattan and no experience yet in raising children. Our adopted daughter, Casey, would arrive a year later.

I don't want to believe that death is forever. I want to tell David that he has not yet died on distant stars nor has he yet been born in the dark reaches beyond our faint light, which has yet to deliver the news that any of us have been here, have come and gone. The senseless universe thunders on in silence, and only we, stranded here in webs of memory, know that David is gone.

Anna's voice brought me back to the present moment. "Maryellen said that they are planning a memorial service at Fordham University. She would like you to attend and say a few words." I nodded in agreement.

"Suicide," Anna continued, "is often an act of hostility."

I wondered who or what would have been the target of David's hostility. We, the cousins, who were, in David's opinion, guilty of neglect of our cousin's family? Himself? The largely imperfect world that suddenly springs back into existence as soon as you leave those quiet hills near Albuquerque?

At Fordham University where we remembered David, we all remembered to forget what we all imagined had really happened. We prayed for David and for the peace that had eluded him. I also said a prayer for Aunt Helen, whose dementia shielded her from the painful reality of the death of her only child.

Finally I prayed for Uncle Charlie and wondered if the only negative comment I had ever heard about him was true. Had his son, David, succeeded where he had failed? Had David found a way to say what neither one of them ever could? I could hear Uncle Charlie's soft voice murmuring from a faraway corner of the room. Too soft, too faraway to be understood.

It was an extremely warm morning in early July, as Anna and I left our apartment in Greenwich Village. "What are you up to today?" she asked.

"I have a meeting with Tom Lester," I said, "and then lunch at Fraunces Tavern."

"Have a good time with Tom Lester, if that's possible," she said. "I will meet you at six thirty in front of the Y. Don't be late. Dinner at Christine's at seven."

"OK. No problem. I'll be there. Have a nice day."

Tom Lester was an important, if difficult, customer of mine at Bankers Trust Company during the mid-1970s. He prided himself on being taciturn and tough. He rarely smiled. When he did, it was usually upon hearing about some perceived rival's misfortune. From a business point of view, however, it was essential for me to be accommodating to him, even if it was sometimes very difficult, even distasteful.

Tom Lester had admiration for the strangest things. He had once worked for US Steel and was in awe of their creative approach to firing thousands of people in a single day. He had been a first-line manager in their IT department. On a certain day, he was told to convene a meeting of his direct reports at nine thirty in the morning to tell them that they were, as of that moment, no longer employed by US Steel. Good-bye and good luck.

At ten that morning, Tom Lester's phone rang. He was summoned to a meeting with his boss, a second-line manager, along with that manager's other direct reports. At ten, Tom and his peers were told by the second-line manager that they, too, were no longer employed by US Steel. More good-byes and more good luck.

At ten thirty that morning, the phone on Tom Lester's boss' desk rang. He was invited to a meeting with his boss, a third-line manager...So it went for most of the day at US Steel, where top management was able to creatively have thousands of employees fire each other in an orderly fashion in a single day. Tom Lester was beside himself with admiration and laughter whenever (which was often) he recounted this tale of self-destruction.

And whenever Tom Lester related this event to me, I could not help thinking of the film, *Casablanca,* when Bogie, - to prevent the arrest of Victor Lazlo, the anti-Nazi hero - points his gun at Captain Renault and says, "Remember, Louis, this gun is pointing right at your heart." To which the seriously-lacking-in-compassion-just-like-Tom-Lester Louis replies, "My least vulnerable spot."

Anna knew Tom Lester very well. We had once been invited to his home for dinner, an unwanted but unavoidable invitation. We went to his rather-upscale home in New Jersey and met his wife, Joanne, who was quite shy and quiet. They had no children. We were invited into the living room. After we had been seated and had chatted for a while, Tom asked if we would like something to drink.

As soon as we replied in the affirmative, Tom snapped his fingers, and his wife jumped from her chair. She asked us what we would like. I dared not look at Anna and prayed that this was just another example of Tom Lester's twisted sense of humor.

It wasn't.

His wife robotically took our drink order and left the room. Still avoiding eye contact with Anna, I tried to continue the conversation as if nothing unusual had happened. After a few minutes, Tom Lester's wife returned with our drinks. She drank nothing. Our reality-avoiding conversation continued, dragging on until Tom suggested another drink.

I said yes, hoping that the finger-snapping game would end and Tom would admit it was just one of his weird jokes. Unfortunately it wasn't a game. Once again his wife jumped up, took my empty glass, and left the room. I felt awful for putting her through this nonsense a second time. Anna and I silently decided to drink no more that evening. Tom's wife served dinner mechanically.

Despite our numerous compliments on her cooking, the sad expression on her face remained frozen in place. We managed to delicately and diplomatically leave soon after desert. We thanked them again for their hospitality, got into our car, and left for home.

We remained silent as we drove home until Anna finally said, "I cannot believe what we just saw. Are you sure this wasn't just a sick charade?"

I told her that I wished it had been, but knowing Tom Lester, I doubted that it was. "That was the real Tom Lester, the guy who snapped his fingers for a wife whose only choice was to obey or run away."

When I told Anna that morning that I was having lunch with Tom Lester, therefore, she was sympathetic and understanding. I had no choice. When I reached the office, I called Fraunces Tavern to make a reservation for lunch. That turned out to be impossible. It was July second, just before the July fourth weekend. It was also the bicentennial year, 1976. Fraunces Tavern, with its history of hosting General George Washington for his farewell address to his officers, was more popular than ever. A table for lunch was out of the question.

Plan B was a very pleasant restaurant called Saint Charlie's, just across the street from the Bankers Trust building on Liberty Street.

I made a reservation for twelve thirty that afternoon and so informed Tom Lester's secretary. I arrived at his office just before twelve thirty, and we were immediately on our way. One thing about Tom Lester: he was almost militarily punctual.

We sat down at our table in a very crowded Saint Charlie's restaurant. Tom said he would really enjoy a nice bottle of red wine. I ordered a bottle of California Cabernet Sauvignon. Tom took a large drink from his glass, smacked his lips, and expressed his satisfaction with my choice of wine.

"I think I'm a more-than-one-bottle man today," Tom predicted. "After all," he said, "it is the Fourth of July. It would be unpatriotic not to drink." I nodded in silent agreement with Tom, my most common response to his pronouncements.

Tom launched into one of his lengthy narrations, which were usually a combination of his life story and his political struggles at Bankers Trust Company. Along the way, he would make it clear that he would be most grateful for any negative information I could supply about his competitors back at the office. I usually dodged these solicitations with a combination of wine pouring and joke telling. Tom emptied the bottle and ordered another bottle of wine. It was two o'clock.

Unknown to us, at that very moment there was chaos and death in Fraunces Tavern, which was about a half mile away from Saint Charlie's. A terrorist group, FLPR, the Front for the Liberation of Puerto Rico, had just exploded several bombs there during the lunch hour, their macabre contribution to the celebration of July fourth.

Six people were killed, and many more wounded. The restaurant was seriously damaged. Among the dead, I would later learn, was a young man named Frankie Connors, who had been my next-door neighbor in Washington Heights during our teenage years. Frankie was thirty-three years old, the gentlest soul in the neighborhood.

Our second bottle of California Cabernet Sauvignon arrived. Tom filled our glasses and continued our one-way conversation. I wanted to ask him if his finger-snapping wife control was a contrived performance for our benefit. But I was afraid to find out that it wasn't. Believing that it might have been simply his strange idea of a joke made it easier to accept. Tom filled our glasses again, even though I had hardly drunk any wine from the previous pour.

At about three thirty, Tom ordered our third bottle of wine. It was an unwritten rule at IBM that you never let the customer drink alone. If you did, the customer might become a bit paranoid, thinking that he is letting his guard down and you are taking advantage of that. So, "Bottoms up, Tom." I tried to drink a lot of water while only sipping the wine. I did not want to get into trouble later with Anna for having drunk too much before we even arrived for dinner at Christine's home.

Tom finally put down his wine glass for the last time. "That was good, and I think that it was enough," he said. I agreed. It was about five fifteen. Tom got up from the table and told me he would see me on Tuesday. Without even waiting for me to pay the check, he ambled out the door, crossed the street, and headed to the World Trade Center for the PATH train to New Jersey and home.

I paid the check and took the subway up to the Y on Twenty-Third Street. I sat in the steam room and tried to drain the Cabernet from my body. That was when I learned of the bombing of Fraunces Tavern. It was six fifteen. I took a cold shower and hurried downstairs, where Anna was parked illegally, waiting for me.

Anna was furious. "Where were you? I called your office a hundred times this afternoon. Nobody knew where you were. The last thing you told me this morning was that you were going to have lunch at Fraunces Tavern. Then I hear that it was blown up by terrorists. What was I supposed to do? I was going crazy with worry."

I told Anna that I had been unable to get a reservation and had taken Tom Lester to another restaurant. I had only recently heard about the bombing. "If I had known, I would have called you," I said.

"Why didn't you get my messages this afternoon?" Anna asked.

I couldn't tell her that I was drinking wine all afternoon and never called the office. It was at that moment that I realized for the first time that having a customer like Tom Lester could, on occasion, be a good thing.

"You remember that I was having lunch with Tom Lester. You know how difficult he can be. When we finished eating, he insisted on reviewing a report he was creating on everything that IBM was doing wrong at Bankers Trust. I had to sit there and listen. I had no choice. He's the customer. If he's unhappy with me, it will be bad for business. And if it's bad for business, it will be bad for me."

Anna calmed down. In silence, we drove north on Eighth Avenue to Christine's apartment on West Ninety-Fourth Street.

When I later heard the sad news about Frankie Connors, I could not help wondering then—and still can't now—if Frankie had gotten the table that I couldn't get that July fourth weekend at Fraunces Tavern.

Relationships seem to have a center of gravity, a common interest, point of view, goal, profession or neighborhood. The center of gravity in my relationship with Frank was running. And not just running, but running that was almost always followed by a few beers, some old jokes, and a lively discussion. There was, however, one common, guy-talk topic we never discussed - home-improvement or repairs of any type. We were both essentially helpless when confronted with those types of challenges.

In my small universe of friends and acquaintances, Frank was the first person I knew who actually ran a marathon, twenty-six point two miles.

"Don't forget the point two," Frank would always say.

The year was 1973, before marathons became popular. Running a marathon had always seemed to me to be an impossible feat. But once Frank had done it, it suddenly became possible, not just for me, but for other friends of Frank. He was our inspiration. For some of us, years of running together and training for marathons followed Frank's breakthrough accomplishment. Many of those runs took place in the Pocono Mountains where Frank and I both had weekend homes.

Anna and I had sold our first Pocono house in the late 1980s and built a new one about a mile away, just before our daughter, Casey, came along. Several years after moving in, however, I was still working on the landscaping. I thought it might be a good idea to line our semicircular driveway with railroad ties, a task that required more muscle than skill, a task perfectly suited to a city boy like myself.

I wasn't handy at all. I never felt comfortable in a hardware store or a lumber yard. I would need some assistance, so I naturally turned to my friend Frank when he and his wife Kathy came to dinner at our home in the Poconos one spring weekend. Frank very much enjoyed doing outdoor work as a way of relaxing. On Saturday morning, Frank and I drove to Kramer's Lumber Yard, about five miles away, to pick up some railroad ties for the driveway.

The Pocono Mountains are in a rural region of Pennsylvania, well populated with can-do men. Every native-Pocono male I had ever met could build a house, fix plumbing, install electricity, and rebuild an automobile engine.

But I knew my limitations. Consequently I had in our house a tool kit with only two items - a hammer and the Yellow Pages. If I couldn't fix it by bashing it, I called for help. Frank was similarly endowed and, therefore, capable of performing the all-muscle and no-skill task of installing railroad ties. We were comparing notes and joking about our lack of skills as we pulled into the parking lot of Kramer's Lumber Yard.

We went into the office, and I told the manager what I wanted. He asked me for the dimensions of the driveway, which I unhesitatingly rattled off to him. Frank, well aware of my limited skill set, was impressed to no end. His reaction was understandable, since on a previous occasion in the Poconos, he had accompanied me to Sears to buy a storm door, a simple purchase that became suddenly and unexpectedly complex. Everything had been going well until the salesman asked which way the door should open, from the right or from the left. I was stumped.

The storm-door display had two storm doors side by side, with one opening on the left and the other on the right. For the next ten or fifteen minutes, I walked back and forth to the doors, hoping to instinctively reach for the correct side of the door. Even Frank took a few tries, without any conclusive result. I finally had to guess, and the guess turned out to be wrong. That event went into Anna's book of Marty-can-do stories and explained Frank's stunned look when I rattled off the dimensions of my driveway.

A workman began to bring out the railroad ties. Frank and I lifted them onto the roof of my 1986 Toyota Cressida. When we put the third tie on the roof, the roof started to sink. I realized too late that we should have had some kind of roof rack or at least a small tarpaulin. As we continued piling the railroad ties onto the roof, a number of lumberyard workers began emerging from the warehouse and workshops. They seemed unduly interested in what we were doing.

As we loaded the last tie onto the roof, I prayed that it wouldn't collapse and break. It didn't, at least not immediately. The next job was to secure the railroad ties to the roof so that we could drive them home. I had brought along several lengthy pieces of strong rope. Again Frank was impressed with my foresight.

As Frank and I wrapped the ropes around the railroad ties, we threw the ropes to each other through the open front- and rear-door windows of the car. While doing this, I noticed that the group of lumberyard employees that had been watching us had swollen into a crowd. Everyone who worked at Kramer's Lumber Yard must have taken a break to watch us load railroad ties onto the car.

When we had finished, we went back into the office with the manager, and I paid the bill. As we came back outside, I realized that nobody had gone back to work. All the lumberyard employees were just standing there in silence, seemingly waiting for us to get into our car and drive away. We soon realized that our getting into the car was the focal point of their interest.

Frank went around to the passenger's side of the car, and I to the driver's side. We both pulled on the front doors. When they didn't open, we heard laughter and snickers, followed by loud guffaws, as the lumberyard employees awaited our solution to the crisis. We had sealed the doors shut with the ropes binding the ties to the roof of the car.

With no other choice, Frank and I climbed headfirst into the front seat of the car amid sounds of yelling, screaming, knee slapping, and roaring laughter. As soon as we could rearrange ourselves into an upright position, we drove off, blowing the horn, smiling, and waving to the laughing crowd through the open windows of the car.

Against all odds, we made it home without losing a single railroad tie along the way. As Anna and Kathy looked on, Frank and I tumbled out the car windows. We untied the ropes; pulled them off through the car windows; and one by one, we removed the ties and laid them along both sides of the driveway in the shallow trenches that I had dug earlier. With the last tie removed, the roof of my car magically popped back into shape. The ties had done no lasting damage.

Around this time, I began to experience the negative effects of years of running, which had done irreversible, arthritic damage to my knees. Unlike my car's self-healing roof, however, I couldn't bounce back. I ran less and less. Finally, I stopped running altogether. Running had been the center of gravity in my friendship with Frank. In my case, bad knees were the unexpected price to be paid, a price well worth the friendship, no matter how loosened the ties might ever become in the future.

I switched to swimming. Frank, however, remained physically unscathed by years of running. He ran a marathon every year, his string of marathons interrupted only once or twice by an injury. He and I continued to meet periodically at the YMCA and to have a few post-workout beers together, but the ties had loosened with the loss of running.

I have often thought back on that day at Kramer's Lumber Yard. I can still see all the smiling faces in the ever-swelling crowd of workers. I feel the steady focus of more than a hundred pairs of eyes as they watch us bind the ties to the roof of the car. I can still sense their cheery anticipation, as they await the inevitable outcome. Then I hear the howling, raucous laughter as we try to open doors we have sealed shut. But that day, in the face of that obstacle, we didn't loosen the ties. Together, we dove in, head-first.

Third Avenue has always had a lot of bars and restaurants, many of them temporary. For years, the southeast corner of Twenty-Second Street and Third Avenue was a place of constant change. Restaurant and bar after restaurant and bar had successively opened, struggled, and failed on that corner. Then in the seventies along came Rolf's and the era of stability and success.

Survival, let alone success, is no small feat, particularly for a German restaurant and bar, a once-common local species in Manhattan, but one that in recent years had become nearly extinct. Defying that historical trend, Rolf's German Restaurant and Bar came, stayed, and brought an end to the constant change on the southeast corner of Twenty-Second Street and Third Avenue.

Inside Rolf's, it was always harvest time. Suspended from the ceiling in nets were fallen autumn leaves, orange, yellow, and red, whose colors echoed in the mirror behind the bar. The mirror itself was draped in lights that silently whispered, "Merry Christmas," all year long. The overall effect was a cozy, timeless, comfortable, and predictable ambience, qualities that probably were at the heart of Rolf's success.

Fittingly from a seasonal point of view, Anna and I were in Rolf's on a Sunday afternoon in October 1987. We were sitting at the small, separate bar along the window looking out onto Third Avenue. The autumn day was mild as the sun dipped behind the buildings to the west and the late afternoon began its subtle transformation into early evening.

Anna and I had just toasted each other when, without any prelude, she put down her drink and said, "I would like to adopt a baby. What do you think?"

Before I could think what I thought, I said, "That's great. I would love to adopt a baby." I finished my half-empty glass of beer and looked out the window at the passersby on Third Avenue. Everything looked different than it had just moments before.

"When did you decide that you wanted to adopt?" I asked.

"Oh, I have been thinking about it for quite a while. I didn't mention it to you because I had to first come to terms with it myself. It is a big decision."

I could not agree more, I thought. Perhaps I, too, had unconsciously ruminated about this for a very long time myself, perhaps years, and had come to a decision-in-waiting, should Anna ever want to do what she had just said she would like to do. We were both ready. We ordered another drink and began the process of adapting to virtual parenthood.

The path to adoption would present some obstacles for us, primarily because of our ages. We had already been married for sixteen years, which, in the opinion of most adoption agencies, would put us far down on the lists of suitable, prospective parents. But past good deeds and the goodness of lifelong friends would conspire together to carry us along into real parenthood.

Before Anna pursued her PhD in clinical psychology, she had been a social worker at an adoption agency in Brooklyn. She had helped many children and parents and knew how the system worked. In addition, our dear friend Bonnie had worked at the Foundling adoption agency and had many contacts there. Assuming the odds were against us, we would try every legal path to a successful adoption.

Eighteen months passed. Nothing happened. Then a phone call. There was a newborn baby boy for whom the biological parents had just signed a release. For twenty-four hours, we were ecstatic. Then the phone rang once more. The mother had changed her mind. Yesterday's up became today's down. Two more months passed before the next call came.

I was away in Florida on a business trip. Anna called me and asked if I was sitting down. A baby girl, eight months old and in foster care, was available for adoption. "Great!" I yelled. "What do we have to do?" The Foundling arranged a meeting for us with the baby girl and the foster parents. It was love at first sight.

There was one small problem that the Foundling expected to be resolved in the near future. The mother had signed the release, but they could not find the father. A process of due diligence would be required before we could legally adopt. That process could take eighteen months, during which time the father could reappear and legally demand the return of his daughter. If they were unable to find him during that time, however, the biological father would lose his rights and we could legally adopt.

We said yes. The next day I made the first of hundreds of phone calls to our adoption lawyer, Harold Warren. He finally told me politely that there was no reason to call him. He would call me as soon as he had some news about the father. While Anna immediately went shopping for baby clothes, I called Joseph and asked him to meet me for lunch.

Joseph was my little brother in the Catholic Big Brothers program, which had matched us up three years before when Joseph was nine years old. Joseph had become part of our family. I wanted him to know about our new daughter before anyone else.

I picked Joseph up at his home in Queens, where he lived with his mother and two sisters. We went to a MacDonald's drive-through and bought some hamburgers and fries. I parked the car across from Calvary Cemetery.

"You said you had some news to share with me," Joseph began. "What's up?"

"Anna and I are going to adopt a baby," I replied.

"Boy or girl?" Joseph immediately asked.

"A girl," I answered.

"Great, that's great," Joseph said with a big smile. "I can't wait to meet her."

We finished our hamburgers, and I drove Joseph home.

"What's her name?" he asked as he stepped out of the car.

"We don't know yet," I said. "We're thinking about it."

On June 30, 1989, we drove to Long Island City to pick up the nine-month-old baby girl whom we would later baptize Casey Rose. Her godfather would be a twelve-year-old boy named Joseph and her godmother, our dear friend Bonnie. We placed our daughter in the brand-new baby seat in the back of the car.

Driving for three hours from the Foundling in Long Island City to our weekend house in the Poconos was the most nerve-racking drive I had had since the day I passed my driving test many years before. I never left the right lane nor went faster than forty miles per hour.

During the month of July, Anna remained in the Poconos with Casey while I went back to work in New York City, returning to the Poconos on weekends. In August, we reversed roles, and Anna returned to work. I can still hear the fading sound of the car as it turned the corner at the end of our street, leaving me with the sudden realization that I was alone and responsible for a ten-month-old baby girl.

I was so afraid that I would not hear her cry or somehow need my help that I was unable to fall asleep until about five in the morning I just sat there listening for a sound and continually checked on her breathing. At six, I was awakened from my brief sleep by the sound of crying. I rushed into her room to make sure she was all right and grabbed Anna's written instructions on the table next to the crib.

"Change diaper," I read. I had practiced and changed the diaper immediately. "Warm bottle" was next on the list. I picked Casey up and carried her to the kitchen for a prepared bottle, which I warmed up. Then I walked around the house with her, patting her back. She quieted and leaned her head against my chest. I sat down in a chair and tried not to fall asleep.

"Put her back in the crib at ten," I read. At ten, I followed instructions. She quickly fell asleep. I was so tired that I did not want to waste the five seconds it would take to get from Casey's bedroom to mine, so I just lay down on the floor next to her crib and fell asleep. Finally I was a real father.

The eighteen months during which the father was sought dragged on. But as slowly as those months passed, just as quickly our attachment to Casey grew. We realized that there was no way we could ever give her up if the father appeared and wanted her back. I made contingency plans to take her to Europe, where I had friends and connections that would enable me to work and care for her. Anna, who had a private psychotherapy practice in Manhattan, would visit as often as possible. In retrospect, this scheme seems somewhat crazy, but we were absolutely determined to never give up Casey.

The father was never found. Soon the bottles were gone, schools began, and friends were made. We moved out of Manhattan to the small village of Bronxville, just north of the city. New school and new friends for Casey and, for us, a new life. Boys started showing up, and soon Casey went off to college. It all happened so fast.

As I write these lines, I am once again on the southeast corner of Twenty-Second Street, sitting in Rolf's for the first time in many years, gazing out the same window onto the passing scene on Third Avenue. It is another Sunday afternoon in the early fall. Casey is a grown woman, happily embarked on a career in environmental conservation.

Sadly Anna, the love of my life and wife of forty years, passed away over three years ago. I am alone, but I have been inoculated against loneliness by my love for Anna and Casey.

It seems that everything has changed, except the southeastern corner of Twenty-Third Street and Third Avenue. Rolf's is still here. It is still autumn, inside and outside. It is even Sunday afternoon.

It is all the same. It is all different.

TAKING THE MEASURE

I remember very clearly opening the letter from Claude, my friend in Paris, on that January afternoon in 2002. His daughter, Florence, had succumbed to cancer at the age of thirty-two, leaving behind a husband and an eighteen-month-old daughter. Florence was a beautiful young lady, a burgeoning writer, a woman full of life, good humor, and boundless creativity. Anna and I had met Florence when she and her mother, Nicole, had accompanied Claude to New York City to witness his participation in the New York City Marathon.

Claude and I had literally run into each other in Paris just weeks before while running in the Bois de Boulogne. I was on a business trip to Paris and planned to run in the New York City Marathon. A long run every few days was part of my training. On a cold and damp late-September afternoon, I set out to run fifteen miles through the Bois de Boulogne, a beautiful Parisian park in which it is possible to run seemingly forever but at the risk of easily becoming lost.

Due to the weather, I saw very few people as I began my run. Before I had completed a mile, however, another runner approached me and asked in French if it would be all right if he ran with me. "Of course," I responded. Claude and I were well matched, and before long, we were in a mutually supportive groove. I have always found it easier to run with another person, particularly one who runs at my desired pace or even a bit faster.

Claude did not speak English, but we were able to carry on a conversation as we ran through the chilly drizzle. I asked if he was a native Parisian, and he said he was. I told him that I was from New York City. "Ah, New York! I am training for the Marathon." Quite a coincidence, I told him, because I was, too. Claude was in the printing business and had inherited a company from his father, who, Claude related, had printed road maps for General Patton as he charged across France in 1944. In that same year, Claude had met his first American, a GI in a tank that rolled through the village where he was living with his grandparents, safe from the battle in Paris.

In late October, Claude arrived in New York aboard an Air France 747, which carried over 250 passengers and crew, all of whom were registered to run in the New York City Marathon. In the Verrazano Bridge chaos that precedes the start of the Marathon, Claude and I were unable to find each other, but we did meet for lunch the following day. Claude was accompanied by his wife, Nicole, his oldest daughter, Sylvie, and his middle daughter, Florence, who was about thirteen years old at the time. His youngest daughter, Marie-Laure, had remained in Paris.

Lunch that day was the beginning of a friendship that continues into the present. Nicole invited us to visit the family next time we were in Paris, which we did and continued to do over the years. Claude and Nicole visited us from time to time in New York as well. As I came to know Claude better, I discovered that the professional printer was, in fact, a Renaissance man. Claude was a wine collector and connoisseur, a painter, a talented cook, a photographer, a weekend fruit farmer, and an adjunct professor of courses on methods of fruit cultivation at a local branch of a Paris university. It was not surprising that this creative energy had been passed along to Florence.

Florence had inherited her love for literature from her mother, Nicole. Discussions of books were common on our visits to Claude's home in Paris, as we sipped fine wines from his cave, which was filled with countless bottles from Bordeaux and Burgundy. After finishing college, Florence had traveled and lived in Canada for several years. Eventually she found a job writing for a magazine in Paris while she embarked upon authoring a book of short stories, some of which she would send me, from time to time, for my thoughts and comments.

Florence married, and within several years, gave birth to a daughter, Stephanie. Our correspondence continued, the short stories kept coming, and Florence seemed blissfully happy to be a mother. Then came the diagnosis of breast cancer. Radiation was initiated, apparently successfully, as Florence's cancer went into remission. Tragically that proved to be only temporary, as the cancer returned, more virulent than before. Florence's last letter to me spoke of the pain and the vomiting and of both her love and fear for her daughter, who would be left without a mother.

It is impossible to understand someone's grief unless you have suffered similarly. Nothing could be worse than losing a child, so I could only imagine, not really know, what Claude and Nicole were suffering. I telephoned our condolences to them and sat down to write them a letter. It was impossible. Every word I put down on paper seemed trivial and inadequate to the point of meaninglessness. The reality of the grief was so far beyond the range of language, at least of my language. In many ways, Florence's life had been all about words, and now ironically words proved to be artificial, petty, and useless when I attempted to use them.

Fewer than ten years would pass when once again, and even more painfully and poignantly, I would find myself struggling with the same total inadequacy of language. Anna passed away on June 23, 2011. The bottom fell out from under my world. Without my daughter, Casey, I would have tumbled out into the void. Anna was the gravity that held the stars in place, that prevented the oceans from spilling their waters off the sides of a spinning Earth. Without the force that was Anna, connections strained, elongated, and attenuated until they were gone. Relationships collapsed. The crowded world emptied. There was pain and anger everywhere. I became a mute in a senseless world of words devoid of meaning.

Casey and I struggled, often unsuccessfully, with our loss of Anna. I had an inkling of what Claude and Nicole must have felt when they lost Florence. Despite the terrible pain with which it is experienced, grief, I came to realize, was something that I did not want to give up. It became my deepest, strongest connection to the woman I loved, the woman that I could no longer see, hear, or touch. Grief and pain were the closest I could get to a living Anna. Getting beyond grief, losing and forgetting pain, would be like losing Anna a second time. I would not say good-bye to her or to the pain that connected me to her.

One night I had the clearest, simplest, nonchaotic, and easily remembered dream of my entire life. In the dream, Anna, Casey, and I were walking through a quiet, charming, residential neighborhood of three- and four-story brownstones. We were near a park. I thought we might have been in Park Slope in Brooklyn because it resembled the neighborhood in which one of Anna's colleagues had lived many years before, near Prospect Park. It was early on a summer evening. There was still some light in the sky. We had not had dinner yet, and I suggested that we find a nice restaurant.

In the distance, near the corner of the park, I saw some lights streaming from the ground floor of a brownstone. It looked like it might be an electric sign, and I thought that it could be a restaurant. It was too distant to know for sure, so I asked Casey to walk over there and find out if it was, in fact, a restaurant. She walked off in the direction of the lights while Anna and I waited in the growing darkness.

Some minutes later Casey returned. She confirmed that it was a restaurant. I asked her what type of restaurant it was. "French," she responded. "It's called Au Revoir."

Anna suggested that we go over and have dinner there. I said that I did not want to go to that restaurant.

"Let's eat somewhere else. Or let's get back in the car and drive home to Westchester. We could buy a pizza on the way home," I strongly suggested. Anna was silent.

We made our way back to where I had parked our car. As we drove off, I once again suggested pizza. Anna became furious.

"Why didn't you want to go to that restaurant?" she asked angrily.

I told her that I didn't really know. Anna had a look of uncomprehending, annoyed frustration on her face.

As we continued driving home, enveloped in an uneasy silence, I suddenly woke up, sad and disturbed. The dream had been so real. Anna so alive. Consciousness had now taken her life once again. I wanted to go back to sleep and return to my dream.

I could not take Anna to a place of good-byes, even one that implied the hope that we would see each other again. Doesn't death destroy all "agains"? Going to that restaurant would have been accepting what I could not yet accept.

It has been a long time since I received that letter from Claude. Have he and Nicole accepted the unacceptable death of Florence? I don't know. But I no longer say "*Au revoir*," even in Paris, even to Claude.

We had just left the doctor's office and were driving home.

"You should find someone else. You should not be alone." Anna's words cut through the protective bubble of silence that had enveloped us since the awful news just moments before. Stage-four colon cancer had metastasized to her liver. Silence rushed back in, filling the vacuum left by my inability to respond. Her first thought, evoked by the last sentence anyone would ever want to hear, was of another, of me. That was Anna. That was the way Anna was. She was incapable of being otherwise.

As the Westside Highway slipped beneath the wheels of our car and the gray-green Hudson bounced the sunlight back to the sky, the George Washington Bridge, in the distance, reached its strong, cabled arms across the river. Suddenly, desperately, I wanted to drive across that bridge onto Route 80, the road we had taken almost every weekend for so many years, and continue driving, on and on, nonstop, all the way back into the past, until the world that used to be might emerge before us on the other side of the windshield.

Out in front of the car hood, I could see Route 80 rolling ahead like an asphalt carpet, unraveling its way from the Atlantic to the Pacific, from New York City to San Francisco, from the George Washington Bridge to the Golden Gate, a coast-to-coast runway tempting us, like Kerouac and Steinbeck's dust-bowl farmers, to drive to the dream that is California. But Anna and I would only go as far as Pennsylvania, for weekend visits to our house in the Pocono Mountains.

Friday nights usually meant getting into the car, driving up Tenth Avenue to the always-crowded Lincoln Tunnel, onto Route 3 in New Jersey, and north to Route 80, where a sea of cars, trucks, and buses would drain, like a tide, out to the west. Big tractor trailers stuffed with cargo and buses packed with tired workers would ignore beeping horns and impose their will on small cars like ours.

But it didn't matter, at least to us. It was Friday, and we were on our way to a weekend in the country. Despite the rush-hour traffic, it was always a welcome time, not just because it was the weekend but also, and primarily, because it was a chance to spend time together after separate, busy workweeks.

We built our first house in the Poconos in 1972. A house in the country was a great novelty since neither Anna nor I had lived anywhere other than in an apartment in a city. Figuring out how to pay for it was the first challenge. Everything we could do ourselves, limited as it was, we did, rather than paying someone else to do it. That meant painting, staining, finding, buying, and moving furniture.

We had a new red VW Super Beetle, vintage 1971, which we purchased with wedding gifts. It wasn't exactly a moving van, but we made it do wonders. We once transported the living-room carpet tied to the roof. The carpet was so big and the car so small that the carpet draped over the roof, from the front bumper to the back bumper. I had to sit at a forty-five-degree angle to see through the windshield. It wasn't the only *Grapes of Wrath* trip we would make to Pennsylvania.

The builders and contractors presented a more significant challenge because they quickly realized that I knew absolutely nothing about building a house. Anna, in fact, knew a lot more than I did. But the local Pocono mores dictated that the builders and contractors talk to the man of the house. Whenever I questioned the reason for delays in the schedule, for example, their explanations usually involved pumps, drains, two-by-fours, or four-by-eights, as well as delivery delays of building materials that I had never heard of. Confronted with my silence and glazed-over eyes in response, they knew they had won the argument and had explained away the delay.

To compensate for my ignorance about home construction and to restore my sense of dignity and competence, I decided to build a wine rack for the new house, to prove that I had learned something about building. With the indispensable help of a neighbor, I built a wine rack that could hold 140 bottles. I thought that the Pocono climate and the basement of our house would happily and cooperatively combine to nurture young wines into pleasant maturity.

A fairly extensive period of acquisition without consumption, however, would be required. Unfortunately consumption kept pace with acquisition, leading me to refill the wine rack with empty bottles. This artificial collection looked impressive to the casual visitor, but it was a metaphor for the mask I tried to wear with the local workmen.

For nine months, Anna and I traveled back and forth to Pennsylvania almost every weekend until like a sudden miracle, the house was actually finished. And then a real miracle happened. We had wanted to build a loft over the kitchen, but it would cost another $400, and we were at the end of our shoestring.

Fortunately as was my annual custom, I had made a three-dollar bet on a long shot in the Kentucky Derby. His name was BBB. On the day of the race, it rained in Kentucky. There was a lot of mud on the track. Happily BBB turned out to be what they call a "mudder." He won, paying $400 to my three-dollar bet. We had our loft. After several more weeks of painting and staining, we finally moved in.

During those nine months, we learned something more than the challenges of building a house. We learned the value of the time we spent together on Route 80. Driving along a traffic-jammed highway for two and one-half hours in a confined space presented those opportunities for giving, taking, and sharing that had escaped us during the preceding workweek. The intimacy of the car enabled unhurried sequences of words and silence, an unpressured pace of exchange connecting us the way Route 80 connects the coasts, at varying speeds and distances, across changing terrain. To begin our conversations, sometimes composed of words, sometimes of shared silences, all that was required was a Zen-like dismissal of schedules. "We get there when we get there" was the attitude that opened the door to the unshared moments of the past week.

As we chatted, our little schnauzer, Pumpkin, slept quietly in the back seat. Pumpkin loved the Poconos and would be the first one in the car on Friday nights. I had bought him for Anna as a one-month wedding-anniversary gift. He was a lovable little guy, even though he had failed out of obedience school. We would never successfully reverse this failure during the ensuing sixteen years of his life, a life nearly coeval with our first Pocono house, which we would sell several months after Pumpkin passed away.

During those years, we commuted weekly to our A-frame house, which was located on a little cul-de-sac called Lehigh Circle, part of a development called Pocono Farms, just a few miles north of the town of Mount Pocono. Although a native of Wyoming might consider Pocono Farms as crowded as the New York City subway, for us it was the quintessence of rural.

In reality, it was rural with amenities like a clubhouse with a restaurant and bar overlooking a private lake, tennis courts, and a golf course, on which we would build our second house in 1988, a year we would later refer to as 1 BC, the year before Casey our daughter came along. But that's another story.

During our commute, Anna, who was a psychotherapist and the most caring human being I have ever known, would sometimes talk anonymously about one of her patients, give me some background, and ask for my objective opinion as an outsider and a layman. She said it was refreshing to get the point of view of someone who only knows some facts and not the patient. She respected my opinion, and I was flattered whenever she asked for it.

Except in the company of acquaintances whom we did not know well, Anna rarely called me by my name, usually addressing me instead as "Big Guy." In turn, I almost always called Anna "Tootsie." Whenever we did call each other Marty or Anna, we knew there was a problem or, at the very least, that something quite serious was about to be said. Rare were the occasions, in the close confines of our car, when we addressed each other with our real names.

When the Training Institute for Mental Health, of which Anna was at the time the executive director, moved to a new location on West Twenty-Seventh Street, Anna had the dual responsibility of designing the new space and closing down the old. When she turned off the lights for the last time at the old location, Anna penned a few lines on her parting thoughts:

> A thousand journeys began in this place. What magic has occurred here! What marvelous beginnings have these rooms seen. What joy have so many felt, what wonder to see things clearly for the first time, what shy glances, what triumphant grins, what shared laughter, what decisions have been made, what sorrow expressed, what souls reclaimed, what gifts have emerged, what lives have been saved in this humble place.

"This humble place," like Freud's apartment at Berggasse 19, reminds the visitor to look within, that what is to be seen is to be found on the inside, not the outside, to close off, if just for a while, the distracting world around us, as did Somerset Maugham with his boarded-up window in the hills above Nice.

I have been back to those hills above Nice a number of times since my visit to the office of Dr. Freud but not since Anna passed away. Every time that Anna and I returned there, I always thought of Somerset Maugham and his battle between outside and inside. It seems to me that art is easier for landscape painters, who need the outside to evoke the inside. For them, listening to a symphony of colors is not a distraction. It is an inspiration.

Writers, on the other hand, like psychoanalysts, must wander searchingly about interior landscapes before they can finally stop, focus on the scene, pick up their ink-tipped brush, and write the words that faithfully depict the scene they hear.

During her more than thirty years of practice, Anna had the same painting hanging in her office behind her chair. It was a view from the interior of a room, quite like her office, looking out through a big picture window onto a garden of sunlit, multicolored flowers. The window was always open.

When we used to commute to the Poconos on the weekends, we would listen to music on the radio, with stations fading in and out as we drove out of the reach of radio stations in New Jersey and into the reach of those in Pennsylvania. Later our music came from tapes and then CDs: Joe Cocker, Rod Stewart, the Beatles, Eric Clapton, Jim Croce, Linda Rondstadt. Even now when I listen to "Maybe I'm Amazed" by Paul McCartney or "Long, Long Time" by Linda Rondstadt, I find myself back on Route 80, looking west through the windshield, heading to Pennsylvania.

But at that moment, in silence, I was on the Henry Hudson Parkway driving home, north to Bronxville, Anna beside me, seriously ill. I didn't want to get to where we were going. I wanted to keep driving with Anna until we could reach a place where her illness would disappear. I just didn't know where that place might be. What I did know was that I did not want to find someone else.

Among her many talents, Anna, with her fine eye, elegant taste, impeccable judgment, and unhesitating decisiveness, was a born interior decorator, a creative escape from her practice of psychotherapy. She completely furnished and decorated three just-built houses, four apartments, and three offices. She had the uncanny ability to imagine in detail the formless, barren space she saw before her as a beautiful, welcoming, lived-in home.

Furniture, fabrics, carpets, tables, lamps, pictures, and prints would all come together in her mind, simultaneously spreading across that space like forms and colors on a canvas. Invariably the result was a warm, colorful unity that was so natural, so permanent, and so seemingly incapable of being otherwise that it was impossible to remember the emptiness it had filled.

I was at the other end of the spectrum when dealing with empty spaces. I can remember measuring the height of two living-room walls in my first apartment. I came up with two different measurements. Even more significantly, not only did I find nothing unusual in those differing measurements but I went ahead and ordered two sets of drapes of different lengths for two walls which, being in the same room, had to be the same size.

It is no wonder that my daughter Casey now regards me somewhat suspiciously as I help her take measurements in her new apartment. I sense that it is less that she needs my help than it is that she knows that I want to be needed to help her. So here we are in her new, empty apartment, taking measurements of doorways, hallways, and rooms in preparation for furnishing them. We work together in a sort of industrious silence, serious about what we are doing but even more serious about trying to ignore Anna's absence. This shared attempt to forget fails, leaving us, in our unspoken sadness, to take measures of each other, furtive counterpoints to shouted numbers.

Neither Anna nor I had ever lived in a house before, so it was a major undertaking when we decided to build a new weekend house in the Poconos soon after we were married. Within weeks of our marriage, she had already completely redecorated my Greenwich Village apartment, but taking on an empty house that we had just built was a challenge of a different order.

Anna was an unstoppable, creative force. I trusted her judgment implicitly, followed her direction, and supported her efforts by arranging financing, negotiating with the builder, and, in general, supplying more stamina than skill to the project. Weekend after weekend, we drove to the Poconos along still-being-built Route 80, our new red Beetle stuffed and loaded with items for the new house, including large, flexible pieces that circumflexed over the roof, from the front to the rear.

During the cold and damp spring that year, Anna and I painted and stained the entire house. We then laid down the carpeting, rented a truck, and transported all the furniture that Anna had acquired while the house was being built. With help from friends, we moved all the furniture into the house. In twenty-four hours, our new house was completely furnished and decorated.

More than a few times would we repeat this process with other new weekend houses, as well as apartments and offices in Manhattan. In every case, the result was always another creative tour de force, a burst of color, warmth, and surprise. No wonder that I feel inadequate as I try to help my daughter measure the dimensions of her new apartment. This is what her mother did unerringly, furnishing and decorating in her mind while she jotted down lengths and widths.

Anna is gone, and Casey is moving to her first apartment without a roommate. She is alone, and I am alone. We are alone together, painfully aware of our own dependence on Anna and each other, as we try to take the measure of this new, empty space that asserts Casey's fledgling independence.

In every extension of the tape measure, I see other barren spaces, the rooms and walls of the homes that Anna had furnished and embellished. I see the barrenness washed away by floods of color and fabric. I feel plush carpeting beneath my knees as I kneel on the wooden floor. I hear Anna's voice as Casey shouts, "Eighty-four inches!"

All the homes of our past come crowding into this empty living room. I feel I am trying to measure an immeasurable space between Casey and me, between Anna and us. We grasp opposite ends of the tape measure, anchoring an almost umbilical connection, in our attempt to define the ever-present dimensions of Anna's absence.

My limited competence must remind Casey of the mother who isn't there to help her and guide her in tasks she knew so well. Casey must know that Anna would be decorating as she measured, shopping for furnishings in her mind. She would trust Anna's judgment and follow her advice. "Seventy-six inches!" Casey yells, as I quietly wish that a father could, just for five minutes, be a mother, too.

Several years after we were married, I became the director of a computer center at NYU and was given a very large office in a very old building on Washington Street, just a block from Washington Square. I was promoted on a Friday. Anna and I celebrated that evening. The next morning Anna suggested that we redecorate my new office. During the next thirty-six hours, we painted, hung drapes and prints, and reorganized the space. On Monday the staff was stunned by the transformation and admiring of the results. I would like to perform a similar miracle for Casey, but Anna isn't here.

Three years after Anna's death, again with the help of friends, I was able to slip through the wall of grief that had immobilized me. I refurbished the basics of the Bronxville apartment, into which we had moved sixteen years before, with new windows and air conditioners. The living room and dining room were replastered and repainted with the same colors that Anna had chosen. Both rooms were restored exactly as Anna had decorated them. The drapes, carpets, and furniture throughout the apartment were cleaned and reinstalled.

By that time Casey had already moved into her second apartment in Dobbs Ferry with several roommates. A dear friend of ours, Peggy, suggested transforming Casey's former bedroom into an office, furnished with a new convertible couch that would allow the office to still be used as a bedroom. I filled Casey's old bookshelves with all my books, including Anna's large collection of cookbooks, which are a mystery to me, bittersweet memories of Anna's magical powers in the kitchen but also a continuing, soothing presence.

"We are going to need a very long carpet in the hallway," Casey remarks. "Do they make carpets eighteen feet long and three feet wide?"

Another question that I can't answer. "I am sure that we can find something," I reply, with a transparent combination of ignorance and hope.

"I would like to get a new set of dishes. Maybe I could host next Thanksgiving here," she muses.

"That would be great. We could cook the turkey together," I say, and Casey smiles back at my good intentions.

"You can be a big help in a lot of ways," she replies warmly.

We once hosted Thanksgiving in our second Pocono house, which Anna had designed. The kitchen was her favorite room in that house, with two ovens, eight burners on the stove, a big butcher-block island in the middle of the large space, two sinks, and a long sitting bar, across which Anna could see and relate to everyone in the dining room.

The kitchen, like all rooms but the bedrooms, was on the second floor, which was walled-in glass. We could see the trees and fairways of the golf course next to which our house stood. As Casey and I spoke of cooking a turkey together, I thought of that Thanksgiving in the Poconos. Casey and I would join forces to fill another holiday vacuum.

"What do you think about drapes?" Casey asks.

"I don't know, sweetheart. I really don't know." My confessed ignorance is another metaphor for Anna's absence. "Mommy would have known," I say silently.

Casey's eyes lock onto mine and read what I am saying to myself. In hers, I read, "That's OK, Daddy. I love you very much."

"Thanks for all your help," she says generously.

"It was nothing, my love."

She doesn't know how sincerely and literally I mean those words. "Let's go to lunch," I suggest. "I'm really good at that."

As Casey and I hug each other, I look at the bare walls behind her. They are all the same size. I realize that this time around I could probably take their measure correctly.

Anna loved Waterford crystal. When returning from business trips in Europe, I would always include a stopover at Shannon, Ireland, so that I could pick up some more Waterford crystal for her. Years before I met Anna, I had been introduced to Waterford crystal by Nancy Hummel, my girlfriend of several years, a gorgeous young woman, a psychiatric nurse, and a wonderful person.

But despite those attributes, Nancy and I broke up. She was faultless, except for her understandable wish to get married. We were both in our late twenties, but I could still not imagine myself ever being married. It was another failed relationship.

Compounding my unmooring after that breakup, I took a leave of absence form my job at IBM to return to graduate school. I was feeling lost, lonely, confused, and adrift, cut off from the rest of the world. In a word, desolate. So desolate that I was devoid of the good judgment that would have prevented me one Sunday afternoon from turning to Ingmar Bergman for distraction and escape.

The movie theater on Third Avenue and Sixty-Seventh Street wasn't very crowded that afternoon in 1968. In retrospect, I suppose that was understandable. The theater's double feature was a Bergman one-two punch, *Persona* and *Wild Strawberries*, a program capable of disturbing even the most grounded and integrated psyche

I saw a lot of gray sky and experienced no comic relief during the next four hours in the black-and-white world of a sparsely populated island off the coast of Sweden. That entire country was buried beneath a monotonous shroud of faint, cloud-diffused sunlight. After so many big decisions, that double feature proved not to be the wisest choice.

Persona seemed to be an exercise in mutual exorcism, as two women, an actress suffering a nervous breakdown and the nurse caring for her, gradually and subtly exchange personalities, each becoming the other or perhaps the person they both are. *Wild Strawberries*, although concluding with the hero's redemptive acceptance of both his life and his death, was an equally painful, emotional trial.

When the theater lights came on after the second feature, I was surprised to see people getting out of their seats to leave. I felt no need to leave. On the contrary, remaining in my seat and starving to death seemed more reasonable and appealing, a surrender to the gods of the gray Bergman skies. But that was not an option. I had to go to work.

For months, I had been driving a cab at night to support myself in graduate school. That evening while driving through Hell's Kitchen, I was hailed by a middle-aged woman. She told me that she was late for work at a theatre near Times Square. Despite the pressure she was under, she spoke in a soft, gentle voice. Taxi driving, I was learning, was a valuable way to study one's fellow man and the society that we all share.

From her dress and the neighborhood in which I picked her up, I knew she would offer me a generous tip. That was the way it worked. Tips were inversely proportional, socioeconomically speaking. The lower the passenger was on the socioeconomic ladder, the bigger the tip. The consistently worst tips were from passengers whom I either picked up or dropped off on Park Avenue.

As we drove east toward Times Square, I saw in the rearview mirror a face whose expression could only be described as serene. It wasn't the serenity of an infant, undisturbed in its innocence, but rather the serenity of a woman who was at peace with herself, despite the absence of innocence and the unavoidable presence of life's problems.

When we stopped at a red light, she leaned forward and asked, "What do you think of this?" I turned and saw a beautiful Waterford decanter that she was holding up for me to see. "My friend is getting married, and this is my gift. I have had it for years, and I will miss it. But in a way, it takes part of me with it and into my friend's life forever. Separation doesn't have to be a bad thing."

She told me that she worked as a hat-check girl at the theater and had worked there for a number of years. We arrived at the theater in just a few minutes. She paid the three-dollar fare and, predictably, handed me a generous tip. I thanked her but insisted that she take back the two-dollar tip she had given me.

"No," she said. "I am sure your job can be tough sometimes. So please take the two dollars. Say a prayer for me."

That's what the Christian Brothers used to say. "Say a prayer for me." But as with this woman, their request always seemed unnecessary. The Christian Brothers lived in a brownstone on Ninety-Seventh Street between Columbus Avenue and Central Park West, a beautiful building, with a long stoop sloping up gracefully from the street to the second-floor entrance. It was a house of peace, silence, serenity, and spaciousness. A world apart, separated from the world I lived in. I loved going there.

Like this woman, they were good people, devoting their lives to helping others. They didn't need prayers. She didn't need them, either. But I said yes anyway. I was happy to help, if she believed that I could. As she entered the theater, she turned and smiled, clutching her decanter. She seemed blissfully fulfilled by a life that appeared to lack any fulfillment. I nodded to her and smiled back.

Above her, the blinking lights of the theater marquee promoted a cheery musical. I was glad to be out of Sweden. For the first time that Sunday, I felt upbeat. I drove off into the evening's eastbound traffic, looking for my next fare, harboring the lingering awareness that I would never forget that woman whom I would never see again.

"Separation doesn't have to be a bad thing," I said to myself.

After graduate school, I turned in my taxi and returned to IBM, where I discovered that I had a hitherto untapped and unexplored attraction to show business. I soon became very involved in creating the entertainment for sales rallies and teamwork meetings, writing scripts, and making films and videos. Anna was my biggest fan and supporter, as the scripts and productions became increasingly elaborate and complex. She had such a good eye for the right touches to scenery, props, and costumes.

Anna loved beautiful things, objects that would delight not only her but others with whom she could share them: paintings, prints, jewelry, scarves, furnishings, and accessories of every type. Since she loved to cook and entertain, Anna purchased multiple sets of beautiful dishes and crystal. Even as she collected new sets, she found it impossible to separate from the old. There would always be precisely appropriate sets for particular occasions and gatherings.

When entertaining, she would use different sets of dishes and crystal, depending both on the foods and wines to be served and the colors involved. The resulting presentation would itself be a work of art, transforming the simple act of serving and eating into a thing of beauty.

One afternoon I was at the home of my IBM colleague, Jim Martin, working on a short film we had made along with another IBM colleague, Gene Cronin. Jim was a talented musician and singer, who added a finer, more professional dimension to what would otherwise have been the unadorned, slapstick comedy that Gene and I very much enjoyed doing. That afternoon we were putting the finishing touches on the film as I began to do the final voice-overs.

A world I had never before experienced inexplicably materialized, as I spoke into the microphone. A feeling of complete fulfillment, a desire for nothing else, a sense of blanketing serenity enveloped me. Reeling off the words of the simple script of our little comedy, I was transported somewhere I had never been before. Once there, I wanted to be nowhere else.

Nor was there anything else that I wanted to be doing at that moment other than what I was doing. There was nothing in the world that was missing. There was nothing else in the world that could have made that moment more complete. There was nothing but a sense of serenity. Everything that had been separate came together, became one, words with music, sound with sight. It was only a voice-over, but it was everything, one complete, integrated whole.

At that moment, I saw once again that woman from Hell's Kitchen, the hat-check lady, standing in the doorway of the theater, smiling her peaceful smile. For the first time since that evening, I felt I understood her. For a fleeting instant, we traded joy and shared peace, unlike the two women in *Persona,* who trade grief and share pain.

As I packed up yet another set of Waterford crystal for my daughter, Casey, to use in her new apartment, I remembered the evenings of entertainment from days gone by and imagined Casey's entertaining in the years to come. I had washed every one of those glasses many times. That was my job, my sole permitted responsibility in Anna's kitchen. I knew every piece in every set of Waterford crystal that we owned, including how many there were of each type.

I felt I was transferring Anna from our past to Casey's future. It was a good thing, despite a contradictory mix of pride and sadness at Casey's independence. In passing along those sets of crystal, Casey and I were acknowledging the woman who had been and, in so many ways, still was at the center of our lives. It was a moment of peace and serenity, of giving away while retaining, of sharing without diminishing. Instead of either-or, it was a moment of both.

"Separation doesn't have to be a bad thing," I heard the hat-check lady say, clutching the Waterford decanter she was about to give away.

GOING AWAY

For the first time since Anna's death, my daughter Casey prepared Thanksgiving dinner in her new apartment. Some friends and I were the hungry and fortunate guests. And for the first time, she used her mother's favorite set of dishes. As we waited expectantly for the arrival of the turkey, I was captivated by the rich, lush-green, and bright-white curved lines floating across and over the sides of these dishes, echoing the green of the dining-room chairs and the white of the tablecloth.

The lines of the mesmerizing pattern seemed to start out as single lines that gradually, almost imperceptibly, moved apart, going in different directions, each becoming more separate and defined but yet continuing to resonate the contrasting connection that they had, one to the other.

Anna bought these dishes in Austria in 1983, at the factory where they were made. We had been vacationing with our friends Les and Peggy on the shore of an Alpine lake, the Wolfgangsee. The lake was surrounded by mountains, some of which Les and I climbed during the week we spent at the Weissen Rossl Hotel on the edge of the lake. We would set out for a different mountain each day, returning in the late afternoon with time enough to quench our thirst at one of the several lakeside biergartens before returning to our hotel.

While Les and I hiked in the mountains, Anna and Peggy drove around in our rented car, exploring the countryside surrounding the Wolfgangsee, which is about twenty-miles east of Salzburg, Mozart's birthplace. We had tried in vain to get tickets to the annual Mozart Festival in Salzburg. The positive side of that failed attempt, however, was that we were able to spend more time at the Weissen Rossl.

One morning Les and I decided to climb a mountain called Der Ringkogel, which proved to be the most challenging mountain that we had yet attempted. We were hikers rather than climbers, lacking technical climbing skills and consequently cautious.

When we approached the top of Der Ringkogel, we discovered a flat wall with a ten-foot cable that we would have to climb in order to get to the top. We paused to reconsider getting to the top.

The problem wasn't the ten-foot cable. The problem was that the ten-foot cable didn't reach the top of the thirteen-foot wall. Three feet of wall would have to be scaled, going up and coming down, without the aid and safety of the cable. For those three feet, we would have to separate ourselves from the cable and make it on our own. That challenge encouraged us to take a break and have lunch while we pondered what to do. After lunch, decision made, we started our trip back down the mountain, never having reached the top.

We later learned that Anna and Peggy that same afternoon had discovered a little village called Gmunden at the other end of the Wolfgangsee. The village was famous for manufacturing beautiful dishware. Anna and I really did not need any more dishes. At home and in our weekend house, we already had eight or ten different sets of dishes, with complete place settings for eight people.

But as far as Anna was concerned, there was always room for one more set, if it was beautiful. And it was. Soon after returning from Austria, we received several large boxes from Gmunden. We packed the boxes in our car and brought them to our weekend house in Pennsylvania, where we would use them for entertaining during the Christmas holidays.

For nearly thirty years, we used these green and white dishes from Gmunden in every house or apartment in which we lived. Anna loved to cook and to entertain. Our Gmunden dishes are those that I most associate with those loves of Anna.

I listen to the conversation at the table, but my thoughts wander back to the first time we used these dishes, Thanksgiving 1983. Casey had not yet been born. Now she is in the kitchen doing, for the first time, what her mother had always done.

Casey and I are living through the fifth year since Anna's death. Every holiday, perhaps Thanksgiving especially, collapses those years into a just-happened yesterday. To do what your mother always did without your mother being there to guide you is a difficult, sometimes crushing, reminder of her absence. Where can Casey turn for guidance? Not to me, as is often silently and painfully obvious to both of us.

For the first time, Casey is living alone in a new apartment, a decision she reached on her own after four years of sharing apartments and houses with roommates. Hosting Thanksgiving is another significant step. I try to help in whatever way I can. I even make an appetizer that is universally enjoyed, which apparently is proof positive to everyone that I really could not have made it myself.

The conversation continues as Casey emerges from the kitchen with a big, golden-brown turkey atop an even larger, white serving platter. Casey displays the turkey to everyone at the table and graciously accepts their compliments.

Before returning to the kitchen, Casey asks, "Dad, do you think you can carve the turkey for us?"

Of course I reply, "Certainly, sweetheart," even though this will be my maiden voyage in carving a turkey, a task Anna always insisted on doing herself.

I follow Casey back into the kitchen, and she hands me a large carving knife. I try to look experienced, but she knows the truth.

"Go ahead, Dad. This is my first turkey, and this is your first opportunity to carve."

We are filling the vacuum that we acknowledge by our mutual, unspoken consent to avoid discussing it. In the kitchen, we hear the sound of laughter at the table as my carving skills are discussed. Casey and I smile at each other. We are each doing something for the first time, on our own.

We bring the potatoes, the broccoli, the cranberries, the stuffing, and the salad to the table. I pour the wine and the water. Casey asks me to say grace, which I do and conclude with a toast to Anna, the first time her name is mentioned, although her absence has been present all afternoon. We drink to Anna's memory and all the happy times that we all shared together.

The turkey has been perfectly cooked, which evokes a steady stream of compliments. Casey blushes gratefully. Unsurprisingly the results of the carving receive more good-humored criticism than praise. The table becomes a bit quieter as everyone enjoys the Thanksgiving feast. When dinner is finished, several of us clear the table for dessert and coffee, which Casey brings from the kitchen. I refill the wine and water glasses.

The conversation turns to Thanksgivings past and, inevitably, to Anna, the peerless cook. Cousin Angela asks about the dishes, which she says she has been admiring all afternoon. Peggy responds with the history of the purchase in Gmunden, Austria. As Peggy speaks, I sip my wine and observe the water pitcher before me, with its green and white pattern of lines that begin joined together before separating.

As I turn the water pitcher around, the lines converge again, closely but never quite rejoin, only to separate once more. It is like a dance of line and color, attraction and rejection, first together and then apart. I am reminded of Dante's description of the Tigris and Euphrates Rivers, which, having begun at a single source, "separate slowly like old friends saying good-bye to each other."

Perhaps this is another thing that Casey and I are doing together for the first time, saying good-bye, separating slowly into a new way of being together, like the two rivers with a solid, earthen bond between them, like the green and white lines on the water pitcher that dance around and around, now near, now far, but always together, moving rhythmically, like the inhaling and exhaling of life-giving breath.

I hear Peggy speaking warmly, nostalgically of that afternoon long ago in the small village of Gmunden on the shores of the Wolfgangsee. I see Casey listening attentively. I watch the water pitcher come alive while Peggy tells the old story that I seem to be hearing for the first time. I feel Anna entering the room. She smiles. For a brief moment, the green and white lines on the water pitcher, the Tigris and Euphrates Rivers, Casey, Anna, and I, everyone present, and everything around us end our separation. We are back together as one.

Driving home later that evening from Casey's apartment, I think back to Der Ringkogel. But this time, I imagine that I grab the cable, climb up, reach out for the ledge, and let go, filled with the same hope and confidence that I felt years before when faced with my own illness.

Lying there on the morning of my first treatment, I prayed to be blessed. Above me, almost close enough to touch, was an azure-blue sky, sprinkled with bulbous blotches of bright, white stars pouring their light down on the table on which I was lying. This cheerful, curved ceiling reminded me of the sky painted by Dante's words early in the *Purgatorio,* the sky of hopeful, guiding light that he sees when he emerges from the depths of hell. Light, the dominant metaphor of the *Divina Commedia,* enables us to see the beauty of the world and of others, through which and through whom we connect to the source of beauty.

It is no accident that the *Inferno,* the *Purgatorio,* and the *Paradiso* end with the same word, "*stelle*" (stars), those celestial lights that dispel the desolation of darkness. Radiant light brings warmth, grace, inspiration, love, and, sometimes, healing. Healing was what I was hoping for each of those mornings at seven, Monday through Friday, for eight weeks, as I lay on that table receiving radiation therapy, looking up at those stars, thinking of life, death, cancer, and, most of all, a cure.

Eighteen months earlier I had been diagnosed with prostate cancer and had had surgery. Unfortunately the surgery had not entirely eliminated the cancer, compelling me to have radiation. After eight weeks of radiation, however, I was blessed with being cured, at least as cured as one ever is from cancer.

Three years after my radiation treatment, Anna and I left her doctor's office and got into our car. I turned the key and stared straight ahead. Anna had been told that she had a terminal illness, and we were sharing the same thoughts in silence. Despite this terrible news, Anna was not capable of feeling sorry for herself. Caring, giving, enabling were the steadily flowing, abundantly overflowing, streams in her life. They were the vital core and applied purpose of all her talents, her decorating, her cooking, her entertaining, her teaching, and practice of psychotherapy. She was my Beatrice.

We would have only one year. We didn't know that. We didn't ask, and the doctor didn't say. We didn't want to know. We only wanted to hope. For six months, we said nothing to anyone, not even to our daughter Casey. We were waiting for the good news that never came, good news in which we could distractingly wrap this terrible truth, like an unwanted present in a beautiful box.

In the coming months, we would avoid discussing the future, concentrating instead on the logistics of chemotherapy, doctors' visits, and, on very good days, the possibility of going on a cruise one day, a cruise we would never take. Loyal friends like Geri and Eddie would drive many miles every week just to bring us home-cooked meals that I couldn't manage. Casey had just graduated from college. Her new world was beginning as we were struggling with our old world ending.

Anna had not stopped working and continued her normal schedule, seeing patients whenever she could, working around the requirements of her treatment. Eventually, however, neither her profound inner strength nor her commitment to her profession, the job she loved, could prevent her from succumbing one afternoon to the relentless onslaught of her illness.

I took the train into the city and went to Anna's office on Thirty-Fourth Street and Park Avenue. She said she was very tired. We drove home in silence. When we arrived, Anna wanted to rest.

She went into the bedroom and closed the door. For the first time since she had received her diagnosis, I felt hope beginning to slip away.

That day, with discordant irony, was a painfully beautiful day in late May, not unlike the other beautiful May days that we had shared together over so many years, including our wedding day, the fortieth anniversary of which we had just celebrated two weeks before. Through the living-room window, I saw a world filled with trees and birds and blue sky, a day like the day Dante meets Beatrice once again in the Garden of Eden. It seemed a gorgeous fantasy, a memory dropped like a multicolored veil over the present world of empty gray.

I thought of something Anna often mentioned during the years of our marriage. As a young girl, she had loved to ride her bicycle around her native Yonkers, the eastern edge of which I could see on the far side of the Bronx River Parkway. Bicycle riding gave Anna a sense of freedom and escape from her heavy responsibility of attending to a difficult mother, a responsibility that a faithful daughter could not avoid. In my mind, I saw a ten-year-old girl, a skinny little Italian girl, on a bicycle. I wondered what her thoughts were as she pedaled tirelessly up and down Yonkers's uncountable hills.

As I looked out on the hills of Yonkers that afternoon, imagining this skinny little Italian girl on her bicycle, I spoke in silence to Anna, who was sleeping in the bedroom: "You are so slight and so alone, a sight that might be sad if you weren't so free. But you are not without a burden, a weight you are learning to carry, even though it is not yours. Someone must carry it or the world will collapse.

"You ride around and around, as your pedaling body flees a mind it cannot leave behind. You want to go anywhere but home. Every turn, left or right, invisibly maps the shapeless burden you bear, wrapping that weight in a string of circular thought far beyond your girlish reach. Why can't you describe your pain? Only your bicycle takes it away, letting thoughts whir about like spinning wheels that go nowhere, until you turn, tired, toward home.

"You can never ride far enough or long enough, Anna, to escape the responsibility thrust upon your bony shoulders. You are the daughter, and men need not be responsible for the problems of a woman. That is women's work. You are too young to find answers, only old enough for dreams or despair.

"Perhaps during these hours on your bicycle, pain will couple with innocence, you will conceive new eyes that will see what others won't, new ears that will hear what silence sometimes says. You will begin to understand what was misunderstood. In your young ten years, you have already unleashed a power to cope that will become the power to heal. And you, Anna, are still only a skinny, little, Italian girl on a bicycle."

But Anna was no longer riding up and down the hills of Yonkers. She was lying in bed, dying. I turned from the window to the interior universe that Anna had created, our world within a world, a world of lamps, chairs, drapes, and tables held and connected each to the other by the gravitational pull of harmony. Anna knew how to create harmony. It became her life's work to bring harmony into the lives of others. How empty the world had become. Our life together, our shared joy and pain, now seemed like a dream from which I was sadly awakening.

"I remember," I continued silently in my mind, "you told me what you once felt, as a young girl, when you gently stroked the face of a horse that stood obediently next to a farmer's fence on the edge of a country field. You said his big brown eyes—eyes like yours—looked innocently, so innocently into the distance as you gently patted his head and softly stroked his face.

"It seemed, you said, that his only understanding was that now, right now, was good. And if his whole life remained now, his whole life would be good. Those big, brown eyes carried no past and saw no future, just now, forever now, innocent and unknowing.

"All directions in your life were really only one, Anna, always toward the horizon, toward the sunrise, a harbinger of the future day, yet a vestige of the past night, the glimmer of more than now, the yes to other than you knew, experience in the offing, knowledge not yet known, your path to helping and healing others."

Several years after Anna's death, while sitting at the far end of the table in the Training Institute's conference room, I have a perfect view of Anna's picture, mounted high on the wall at the other end of the room. I am a member of the committee of the Anna Keefe Women's Center, which was dedicated in her memory not long after her death. This conference room, like every other room and office at the Training Institute, was modeled and constructed under Anna's direction, a voluntary labor in addition to her responsibilities as executive director of the Training Institute and her full-time practice of psychotherapy.

Anna's smiling face oversees our discussion of upcoming events at the center. Her presence, like her picture, lingers here, a continuing inspiration to her colleagues of many, or merely a few, years. Anna's warm smile assures us, inspires us, and continues to guide us.

I think of Anna lying in her hospice bed, sleeping more and more each day and asking for less and less. Eventually an uninterrupted silence descended on our home, except for labored breaths that, in turn, slowly faded away at three thirty on a Thursday morning. Casey and I were suddenly alone, without Anna, alone with each other.

Patches of light were painted on that night's clear sky, which curved down toward the horizon, like the azure-blue, curved ceiling in the hospital, above the table on which I had received my radiation. Dawn broke soon after. The world filled with radiant light, but we remained in darkness. There had been no rays of light that could save Anna the way they had healed me. Even love could not hold onto her tightly enough. The celestial flames had been extinguished.

Anna, the skinny little Italian girl on a bicycle, the little girl who never wanted to go home, had vanished, like Beatrice, with the stars of the night sky.

35473362R00148

Made in the USA
Middletown, DE
04 October 2016